DO IT YOURSELF NUMEROLOGY

Sonia Ducie Dip. AIN, MAR, has been working in the field of healing and personal development for seventeen years, and has explored many forms and ways of healing the mind, body and spirit. She originally trained as a reflexologist and is the author of *The Self-Help Reflexology Handbook*.

However, Sonia was fascinated by the power of numbers and subsequently trained as a numerologist at the Connaissance School of Numerology in Hertfordshire, England. She has been a practising numerologist for more than fourteen years. She leads business and personal workshops in numerology, as well as giving private chart readings.

By the same author

The Self-Help Reflexology Handbook

The Principles of Numerology

Numerology: Your Love and Relationship Guide

Numerology: Your Personal Guide to Life

The Complete Illustrated Guide to Numerology

The Lucky Numbers Oracle

Numerology Directions

Sonia Ducie's Numerology Secrets

DO IT YOURSELF NUMEROLOGY

How to Unlock the Secrets of
Your Personality with Numbers

SONIA DUCIE AIN

WATKINS PUBLISHING

LONDON

Distributed in the USA and Canada by Sterling Publishing Co., Inc.
387 Park Avenue South, New York, NY 10016

This edition first published in the UK and USA 2007 by
Watkins Publishing, Sixth Floor, Castle House,
75–76 Wells Street, London W1T 3QH

1 3 5 7 9 10 8 6 4 2

Designed by Jerry Goldie
Typeset By Dorchester Typesetting Group

Printed and bound in Great Britain

Manufactured in the United States of America

Library of Congress Cataloging-in-Publication Data Available

ISBN 13: 978-1-84293-134-9
ISBN 10: 1-84293-134-2

www.watkinspublishing.com

For information about custom editions, special sales, premium and
corporate purchases, please contact Sterling Special Sales
Department at 800-805-5489 or specialsales@sterlingpub.com.

CONTENTS

Learning More About Numerology

Acknowledgements

Thank you to all my family and friends for being a part of my personal development, and therefore indirectly, but essentially, contributing to this book, and to my life.

INTRODUCTION

NUMEROLOGY AND YOU

THE SCIENCE, PHILOSOPHY AND PSYCHOLOGY OF NUMBERS

Numerology is the science, philosophy and psychology of numbers. It is an ancient method which can help you to understand more about life – past, present and future. Life evolves in cycles, or trends, all of which are contained in the numbers 1 to 9. Indeed numbers can be counted as far as your imagination will go (or as far as a computer will add) but each number, no matter how large, divides down to between 1 and 9.

Numerology is scientific in a modern sense. Mathematician and physicist Sir Isaac Newton (1642–1727) believed in 'order': that the sun will rise tomorrow, because it did yesterday and it did today. However, science has since discovered that stability and harmony actually come out of chaos, and that chance and probability affect life on earth. Numerology also brings order out of chaos. By being aware of your numbers you can eventually reap rewards even from experiencing disorder in your life; out of chaos and disorder will come the rewards of new understanding, and experiences which may strengthen you and help you with your life in the long term. Numerology can also help you practically with your personal development.

As a philosophy, numerology contains wisdom about life. It is both a system of thought and a theory of knowledge. The Greek philosopher Pythagoras (c580–500 BC) was an early numerologist whose theories have greatly influenced modern-day numerology. He believed that numbers 'are the essence of all life'.

Numerology is also a form of psychology with which to explore the personality. The pioneering, revolutionary work of psychologists Sigmund Freud and Carl Jung emphasized the importance of understanding the strengths and the weaknesses of personality characteristics. They both spent many years working through their ideas and concepts about how people function, and working on their own personal development as well.

Freud was particularly interested in instincts and desires, sex, and dream analysis; he did a lot of work with the mind. Jung wrote more about the soul, and the paranormal, but he also catagorized personality archetypes.

Psychology is one way of understanding your personality; in numerology all possible psychological characteristics are contained within the numbers 1 to 9.

NUMBERS AND ENERGY

Numbers are simply energy, which is constantly evolving and changing. They contain within them the potential for many different experiences and are attributed many different qualities. Each number also contains physical, emotional, mental and spiritual dimensions, which explains why numerology is such a wonderful representation of life.

Numbers are energy and therefore each number flows into the next and is influenced by other numbers. For example, on 31 August you will be influenced a little by the dates of 30 August and 1 September. During the month of April (the fourth month – 4), you will be influenced a little by March (3) and May (5). Of course the 4 (for April) has the strongest influence on the actual month. You may also notice this effect if you were born just before or after midnight; then you may be influenced more by the Personality Number before or after your actual day of birth.

Numerology works with the cycles of numbers 1 to 9, but you will notice that this book embraces numbers 1 to 31 (for the 1st to the 31st of each month). Each of these numbers divides down to between 1 and 9 so you will see your Personality Number written like a 24/6 (if you were born on the 24th), or a 14/5 (if your birthday falls on the 14th), or a 11/2, and so on. All the numbers in these equations have influences within your life experiences.

In numerology you also find Master Numbers. These have double digits such as 11, 22, 33, 44, which means that they carry extreme qualities of the number they represent. For example, a 33 may bring extreme creativity or, at other times, extreme confusion. It is understood that when you have Master Numbers in your chart they highlight ways in which you can help others, as well as the ways you can help yourself with the gifts that the Master Numbers bring. Sometimes Master Numbers are influenced by the single digit that they divide down or add up to. For example, if your number is a 44, then you may be more influenced by the 8, and so on.

This book is essentially written for you, as an individual, but it is also important to recognize that you are a part of humanity, and a part of the 'collective' or the group living on earth together at this moment in time. Therefore in numerology the 'Collective' numbers have an effect on the overall experiences which you may have. For example, the year 2008 adds up to a 1, so during that year the Collective will be strongly influenced by the qualities of that number.

There are twelve months in the year and you will share the qualities of whichever month you are born into. Take January for example. Everyone born in January is working collectively, with the same focus, towards a common goal. (See page 9, 'How to Work Out Your Numerological Influences'.)

Another example of the Collective influence comes from the country in which you were born, or in which you live. The letters of names have numerological correspondences (see the alphabet correspondence chart on page 238), and the name of a country will embody the particular numerological influences to that country as a whole. Japan, for example, adds up to a 15 or a 6. Whatever your own personal numerological influences are (from your date of birth or names), if you were born in Japan, its language, its culture, its food, its people – its particular energy – will exert a strong influence over your life. Even if you move to another country its influence will still colour your experiences of life to some degree.

YOUR DAY OF BIRTH

Your day of birth, that is the day in the month on which you were born, gives you information about your Personality and your psychological patterns. It reveals your personal trends in your health, romance and sex, your career and in life in general.

YOUR PERSONAL YEAR NUMBER

In life, all your experiences are contained within the numbers or cycles 1 to 9, because after the 9th cycle, you start a fresh 1 to 9 cycle. However, in numerology your Personal Year Number also influences the kind of issues, events or experiences you may be working with during that year. To work out this number turn to page 9 ('How to Work Out Your Personal Year Number').

It's fascinating to see what type of events you draw to you during each Personal Year cycle. For example, in a 5 or 6 year, you will be working on commitments; it may be that you will attract people to you who test your commitments, or those who are also working with commitments in their lives.

The Nine-Year Cycle

In life many things have natural cycles of 7. For example, the 7 chakras or energy centres of the body, the 7 levels of the aura, the 7 colours of the rainbow (or the 7 rays), and the 7 seas. Seven is often closely linked with nature. However, in numerology 7 is the number which creates or destroys nature; it is a catalyst which can bring about synthesis, fusion, production or loss (all in varying degrees). Therefore in your Personal Year Cycle of 1 to 9, the 7th year draws together 6 years of experience, the 8th year of your cycle is for repayment of karma (from your previous 7-year cycle, and all the cycles before that), and the 9th year influences you to think about what it is you need to let go of or take forward into your next 9-year cycle.

THE NUMEROLOGICAL AGES OF HISTORY

THE BEGINNING OF TIME

Numerology is as old as time. Numerology is also as old as a day, because each day brings something new and ends something too. Numerology is modern in that it influences each moment. Therefore the history of numerology contains the past, present and future, all wrapped up in the influence of the numbers 1 to 9. No wonder so much information can be gathered from these little digits, and that they reveal so much about life. However, all history was born out of the zero – the potential for all life.

When you think of history you may conjure up physical events which have coloured the world to date, but history is equally about emotional, mental and spiritual events, or changes in consciousness, which have also taken place. Indeed, taken into a larger perspective, world history has also been coloured by influences from the *whole* universe.

Every time mankind takes a leap forward – as happened with the Industrial Revolution of the 18th and 19th centuries, and the landings on the Moon and Mars in the 20th century – the leap occurs because mankind is being influenced by new qualities from the numbers that have now become available to them. When mankind moves forward it is because there has been a change of consciousness and a change of numerological influences. For example in recent years a 13th astrological sign called Ophusius was 'discovered', situated between Scorpio and Sagittarius. This planetary sign or constellation probably existed all along, but until the time came when humanity could recognize its qualities and influences it was of no use to mankind. Thirteen represents change and transformation so it indicates that in the late 20th century there began to be a change of consciousness on planet earth.

A change in consciousness happens when society changes, and the whole group moves on together in unison. Society changes from within; it is not external events like the deaths of great leaders or natural disasters which create the changes, but the consciousness itself which results in the changes that occur.

Everything in life happens for the best of the group, although it may not seem like this at the time. Throughout history great leaders have advisors to help them make decisions or people to call upon for practical help. But whether they were advised by others or not, they actually make collective decisions because they were subconsciously or consciously connected to humanity, and were working as part of the group. Even when these decisions appeared 'negative' or caused destruction, they were still part of the cycle of birth, death and rebirth, and part of the healing process for mankind. Cultures and civilizations need to break down and then be rebuilt, this is called evolution. In numerology this can be seen through the numbers 1 to 9, as they reveal society's consciousness at any given time.

However, the only way to be sure of changing society is by changing yourself, and working on your own personal development, because each one of us affects the whole group or consciousness. Numerology can help you to do this by bringing awareness about your potential and your strengths, and by encouraging you to have the courage to face the challenges in your life. It can lead you to new levels of awareness, and mirror to you your responsibilities for creating inner peace and happiness within society. By recognizing that you are part of the world team you can feel 'people power' and know that your say counts (even if you don't speak) because of your spiritual connection to mankind.

In life, which is reflected in the numbers, you are always consciously or subconsciously working on your own self-healing, and on the larger healing of humanity as well. Therefore you are healing things which the group before you left behind, and carry the seeds for the future in the inner work, or personal development, which you are doing now. Numerology can help you identify what specific karma (the law of cause and effect in which previous actions influence the here and now) you are carrying from the past, but it also helps to identify the karma from all past generations which the world is collectively 'paying back'. Karma can bring rewards and retribution, and the world you see around you today is the result of all the past karma from the world since it began.

Numbers have evolved in their own way, and although 'history repeats itself' it goes through changes so that each generation re-invents each number and is influenced by them in a different way. The Aztecs may have been influenced by the numbers in a different way, say, to the Egyptians or the Greeks or to how numbers are used today. For example, the Aztecs may have been influenced by the number 5 when developing their oral forms of communication. In the Western world today the number 5 influences more concentrated uses of the mind and the kind of intelligence which has developed computers and telecommunications systems for mass communication all around the world.

Throughout history the numbers 1, 2 and 3 have been commonly used because they are simple units of calculation which can be mastered by anyone. Yet the number 3 is said to be a 'Divine Number' because it contains within it the symbol of the triangle, which represents: the Holy Trinity, the Mind, Body and Spirit, and the Mother, Father and Child. You may have also heard the expression 'third time lucky', as 3 is considered by many to be a lucky number. However, today numerologists use many numbers, ranging from 1 to 81, and sometimes even above that. But the numbers 1 to 9 are commonly used, and are considered extremely potent because they have many especially powerful experiences and influences condensed into them.

Many countries in the world have their own forms of numerology, but in the past the ancient Hindus, Tibetans, Chinese and Egyptians were early developers of numerology. However, the Greek philosopher Pythagoras influenced much of modern-day numerology with the system 1 to 9, which he developed at his School of Mysteries in Ancient Greece, around 500 BC.

METHODS OF NUMEROLOGY

There are many different methods of numerology practised around the world. These include the Pythagorian method, the numeric system of the Kabbalah, Esoteric numerology and various other forms of divination. Some of the methods that are still practised today are fairly crude – such as some methods of African divination – but they all give you information about (your) life. Numerology is applied to find out your potential within certain situations in life, but in divination it is mainly used for prediction.

The Kabbalah and Numerology
The Kabbalah, the Hebrew system of knowledge, focuses on two methods by which to interpret Kabbalistic texts, particularly the Bible. It includes the 'Tree of Life' with its 10 plants or divisions, and the Gemetria, a numerological system in which numbers are translated from the phonetic sounds of the letters of names. The Kabbalah has 22 letters in its alphabet, and Hebrews were said to have changed the letters in their names to alter their significance. These two methods were also used for prophecy.

Esoteric Numerology
Esoteric numerology works with the qualities or concepts 'behind' each number. It recognizes human potential as being related to infinite potential, relating to the moon, the stars, our solar system, and to other solar systems. Esotericists go deeply into the workings of the mind, where they see potential for all life, and numbers for an esotericist sometimes reveal concepts that a rational and logical mind would never think could possibly exist. There have been many esotericists, or 'thinkers', throughout the ages whose knowledge has influenced man. They may have been great inventors, for example, bringing new things into existence that were not conceivable to mankind before their ideas were made concrete. Perhaps the idea that the world is round – when orthodox opinion was that it was flat – came from an esotericist hundreds of years before it was physically proved to mankind by explorers such as Christopher Columbus.

African Divination
With this method a person will usually be seeking a clear-cut answer to a question posed. There are many different things which are read to find the answers. However, in the past an animal was killed and its

intestines were taken out to 'read' the answer to the question within its gut. Instincts are commonly linked to the gut – people also often describe themselves as having 'gut' feelings about something or someone – so this form of divination seems to have a kind of logic to it.

Chinese Divination

The *I-Ching*, or 'The Book of Changes', is a method of divination that was written around 3,000–5,000 years ago, and which is still popular today. Yarrow sticks or coins are used to consult it. In the coin method three coins are tossed six times, and each side of the coin when it lands represents a number or a symbol. The coin lands as either tails, which equals Yin (receptive energy) and represents the number 2, or heads, which equals Yang (active energy) and represents the number 3. These are then placed into a 6-line figure of Yin or Yang, and into a symbol and a number which is explored in the *I-Ching* book of teachings. This book covers all elements of the mind, body and spirit, and is based on 64 divinatory figures containing 64 six-line hexagrams. In numerology the number 64 represents the potential for all life experiences on this planet, like reading an 'open book'.

Tibetan Divination

The Tibetans have many forms of divination. A well-known method involves writing possible answers (outcomes) to questions on a piece of paper. These answers are then wrapped up in dough and put into a Tibetan bowl in which they are spun round and round whilst the recipient holds the question in his/her mind. A ball is then selected. Sometimes the process is repeated many times, using the same question, to confirm the accuracy of the response.

Another ancient method of divination practised by the Tibetans is especially relevant to numerology: it involves dice. The dice are thrown onto a divination board which depicts drawings of possible outcomes to the questions posed, and which also indicates the place of these outcomes within the greater scheme of things.

Pythagorian Method

The Pythagorian method is based on the numbers 1 to 9, and encourages you to develop your intuition by letting the numbers do their own talking – revealing their 'jewels' to you. This book uses this simple method to help you learn more about your personality and your life.

Numerology *is* life, and therefore this book hopes to show how numerology can offer insights which may enable you to learn more about yourself and about the wider world in which you live.

HOW TO WORK OUT YOUR NUMEROLOGICAL INFLUENCES

In this book you will find a chapter on your Personality Number, describing some of the ways in which this number influences your life. In this section you will be shown how to work out this essential number. You will also be shown how to work out your Personal Year Number, which changes every year and influences each individual year of your life. You will also be given information about your Collective Year Number, which explains the general influences of the month in which you were born.

It's essential to remember that you *are not* your Personality Number but that the number *influences* your life. Your Personality Number alone can give you a tremendous amount of information about your life. Some of this information may at first seem to be contradictory but *all* of it is relevant as aspects of the whole. Life isn't black and white; nor are the influences of the numbers.

How To Work Out Your Personality Number
Your Personality Number is the day on which you were born. For example, if you were born on the 8th of any given month, your Personality Number will be an 8. However, each number over 9 has other numbers which influence it as well. For example, if you are born on the 14th, then you should add 1 and 4 to give 5: your Personality Number is a 14/5. Another example: with a 29, you add as follows: 2 + 9 = 11, 1 + 1 = 2; so your Personality Number is a 29/2. By taking into consideration all the digits you can find out more detailed information about your life.

How To Work Out Your Personal Year Number DD/MM/YROf last B-day
To work out your Personal Year Number you add the number of the day on which you were born and the month of your birth together with the year of your last birthday. Each Personal Year influence changes from one birthday to the next.

Example

Sophie Hazlett was born on the 14th of February, 1971.

Let's say that we are in January 2007. So you add Sophie's day which is the 14th (1 + 4) = 5, plus her month (February) = 2, plus the year of her last birthday, which would have been in 2006 (2 + 0 + 0 + 6 = 8. Add 5 + 2 + 8 = 15, 1 + 5 = TOTAL = 6.

Therefore, from her birthday in 2006 to her birthday in 2007 the number 6 is influencing her experiences and her life. From her next birthday in 2007, a 7 will influence her year, and from her birthday in 2008, Sophie will be in an 8 Personal Year, and so on.

PERSONAL YEAR TABLE

Below is a list of a typical quality (there are many) which may influence you during that specific Personal Year.

Personal Year 1 = **Opportunities**
Personal Year 2 = **Balance**
Personal Year 3 = **Creativity**
Personal Year 4 = **Building Foundations**
Personal Year 5 = **Communication**
Personal Year 6 = **Commitments**
Personal Year 7 = **Materialization**
Personal Year 8 = **Rebirth**
Personal Year 9 = **Endings, Beginnings**

WORKING OUT YOUR COLLECTIVE YEAR

To work out your Collective Year Influences simply look up your month of birth in the following list. This shows the qualities and surrounding issues with which you may be working with others in life.

January
Bringing courage to the world.

February
Bringing balance to the world.

March
Bringing joy to the world.

April
Bringing responsibility to the world.

May
Bringing communication to the world.

June
Bringing service and caring to the world.

July
Bringing synthesis to the world.

August
Bringing strength to the world.

September
Bringing faith to the world.

October
Bringing wisdom to the world.

November
Bringing inspiration to the world.

December
Bringing completion to the world.

CLARITY OR CONFUSION?

You can see that there are obviously very many numbers influencing your life. For example, the Universal Date (the current date) also has an influence over your life. Given the amount of data available, you can probably understand why this book will focus on your Personality Number alone!

Remember also that working out your numbers is one thing, but interpreting them is another, and you should allow your intuition or your mind to guide you to 'read' the information between the lines as well as the knowledge you gain from this book.

It may also help you to learn to relax and enjoy working out the numbers because if mathematics isn't your favourite subject, even though these are only simple equations, you may over-concentrate at first. So if you fall into this category perhaps only do a little numerology at a time until you are familiar with the process. Remember, the more you relax the more you will learn and the more you will enjoy this wonderful tool.

1–31

MAKING THE MOST OF YOUR PERSONALITY

Numbers are energy which carry within them immense potential. They, like life, are constantly changing; therefore, by being aware of your Personality trends, you can be aware of the ways you may react or create your reality within an ever-changing world.

THE PERSONALITY

Your Personality or character is largely influenced by the patterns of behaviour which were established in your early childhood (generally the first seven to nine years) and which are set to form the basis of your Personality for the rest of your life. This is called childhood conditioning. However, your Personality can also be influenced by the people around you now and by governing influences such as the changing circumstances you find yourself in during your lifetime.

Your Personality therefore performs an essential role: it is the 'space suit' clothing the inner you and without it you would not be able to function in this world, or be able to learn the lessons which you need to learn. You have choice, and you can say no to the lessons the numbers teach you. For example, if you have a 4, which governs responsibility, influencing your Personality, you may refuse to take responsibility for yourself or conversely take on others' responsibilities instead of your own. Your Personality has a life of its own and it is your wonderful Personality which colours the personal things you may want to do with your life.

YOUR PERSONALITY NUMBER

You will find your Personality Number explored in detail in one of the following chapters (to work out your number refer to page 9). Each individual Personality Number Chapter explores the general trends, challenges (or weaknesses), romance and sex issues, potential physical traits or trends, possible childhood experiences, health or well-being concerns, and possible career choices of those born under that number. Each chapter also gives a relevant example of a famous character analysis, explaining how that character's Personality Number influenced his or her life and death.

NUMEROLOGY INFLUENCES

In numerology you are not your number, but you are influenced by the qualities which the numbers portray. For example, with a 6 Personality you may, at times, be especially compassionate or loving because those are particular qualities offered by the number 6.

Within each chapter for each Personality Number you may find that you identify with some but not all of the qualities mentioned under each heading. If, for example, you have a 26/8 Personality Number influencing you, you may find that some of the characteristics do not seem all that relevant to you at this moment in time. This may be because they are contained within the potential offered by that number, and you may not recognize those qualities within yourself.

During different times in your life you may be influenced more by either the positive or the challenging influences of your Personality Number, and these influences may even vary during different times of each day. Sometimes you may go for many years exploring certain characteristics in more depth than others. You may also 'discover' parts of yourself, or attributes to each number, as you make your way through life. For example, perhaps at the age of 41 you begin to develop the ability to direct others and subsequently incorporate this quality into your life, although it was latent because it was in your chart all along.

You may also note that if you were born just after or before midnight then the number for the day before your birthday or the day after may be more consistent with your Personality. Indeed, in numerology all numbers usually contain a little of the number before and the number after. If, say, you were born on the 21st, then you may have characteristics from the number 20 as well as from the number 22.

Some people believe that the day on which they were born is

their 'lucky number' and if this is so – great! – because your beliefs exert a strong influence over your life.

DOUBLE DIGITS

If your Personality Number has double digits – that is from 10 upwards – then even within your Personality Number you may have one, two, three or four different numbers which, together or separately, influence your personality in a variety of ways. For example, if you were born on the 29th, the 29 divides down into a 2, with the 'hidden' influence of an 11. That is: $29 = 2 + 9 = 11$, and $1 + 1 = 2$. So with a 29 Personality you may be influenced by the 2, the 9, the 11 or the 1 in varying degrees and at different times in your life. The final digit has the most influence.

PERSONALITY NUMBERS 1–31

In each chapter you will find the following sections:

General Trends (for that number)

In this section you will find out some of the positive qualities or patterns which may be influencing your life. It includes information about the physical, emotional, mental and spiritual levels contained within the number concerned.

Challenges

This section explores your challenges or weaknesses, which you can transform into strengths by being aware of some of the possible characteristics which may be influencing your Personality and your life. It is helpful to be able to identify some of your potential challenges in life because then you can – if you choose – work on them by transforming them into positive characteristics.

Romance and Sex

This section on romance and sex offers you a little taster about what kinds of patterns of behaviour you may adopt and the partners you may attract. It also gives insights into possible aspects influencing your sex life.

Childhood Experiences

Whether you can remember much about it or not, your childhood holds the key to your basic personality behavioural patterns. This section gives you information which may help you personally and also help you to relate to children who are influenced by the same number.

Well-Being

At times in your life you may be particularly prone to the health complaints indicated by your Personality Number, than from other aspects of your chart. Sometimes, you may be especially prone to 'visiting' illnesses like influenza, earache or backache, or even more serious illnesses which are not part of your general constitution at all. These may occur during a specific 'Personal Year'.

However, this section contains guidelines which may help you be more aware of possible challenges or weaknesses in your general health.

Career Choice

This section highlights the different career choices that are favoured by your Personality Number.

Famous Character Analysis

This section shows you how somebody has achieved fame by using the characteristics available to them from the Personality Number that influenced their lives. It also looks at their date of death to examine the numbers influencing the completion of their lives.

CONCLUSION

Sometimes, by delving into your own Personality, you may find out more about others as well. For example, by understanding yourself you may understand more about your partner, your parents, your friends, and indeed everyone with whom you come into contact. This is because learning about yourself highlights ways in which you may act, and react, to life.

NUMBER

1

PERSONALITY

GENERAL TRENDS FOR NUMBER 1 PERSONALITY

With the 1 influencing your Personality you have the gift of independence, and a strong desire to use your creativity in pursuit of your goals. You are a very 'upfront' kind of person; you are self-assured and you know what you want. You are incredibly focused and strong; once you set on your path you do not like to waver from it.

You are also self-centred, and have no problem telling everyone, 'I'm great' and 'I'm wonderful'. What a present you are to mankind!

With a 1, you are fearless in pursuit of your goals, and possess masses of physical and mental energy which you channel towards them. You are dynamic, and direct this positive energy into your seemingly endless creativity.

You are self-reliant, and can easily cope with, and enjoy, being alone, and doing things on your own. You may like to withdraw from the world for short or long periods. You are also a thinker, and in the luxury of your own space can concentrate on how to achieve your goals. Those with a number 1 Pesonality do not, as such, think they need people, but are happy to be with people when they choose.

With the influence of the 1, you are always seeking new opportunities and experiences: you are a real pioneer. You may be an entrepreneur, taking and making your own opportunities in every area of your life, and going for what you want. Freshness stimulates your mind, and therefore inputs new energy into your whole life.

You may have an inventive mind, and can easily invent new gadgets and find new ways of doing things. You are also a problem-solver; you realize that by looking at a problem from a different perspective a solution can usually be found. Lateral thinking often helps. Once you have set your mind on sorting out a problem then you like to conquer it. For example, if you are set with an impossible deadline for a project, you will find some way of achieving it. You are headstrong and wilful, and you do not give up easily.

With the 1 influence you can also be unassuming, and you are a typical 'unsung hero', always helping people and seeking no reward. You are a giver, and simply love to help others in a very caring way.

You also enjoy learning and are an intellectual at heart. You are never far from a good book, although you may not always find time to read because you are so busy creating. You are stimulated by your own ideas, and intellectually stimulated by others' ideas too; you greatly respect people's creative talents.

Because you have so much going on in your head you may need to focus some of your time on your spirituality; meditating for example, or listening to beautiful music. You have realized that by developing your spirituality you can reach your inner source of creativity. This can eventually empower your practical creativity and output too.

With a 1 influencing your Personality you are learning to find your own individuality. The 1 brings you great ingenuity, flair and originality. For example, you may decide that you want to make a birthday cake for your partner. Your goal is to make the cake, but you really enjoy collecting fresh edible flowers to decorate the top, making the cake in an unusual shape or colour, and presenting it with great drama and gusto. Then you may love to surprise your partner with it. You are probably not too bothered about whether it tastes nice or not – you enjoyed asserting your individuality, and being creative.

You have a terrific sense of humour, which can lighten your load. You enjoy tennis, gymnastics and aerobics for relaxation, but you may also enjoy a game of chess or watching sport.

CHALLENGES

With the influence of the 1, you have a big Personality which loves to shine and be creative, but this enormous ego can also make you over-bearing at times. You are narcissistic, and like to think that the world revolves around you. You may even create people in your life who dance attendance on you all the time.

Although, typically, with the 1 influence you may enjoy helping people, at the other extreme of this number's influence you may find that at times you do not enjoy giving to others at all. When you do give you think you ought to be congratulated. With a 1, you are self-centred and have a feeling of self-importance, and like to think you are more important than everybody else, particularly your friends and family. In a way this can drive you on, because you need to feel enormously self-confident to be able to channel out those enormous amounts of creativity stored inside you.

You can be destructive, and unaware of people's feelings or how things need to be done. You may break all the rules in pursuit of your creativity because you are self-centred, and may only consider what *your* needs are. For example, perhaps you decide that you don't want to keeping having to ask your boss's permission to hold a meeting. So you just go ahead and organize it anyway.

But sometimes destruction or self-centredness can lead to improved ways of doing things for everybody. Your boss may realize that the meeting was a great success, and tell you that you do not need to consult him or her in the future. With a 1 influencing your Personality you love to be a hero, and such praise from your boss can certainly help to raise your self-esteem!

Like all the 1s (10/1, 19/1 and 28/1), you may sometimes be a lazy person who needs to be drawn out in order to get things done. You may resist your creativity, resist taking a direction, and simply fester and withdraw. With self-image being an important consideration for you, you may need to work especially hard on maintaining your self-esteem. Perhaps you are dependent on others and find it difficult sometimes to rely upon yourself. It is a good idea to set one little task or goal for yourself at such times so that you feel you have achieved something. This little burst of creativity can spur you on to conquer a larger goal next time.

With the 1 influencing your Personality your self-reliance may be taken to an extreme and you may be too withdrawn and feel lonely. You may have an inferiority complex, and think deep down that you are not good enough; when you are withdrawn you may resent others trying to draw you out. At the end of the day you know that only you can dig yourself out of your 'hole' and out of your situation.

You may sometimes find yourself focusing on a goal that is very time-consuming, and you may feel depleted of energy or even may lack the will to go on. These times can seem like major or minor setbacks, but you know deep down that you can overcome these challenges because you are a natural problem-solver.

With a 1 you may be dominant, overpowering, and even forceful until you realize that this doesn't actually help in pursuit of your goals. Force often puts more pressure on you and others, and creates more resistance to achieving your aim. For example, if you keep ordering your partner to do something this puts pressure on him/her, and they may take longer to do it than if you had asked them once. You may react in the same way if your partner tries to order you about too.

Like all the 1s (10/1, 19/1 and 28/1), you may often be unclear in your communication, and as a result can find yourself in all sorts of uncomfortable situations. For example, you may need to ask your tenants to move out of your flat, because no bills have been paid for months. You may indirectly say to them, 'Oh, are you thinking of moving out?' in the hope that they get this obscure message, instead of, 'As a result of … please can you move out in 30 days'. Of course when nothing happens, you end up having an enormous argument with your irresponsible tenants because you did not say what you really meant to say in the first place. With a 1, you tend to feel angry a lot of the time until you can learn to communicate more positively.

ROMANCE AND SEX

With a 1 influencing your Personality you are a dynamic person, with tremendous amounts of energy and focus to give to your relationships. Certainly your partner will enjoy being the centre of your attention. You are also independent in relationships: for example, you may settle down and have children but you will always have that tendency to want to go off on your own and do your own thing. Finding a partner who accepts your individuality is helpful.

You may also be self-centred, particularly about your work, and find it a challenge to 'spare' any time away for others. You might neglect your partner by forgetting to cook dinner when you had agreed, or by not making enough time for romance, and so on. A partner who is also a strong individual will help to complement you, so that you can both lead your own lives 'together.'

You may shy away from intimacy. The 1 influence is that of the intellect and mind; whilst you can easily talk about books and ideas, opening up about your emotions may be 'out of bounds', unless you find a partner who is open with his or her emotions, and who can really help you to feel safe with your own. This, however, takes time and effort, and you may prefer to avoid a partner who requires this sort of intimacy with you.

Sometimes you can be stubborn, and wilful, but this may turn your partner on; some people like a challenge. Number 1s are generally good at leading, but when you are feeling withdrawn and alone, you may also like to be led. For example, if you have been working for days, you may appreciate your partner booking a lovely restaurant for two, or buying tickets for the cinema.

With a 1, you may like to set goals within your relationship – when to date, when to move in together, make a commitment, get married, have children, and so on – although obviously you have joint goals too. You love being creative, so you may come up with all sorts of ideas about how you can make your time with your partner exciting and new.

It is possible that during your childhood your father, or male role models, had a strong influence over your life. Perhaps you idolized your father, or quite the opposite; perhaps you felt intimidated by men. This may mean that you may choose an older man, a father figure, as your partner. It may help you to find a spiritual partner who can help you connect to your inner self too.

Within your sex life, you can really enjoy the creative acts of passion, and enjoy sex in different places or positions. You can either be very willing and giving, and enjoy pleasing your partner, or conversely, be self-centred and just pander to your own satisfaction. You may not like physical affection, particularly if it is outside the bedroom, because you may feel uncomfortable with intimacy in front of others. Whichever, sex may well be an important aspect of your life in some respect.

PHYSICAL APPEARANCE

With the 1 influencing your appearance you give off an air of strength and you will probably look robust. You may be tall, with a medium- to high-pitched voice. You usually have strong teeth, and these, along with your sparkling eyes, are your most noticeable features.

CHILDHOOD EXPERIENCES

As a child you may have possessed a thirst for learning, and you probably thoroughly enjoyed your education at school. At home one of your parents may also have been intellectual, or perhaps like you had a strong will. You may have been hard to handle sometimes because when you set your sights on doing your homework, or focused on playing a game with your friends, you were stubborn and disliked being interrupted. However, you were probably quite prepared to interrupt others' conversations when there was something you wanted to know; even then you were a strong individual. Perhaps you were fiercely independent too, or you learned that relying on yourself was the only way to get things done at home. As a child you may have frequently been told not to moan about life, and to just 'get on with it'.

With a 1, you may have been very close to your brothers and sisters, sometimes as substitute parents, or – at the other end of the spectrum – you may have found yourself parenting them. Your father may have been a strong influence over your life as a child. You probably loved sport, and competitive games which required your focus, but you may also have enjoyed quiet pursuits at home alone, such as reading.

Children with a 1 often need to be encouraged to find their own goals and focus in life, to develop their strong intellect, and to enjoy goal-orientated tasks. If not stridently self-reliant, they may, at the other extreme, be very dependent children, but if given sufficient encouragement, they can learn to stand on their own two feet.

WELL-BEING

With a 1 influencing your health you may be prone to emotional problems, and tend to either repress or over-express your emotions. You may also be open to blood-sugar imbalances, adrenal stress, and digestive problems.

CAREER CHOICES

You are likely to really enjoy earning your own living and being financially and otherwise independent. You love your work and do not work simply for the sake of money, or earning a few extra bucks; creativity is usually your main focus of attention.

With a 1 you may be an athlete, a professional problem-solver, a leader or pioneer in any field, or an inventor. You can be extremely self-motivated once alerted to a cause, particularly education, and you can be a successful leader in that field; you may attract lots of money for your cause with your energy, focus and dynamic will.

FAMOUS CHARACTER ANALYSIS
Marilyn Monroe (Norma Jean) Born 1 June 1926

Marilyn was an enigma. She was a beautiful woman with a big personality and a larger-than-life character. With the 1 influencing her life, she became extremely creative and dynamic, with an extraordinary amount of energy which people found very attractive. She used the 1 to find her own individuality, which she did successfully by inventing her own persona, perhaps unintentionally. She was certainly a humorous heroine, and remains an icon of our time.

Marilyn also exhibited the challenging influences of the 1 Personality: a strong will and stubbornness. She used to withdraw from the world, and refuse to come out. It is widely believed that she felt very isolated and alone at times, and did not always love the attention which her fame and leadership attracted.

Marilyn certainly explored her Personality to the full. She died on 5 August 1962. The whole date adds up to a 31 or 4, so perhaps she found living in the material world too overwhelming on the day she died. The day was a 5, which influences unexpected events; apparently she died of a drugs overdose, whilst lifting the telephone and communicating or asking for help? An unforeseen accident …

NUMBER

2

PERSONALITY

GENERAL TRENDS FOR NUMBER 2 PERSONALITY

With a 2 influencing your Personality you have the gift of balance, and you have a deepest yearning to be able to relate to others. You like to relate to people through your emotions by expressing how you feel. For example, you may say to your friend 'I feel happy', or 'I feel sad …' and through your opening up and expressing how you feel, others can do the same. This inter-relating may take place regularly with you, and is a natural part of your life.

Your life may be based around your ability to 'sense' and 'feel' other people. For example, you may sense that your partner is trustworthy, or that your business colleague is respectful, or you may sense when they are telling lies, and so on. You may be someone who acts upon your gut feelings although they may not always be 'right'. This is because your own expectations of what you want can get in the way. For example, you may sense your business partner is honest, but it may be simply because you want to think that you are working with someone with this quality, even though deep down you feel that they aren't.

With a 2 you are very sensitive, and you can use this gift to help in your life. It can help you to 'put yourself in other people's shoes', and to understand what they need. So, when your friend comes to you for help, you can feel her needs even when she is not clear in her verbal communication. This can then help you to respond in a caring and helpful way.

You are usually sensitive to situations in life which need to be handled tactfully, and diplomacy is one of your key attributes. You can see what both sides are trying to achieve or say to each other. If you find yourself 'in the middle' you tend to remain noncommittal, and diplomatic in your response. However, you are a highly responsive person, and you tend to respond from your emotions.

With the influence of the 2, you are a peace-loving character, and you like harmony. This can mean that you have worked on accepting life's challenges and things that come your way. People you meet are able to sense this inner peace. You may not go around whispering, but you make a real effort to be calm and peaceful in your negotiations. You are placid, contented and considerate to others. You do not feel the need to raise your voice to get your point of view across, to express your feelings, or to be heard. This applies at home, in the workplace and everywhere you go. However, your need for peace and harmony is the greatest in your home, particularly on days when things are not so harmonious outside.

You are receptive and open to life, and so you tend to draw in and gather to you people with 'new' things to say, or new ideas to share, things that can really make a difference. You are good at listening and will genuinely care about what people have to say. For example, as a literary agent, you may need to be open to completely fresh ideas from new authors, at the same time being responsive to the needs of the Publishers you sell to. This is a delicate balancing act, but you can remain 'open' to both sides whilst remaining firmly 'in the middle'. With a 2, you are a decision-maker, but only after careful consideration. Then you may draw upon your instincts to help you make your final choice.

You may feel happiest when problems at home, at work, or 'in politics' (the world at large) are sorted out in a co-operative way. In any disagreement you like to feel that both sides have a chance to win. For example, when your child needs to be picked up from school there is no point arguing with your partner about who will do the rounds. You prefer to make a co-operative decision, even when a compromise is required.

You like to give and receive freely, and to share, and it comes naturally to you. You understand that everything balances itself out and you can never give too much. For example, you understand that by giving you receive anyway, and by receiving you are also learning to give.

With a 2 you enjoy gentle exercise, such as Hatha yoga, meditation, exercising out in the open and, with your moon-like watery Personality, you love water sports too.

CHALLENGES

With a 2 influencing your Personality you may be over-sensitive and emotionally fragile at times. You can be easily squashed by the actions or comments of others.

However, you may also create a lot of this fragility yourself, by sensing things which do not even exist. For example, you may feel that your father-in-law does not like your cooking. However, perhaps this was based on the memory that your own father told you that you had once 'ruined' the roast. Therefore you become vulnerable and emotional about your father-in-law when he may actually love your food. However, these situations are created so that you can get in contact with unexpressed emotion, so that you can 'feel your feelings' and then let them go. Releasing old hurts and emotions can help you to restore balance in your life, and to create more harmonious relationships, particularly with those you love.

Sometimes you may also be 'wobbly' or shaky, and over-emotional. This can result in you expressing your emotions in an unhelpful way; for example, by blaming people and implying that it is their fault that you are feeling that way. Or by trying to make those closest to you feel responsible for your happiness and keeping you feeling OK.

You may also be dependent on others emotionally, and need them to prop you up when you are low. Sometimes you may be intrusive towards your friends and family, and selfishly demand that your needs come first. Eventually you may learn that you need to consider others' feelings and needs too. By learning to give, particularly when you are feeling emotional or vulnerable, or by helping someone around you, you forget that you were angry or sad, and perhaps feel good about helping others instead.

With a 2 influencing your Personality you may be tenacious about others' feelings. You may be manipulative and deliberately hurtful at times, perhaps because you feel hurt yourself and you have not expressed it out. You may also be uncaring and unable to nurture or care for yourself or others.

You may be prone to futile arguments over things that are largely irrelevant to the world at large, and when you do not get your own way you can be very good at sulking. You can even be confrontational; it may seem that you enjoy being at war with another party, always competing against them, and making sure you win. You may cling to your point of view or your feelings about that person. However, occasionally arguments may actually help you to stay healthy, because they air repressed emotions that need to be released; but excessive arguing is exhausting. If you are looking for peace in your life, learning to express and discuss your feelings calmly can really help.

With a 2 influencing your Personality you can be ambivalent about what you want from your life. You can be indecisive for quite a while, not making any conscious choices about what to do. At other times you may prefer others to make decisions for you, because in the end you just can't decide for yourself. For example, you need to choose between going to Australia to live with your partner or staying in your wonderful new job at home. You may find this choice impossible, so you take the advice of your best friend and go abroad. However, things did not work out the way you planned with your partner, and you have lost your job. At this point you may decide to listen to your own advice and make your own decisions next time, although you understand that everything is a learning experience.

You can be manipulative, and put pressure on yourself and others to get what you want. You do this because you feel that this is the only way to get 'heard' or get your needs met. You may also not listen to others or 'hear' them when they are trying to talk to you, particularly when it concerns yourself. By not listening and pressuring yourself and others you add to the disharmony in your life. By listening and expressing your feelings honestly, others will listen to you. Then you won't need to either manipulate or pressure others to get what you want.

With a 2, you may be over-cautious, and tentative about life. You may be fearful of your emotions and instincts, fear your feminine energy (whether you are male or female), or literally be fearful of water. Eventually you may learn that you can turn your fears into your strengths by facing them one by one, and you can also learn to be gentle with yourself along the way.

ROMANCE AND SEX

With a 2 influencing your Personality you are learning to find balance within your life. You do this by experiencing life, and by finding out what does and doesn't work. However, one of the fastest ways you learn about yourself is through relationships with those around you, and particularly with a partner. When you engage in an intimate relationship all your 'imperfections' and buried emotions come streaming out. The closer you get to your partner, the more you learn, and the more you heal those parts of yourself that are preventing you from finding harmony within yourself and in your life.

You are often a caring, sharing human being, who loves to nurture yourself, your partner – and your plants too! You like to lead a peaceful life, and to create harmony with your partner, and to find someone who can also look after you. You are generally placid, except when you are in one of your moods; for example, you may sulk when things don't go your way.

Sometimes you may find that you give too much within your relationship, and you may even smother your partner emotionally. This may be because you have been in relationships before where you did all the taking, and you are now learning about the other extreme. However, giving too much can actually push the other person away. By finding a communicative partner who is able to let you know when you are doing this, you can learn to gently let go of giving too much, and to find a balance between giving and receiving.

With a 2 influencing your relationships, you love to share yourself fully with your partner. You may attract someone who wants to do everything with you: travelling, working, shopping, cleaning and partying. Two is for togetherness and 1 plus 1 equals 2. You may not stop until you find your soul mate; your yearning goes deep, for you may not feel 'complete' until you have found 'that special one' with whom to share your heart and your life.

When you do find that special partner you may be so interdependent that you grow fearful of losing him or her. You may fear losing the security of sharing your life and your most intimate self, and you may get clingy at times. By being aware of your fears and learning to rationalize them and let them go, you can actually let more love in.

You may have a need to be able to relate to your partner emotionally. However, at times you can cut off from your emotions, and not relate on that level in the relationship at all. By sharing your life with someone you are close to, at these times, you can enjoy relating to them on other levels, such as physically, mentally and spiritually.

With a 2 influencing your sex life, emotional security is one of the most important ingredients in this area. You may need a lot of kisses and cuddles, and reassurance from your partner to help allay your fears. However, when you do find a considerate partner, or your soul mate, you can reach a blissful state of contentment. Love and sex becomes balanced as one.

PHYSICAL APPEARANCE

With a 2 influencing your looks you may have a light to medium skin tone, a small nose, and generally look soft, rounded, or fleshy, with a caring, nurturing look in your eyes. Your outstanding features may be your round moon-like face (the moon is connected to the emotions) and soft watery eyes.

CHILDHOOD EXPERIENCES

With a 2 influencing your childhood you may have been strongly influenced by or dependent on your mother. This is because you were, and are, needing to learn about caring, nurturing, feelings and your instincts. (If your mother had stronger masculine energy, then you might have related to the feminine energies with your father instead.) However, you may have adopted strong, mothering instincts from the moment you were born, in which case you may have clashed with your mother or female relatives, and found challenges with them instead.

You may have been a placid child in general, who took life in your stride, but with a tendency to be over-sensitive, and occasionally sulky. Perhaps you enjoyed painting and swimming, or playing quietly with your friends. You probably chose your friends carefully, and you always liked to have one 'best mate'.

With a 2, you may have been very competitive with your brothers, and sisters, particularly for your mother's attention, and for better marks at school. You may also have been ambidextrous, with the ability to write and create with both hands equally, so that you could learn to choose.

Children with a 2 often need to feel like they have choices. You can encourage them to make decisions about what they want to wear, or do (within reason). You need to really listen to these children when they talk about their feelings and instincts, so that they learn to feel safe with them too.

WELL-BEING

With a 2 influencing your health, you may be prone to hormonal imbalances, such as PMT. You may also have a tendency to suffer from insomnia, bronchitis, sinusitis, asthma or eczema, or break out in skin rashes.

CAREER CHOICE

With a 2 influencing your career you may work as a therapist or a counsellor; you enjoy listening to people talk about their problems and their feelings, and you are able to take an unbiased view. You may also work in one of the caring professions, as a social worker, doctor or nurse, or you may be a yoga teacher.

You might also take up a career where you are able to negotiate; as an agent, property negotiator, personnel officer, or in business negotiating deals of any kind. You may also choose a career as a diplomat, bookkeeper, lawyer or mediator.

FAMOUS CHARACTER ANALYSIS
Mahatma Gandhi Born 2 October 1869

Mahatma Gandhi was a 'simple' man, who enjoyed a long and loving relationship with his wife and his closest friends. He was a mediator, a diplomat, a peacemaker and a lawyer, who spent his life relating to people and trying to co-operate with them in a peaceful way. Indeed, Gandhi spent most of his life trying to bring peace and harmony to others' lives too.

With a 2, Gandhi was clearly able to see both sides of an argument, but he was not always diplomatic with his words or in his approach. Sometimes when he was challenged he rose to the occasion and replied with spectacular emotional outbursts. However, he was generally calm and collected, even in the face of adversity.

Gandhi could really 'feel' and 'sense' the pain and suffering of others. He was deeply caring, and even when he was being deliberately confrontational he did it in a giving, caring and often calculated way, to provoke a reaction.

Mahatma Gandhi died on 30 January 1948; he was shot. The whole date adds up to an 8, which is a number strongly associated with karma and rebirth. The day was the 30th or 3, which highlights stillness, and beingness. After his death his family reported that there was a 'strangeness about him that day'. Perhaps he was at peace and complete with his life.

NUMBER
3
PERSONALITY

GENERAL TRENDS FOR NUMBER 3 PERSONALITY

With a 3 influencing your Personality you have the gift of fun and a deepest yearning to express yourself in whatever way you can: by using your body, such as sexually, or through verbal communication, or by using your hands. You may have a particular gift involving your hands, such as painting, cooking, needlework, gardening, writing, massage or healing.

You like to express yourself verbally, and there is no better way of doing this than a night out with your friends, or by getting together in some work or social gathering. You talk at great speed – in fact some people say that you never stop! However, it's a wonderful way to let yourself go, and you are generally a bubbly, outgoing and extrovert person, whose confidence really shines through.

With a 3, you have a mischievous sense of fun and you love to play the odd practical joke on an unsuspecting audience, and you are able to laugh when they do the same to you. Life is for living, and you don't like to take anything too seriously; you simply want to have a good time. You also possess a wicked sense of humour and you love to be naughty at times. You like to clown around; entertaining others is a natural part of your make-up. People find you amusing and you may find yourself surrounded by a crowd wherever you go; you are really able to uplift others and to bring laughter and joy into their lives. Whenever you are 'down' your sense of humour really helps to get you through.

You throw yourself fully into everything, rather than tentatively feeling your way. Your motto could easily be, 'If you're going to get wet, you might as well throw yourself in at the deep end, and then you'll learn how to swim, fast.' For example, you may be working full-time, party five nights of the week, take a night school course on one other night, do art classes and travel at weekends, whilst being in a full-time relationship too. You are also capable of focusing your attention on many different things at one time: for example, you may be baking a cake, talking to your friend on the telephone, and listening to the radio all at once!

You are a relaxed kind of person, and you take life in your stride. You may believe that life works itself out in its own way, and that worrying is a waste of time when you could be having fun. You tend to let worries go, and if you do worry it's often not for long, because you will soon find something else to focus on. You are generally an optimistic person and a positive thinker and you always manage to find something to smile at, or to bring you joy. You like to think that life can 'only get better'.

With a 3 influencing your Personality your life and any decision-making just seem to flow. You may often find yourself with many choices because you create so many opportunities. For example, you could go off to work in Japan, stay in America to study, go and settle down in France. However, in your life the 'right' decision seems to be reached without much direct input from yourself. You may find the college you wanted to go to in America is full, and that the job you applied for in Japan requires that you speak Japanese – and you can't. It may also be that your relationship changes too. Whatever, life sorts it all out for you.

You may be an adaptable person and you happily go along with any changes in your situation. Being flexible means that you can be spontaneous and so get the most enjoyment out of your life. It also gives you the freedom to be able to explore all the possibilities open to you. With a 3, you love to relish every positive experience, and even the not-so-positive ones; you realize that you can learn from these too.

You are someone who can create an abundance of everything in your life: happiness, loving relationships, work, and opportunities for growth. You inspire others with your carefree attitude and generosity. You may also enjoy travel, mysticism and religion, and you might be psychic too. You love any sporting activity, particularly cycling and athletics. You are an active person, and your sense of freedom may take you hitch-hiking around the world, with your rucksack on your back and not a care in sight. You may also enjoy camping or sleeping 'rough' – you are happy to get your hands dirty – and motor cycling.

CHALLENGES

With a 3 influencing your Personality you are a very active person, but you may do too much at times. For example, you may overwork and scatter your energies by focusing on too many things at once. Perhaps you over-exercise and tire yourself out, or overdo communicating so that your voice becomes louder and louder, which people notice. You tend to throw yourself into life but sometimes you can go over the top and take on too much. However, life usually forces you to stop at some point, and helps you to think of ways which may help you to handle situations or slow things down. Perhaps life has already given you clues as to how you can thoroughly enjoy yourself without overdoing it, for example, by giving yourself some boundaries to let you (and others) know when enough is enough may also help.

You may have scattered your energy over so many different areas of your life that you cannot concentrate on any of them. For example, you may stretch yourself between work projects, social activities, lovers, family or friends! However, by realizing that you cannot give to everything and everyone all of the time, you can let go of fretting and do what you *can* do. Some days, for example, you may need to focus more attention on your partner or children; on another day perhaps you need to concentrate on writing an urgent business report. By being adaptable to the ever-changing demands in your life you can learn to manage your energy, and draw it in when it is needed, rather than trying to please the whole world at once.

With a 3 influencing your Personality you are laid back and 'fancy free'. However, you are so relaxed sometimes that you let life slip through your fingers whilst you are lazing cosily on the couch. When under the challenging influence of a 3, you may find that experiences pass you by because you just can't be bothered to make the required effort at the right time. For example, you have been out at a fantastic party until the early hours of the morning – you are an artist, and your time is your own. At 9am the telephone rings with an offer of a meeting with a new art gallery that wants to exhibit your work – wonderful! However, you say you are busy, and you slide back to bed. Some opportunities may never return; eventually you may realize that if you want your life to 'work' you must make the most of every opportunity as and when it arises.

You may be cynical at times, and jaded by life's experiences; perhaps you have tried so many different things, yet nothing seemed to really work out. You may criticize yourself (which sometimes makes you your own worst enemy), and you can constantly criticize others too. Perhaps you find fault with the things that you do, or everywhere you go; at these times you are no fun to be with. However, you have that lovely relaxed and sunny nature which will eventually help you to see the brighter side to life, and which will restore your natural good humour.

With a 3, you may also have an abundant sense of humour which inspires others. However, you can also be sarcastic and use your humour in a nasty way, such as by ridiculing people and making them the focus of your jokes, or by making them look foolish. However, you may soon realize that by using others unfairly for your enjoyment, *you* are the one who ends up looking foolish.

With a 3, you may be a casual person who loves to chat and gossip with anyone and everyone. However, sometimes you may be so casual that you let secrets slip out. You may not always do this deliberately, but sometimes you speak so fast that you lose control of what you are saying. At other times you can be quite venomous, and you enjoy joining in superficial gossip about others. However, gossip has a habit of getting back to the subject of your tittle-tattle, and he or she may end up as a foe. By finding time to talk positively about the good things in life you are contributing towards making others happy, and can keep yourself happy too.

Sometimes you may be unable to express yourself, and feel trapped. By learning to express and enjoy yourself in one area of your life, you can learn to open up to other areas of expression too. For example, if you can express yourself at home with your partner then you may find it easier to say what you really feel at work too. One simple action of expression and creativity leads to the next, which may lead you to abundance in your life.

ROMANCE AND SEX

With a 3 influencing your love life you are a bubbly and 'light' person, full of life and joy. You are also a party animal, who loves social chat and fun. Therefore it may be important for you to attract a partner who loves social gatherings and enjoys going out with the 'crowd'. However, you can be a chatterbox so your partner may need either to be good at listening or to have a strong character with just as much to say as you!

You are usually outgoing and confident, and you have a brilliant sense of humour which draws in many potential partners. You may even double-book your 'dates' sometimes as you struggle to fit them all in. However, on a first date you may try a little too hard to impress your partner with a joke too many; sometimes you want just a little too much attention from him/her. However, you enjoy your date anyway, and you remember not to take life too seriously if it doesn't work out.

With a 3, you can be superficial and prefer not to go in too deep, particularly where your emotions are concerned. Sometimes you may be attracted to a partner who can entertain you, and who looks really neat. This may be great for a first date. However, looks aren't everything and you may be annoyed to discover that the 'perfect creation' didn't quite match up to your expectations. You learn to look a little deeper next time you're choosing a mate.

There is a part of you which likes to flit from partner to partner, trying out different experiences whilst enjoying your freedom. You are often changeable about whom you like, and even when you do decide on 'the one', you may still subconsciously keep your eyes open for other experiences. However, once you do make a commitment in a relationship it may well be with someone who allows you your freedom and who doesn't cling. You may find a partner who is independent and particularly attractive. However, despite the opportunistic influences of a 3, once you have fallen in love or made a commitment you may well find that you do not feel like straying to anyone else, whomever you choose as your partner.

You may like to feel physically close to your partner, when you are standing together you link hands, and when you pass each other you may embrace or offer a kiss. A chance for this kind of loving exchange is rarely missed. You may also love to massage each other with soothing and sensual oils. You may feel instinctually and mutually drawn towards each other.

With a 3 influencing your sex life, you are free with your love and uninhibited about your body, and you like to express yourself sexually in as many different ways as you can. You love sex, and the more you can get the better. At times you may also feel a strong spiritual connection and simply enjoy 'being' with your partner instead of having to 'do' anything, in or out of bed.

PHYSICAL APPEARANCE

With a 3 influencing your looks, you may be of small build, and very muscular, which gives you a sporty look. You may have a short (or upturned) nose, and a very large mouth, or smile, which may be one of your outstanding features.

CHILDHOOD EXPERIENCES

With a 3 you may have travelled around a lot, with or without your parents, and so you may have experience an unsettled childhood. Perhaps you changed schools often. Moving around may have helped you to learn to make friends quickly and easily, and to make the most out of the opportunities that came your way. However, whether you lived in a 'permanent' place or not, your confidence will have been boosted by having a wealth of experiences to choose from, and tales of your journeys.

Perhaps socializing played a large part of life from the day you were born. Perhaps your parents loved to throw dinner parties for your extended family and friends. It is also possible that your grandparents or older relatives were involved in helping to bring you up.

With a 3, you may have spent hours making things with your hands; you were probably brilliantly creative. You may have long periods lost in your self-expression. You were usually a happy child; there was always masses for you to do, as well as a lot of love and affection.

Children with a 3 may need discipline to help bring their sometimes scattered energies down to earth; otherwise they tend to shoot off at different tangents, and accomplish little. Regular routine may also help them to feel settled in themselves. They may find that discipline harnesses their creativity too.

WELL-BEING

With a 3 influencing your health you may be prone to a dry or hoarse throat (from talking too much), or from sexual diseases from careless living. You may also suffer from muscular aches and pains, or circulatory problems.

CAREER CHOICE

With a 3 influencing your career, you may enjoy working in a job where you can express yourself and communicate with others. You may become an artist, writer, entertainer, mime artist, or comedien/ne, or you may work in the entertainment industry. You may become a gymnast or actor, or work as a receptionist or airline steward/ess.

Perhaps you may use your hands in your work: as a physiotherapist or massage therapist, gardener, creative cook or chef. With a 3 you usually love your freedom, and you may willingly work for any company where there is the chance to travel: as a courier, tour representative, travel consultant, au pair, and so on.

FAMOUS CHARACTER ANALYSIS
Mary Shelley Born 3 August 1797

Mary Shelley was the wife of Percy Bysshe Shelley, and was best known as the writer of the classic horror novel, *Frankenstein*, the story of a man-made monster. She was psychic, and very interested in mysticism, not least because her husband was prone to outer-worldly phenomena and delusions. However, *Frankenstein* revealed the depth of her sensitivity. For little did she know that a few centuries later, man would be transplanting internal organs, growing live human tissue, and inseminating one human life into another.

With a 3, Mary's gift was her writing; she kept a journal which was almost religiously filled in every day. In it she often related her deepest feelings, told stories of her travels, or described social gatherings, like visits to the theatre, art shows or dinner parties. Mary loved social occasions; she was very bright, witty and charming, and she thrived on stimulating conversation with those who were attracted to her.

Mary Shelley died on 1 February 1851, having being inspired to explore the depths of her emotions with her husband, and having completing *Frankenstein*. The whole date adds up to a 9, so perhaps she felt it was time for her to close the chapter, and to look for something new. The number 9 is for endings and new beginnings, and the 1st (the day she died) perhaps confirms that she was quite ready to move on.

4

GENERAL TRENDS FOR NUMBER 4 PERSONALITY

With a 4 influencing your Personality you have a gift of determination, and a deepest yearning to feel special. This may be because most of the time you feel 'ordinary', but even feeling 'special' can be ordinary, and everyone is special in their own way. However, life is basically ordinary, and you really connect to the fact that all human beings have the same basic needs to survive: food, water, clothes, shelter, love and sex. Everything else is simply a gift: lots of money, holidays, travel, expensive clothes, a busy social life, and so on. Feeling ordinary may remind you that there is no escape from the monotony of routine, and when it comes to your basic needs each day is more or less the same. You enjoy routine, and you do feel special sometimes.

However, you are working very strongly with things relating to practical issues, your physical reality and your physical body. So learning how to survive is very important to you, and you may work very hard to make sure that all your physical needs are met, and to take responsibility for this. For example, you might work 12 hours a day or work at weekends if it means that you will have more money in the bank, which can contribute to your feeling of security. If you own a home, you see no reason why anybody else 'should' pay your mortgage for you, because it is your responsibility and you are capable of providing for yourself.

With a 4 you like to set realistic goals which you know you can achieve, and you may be prepared to endure many uncomfortable circumstances in order to realize them. For example, you may have a goal of a holiday at the end of the year, in exotic Hawaii, with your partner. You may have barely enough to eat as you put money aside each week. However, you may plod on and on because you know that 'special' holiday at the end of all your hard saving can make it even more worthwhile. You may even spend a whole lifetime working towards a single goal.

Generally you like and need stability. Therefore you may feel more stable in a long-term relationship, settling in the same home for a long time, or working in the same field (or for the same company) for many, many years. You enjoy steadiness and the security of knowing at least a little of what each day may bring. For example, you may like to know that the newspaper is always delivered at the same time each morning, or that the sales person in your corner shop will always be there to greet you with a smile, or that you have a steady income. With a 4, you are a dependable person, but you do not like to rely on anyone else to fulfil your needs.

You are a loyal person and will always endeavour to keep your word. You may have known some of your friends for a lifetime, and you may stick with them through 'thick and thin', and do anything you possibly can to help them. However, you probably take your time getting to know new people, and it may take you a while before you feel safe with them.

With a 4 influencing your Personality you may be a systematic person and love nothing better than using your organizational skills to sort things out, and with great efficiency, so that you know exactly what and where they are. You can help to organize your home, your office or even a whole company if need be; you can help improve others' lives too. Being organized helps life to run more smoothly, or so you believe. You may also like to structure your day (or your life), and break it down into little manageable chunks. Structure and boundaries are very important to you because they help you to feel safe, knowing that everything is in its place.

You are generally a down-to-earth and practical person, and this can help you to materialize your needs, because being 'grounded' means that you have more energy to give to your life. For example, you may be able to devote more energy to your creative skills and earn lots of money from this gift.

With a 4, you may literally love to keep in touch with the earth, by walking, hiking, jogging, or by playing any kind of outdoor sport.

CHALLENGES

With a 4 influencing your Personality you may at times be prone to melancholia because you simply cannot face the physical reality of having to survive. This may not necessarily be because you have no work, little money or no home to go to, but because taking responsibility for yourself day in and day out feels like too much of a strain. However, you learn by your experiences and not every day is exactly the same. When you can accept responsibility for your own survival, you can also accept responsibility for all the good things that come your way.

You may feel that you need material possessions to increase your security. You may always be looking for more, or your may look to others who can 'make' you feel secure. For example, you may own a home with your partner, but you want to provide a second home to build even more security around you. However, neither a person nor a possession can give you security; no matter how much money you have or how many homes you own, you may never feel totally secure, because the feeling comes from deep within. For example, it is possible to feel safe and secure within only a few material possessions. However, material possession can be useful, and it's great for you to enjoy them in whatever way you can, including sharing them with others.

With a 4 you may see life as hard, and you may be durable and cling to a gruelling routine. You may plod on rigidly, with each day mirroring the last, and with no real goals to aim for except getting on with your physical survival. Perhaps you also dislike routine and try to break out of the monotony by being lazy, or creating some drama which may liven up the day. However, routines can help to make your life easier by giving some structure to your day, but they are only guidelines, which can always be changed.

You are generally a grounded person, but without structure to give you some boundaries you may accomplish little. This may be because at times you are lazy and resist life, and you may need some discipline to help you move on. For example, you may be given a chance to travel abroad, to use your writing skills by being an overseas reporter for a magazine. However, you need to submit a feature first, and, even though you really want the post, you may not discipline yourself enough to get the feature written in time for their deadline, so the opportunity passes you by. You may learn from this mistake, however, and in future learn to be realistic, and practical about what you have to do to achieve your dreams.

Sometimes you may not be very clear about setting or expressing your own personal boundaries, and people may 'walk all over you' by either ignoring your needs or simply not knowing what they were. For example, you may need to leave work at 6pm, but only explain to your boss that you 'need to leave early today', as he ignores you by calling a meeting at five minutes to six. Situations like this – in your relationships, with friends or work colleagues – may continue until you are clear about your own boundaries and can express them to others. It can also help you when other people are clear about their boundaries, so that you know where you stand.

Life may seem like a constant struggle, and you may add to your problems by resisting dealing with the challenges that come your way. You may sometimes even ignore problems completely because you are too fearful of change. However, 'burying your head in the sand' may only offer temporary relief, and even though life tends to work itself out, situations still need to be faced. By taking responsibility for your own life you are helping to make things easier by working with the changes, instead of against them. By learning to accept change, life may eventually become less of a struggle.

With a 4, you may like to structure your life, but you may also try to structure others in your mind, by 'labelling' them, and putting them into categories. For example, your husband may be labelled 'provider' because he is a man! Or the receptionist may be labelled 'superior' because he or she is in command. However, people have a habit of breaking your expectations of them. For example, your husband may not at times provide, and the reception-ist may be so disorganized that someone has to 'take command' of him or her from time to time. Life is organic, and people are always changing and growing.

ROMANCE AND SEX

With a 4 influencing your love life, you may be someone who needs commitment within your relationship in order for you to feel secure, and so finding a partner who is happy to commit to being with you becomes essential. You may also enjoy playing around at times, and having fun and games. But you are probably much more interested in a long-term relationship, particularly if your partner is materially secure already. You may need to know that your material needs are going to be safely met. You may be only too willing to do the same for your partner too.

You have a practical streak and you may resist spending money on things like romantic meals with your partner, or chocolate and flowers, although you are happy to on 'special' occasions. At times you may even splash out on a trip to the hairdressers or a beauty parlour, to liven you up and make you feel extra special. With a 4, you may like a partner who is practical too, or at least someone you can trust not to blow all the money in your joint account (if you have one!). However, on occasion you can also be irresponsible too.

In a relationship looks may not be the most important issue on your agenda (although they help!). Finding a partner with whom you can be good friends may be much more important to you than sex. You are a loyal person; even during times of struggle you are likely to invest a lot of effort to make the most of your relationship, and be determined for it to work out.

With a 4 influencing your Personality, you may be a home-maker, and you may enjoy organizing your home (and your family) each day. Perhaps your partner relies on you to organize his or her social life, and other essentials too. However, it is important for you to know each other's boundaries in this respect to help you maintain a happy 'working' relationship. For example, your partner may like you to arrange his or her dental appointment, but organizing his or her lunch appointments at work may be going too far. Similarly you may be asked to do something you simply cannot do.

Generally you enjoy the stability of a regular partner, and you may enjoy the relationship even more, and feel settled within it, when it falls into a simple routine. For example, you may play tennis together on Sundays, go out for dinner on Wednesdays, or rent a DVD at least once a week. Routine may help to give you stability.

With a 4 influencing your sex life, you are an earthy person who likes to get physical by adding a touch of passion to your relationship. Friendship is important here though, and unless you are trying to create new life you may see little need to overdo the time spent entwined in sex. However, you like to be creative, and you enjoy the physical act of making love.

PHYSICAL APPEARANCE

With a 4 influencing your looks you may have heavy eyebrows, small, narrow eyes with heavy lids, and wide cheekbones with an oblong face, be dark-skinned, and you may have a lisp, or stutter. You may also be stocky. Your outstanding feature are your 'staring' eyes, which often attract people's attention.

CHILDHOOD EXPERIENCES

With a 4 influence you may have been a child who had a lot of common sense and who rarely got into trouble. For example, you may have always done your homework, taken extra care when you were crossing roads, and walked along pavements, instead of running, in the ice and snow. You were probably a practical and helpful child too, who happily took part in chores around the home. You may have also possessed an inbuilt sense of responsibility from a very early age, and you may have always been able to look after yourself (in your own way). You may have also felt pressure from your parents to take on more responsibilities sometimes, too.

However, you may have 'broken out' at times, with a deliberate fit of irresponsibility, like 'forgetting' to pick up the shopping on the way back from school. Like any child you could be naughty, and you usually did naughty things to test your parents' boundaries, to see just how far you could go.

With a 4, you may have been prone to bouts of insecurity; perhaps you were hesitant in your actions, and you may have stuttered sometimes. You were probably a hard worker at school who applied yourself towards your goals in a methodical manner. Perhaps you were lazy, and content to plod on with a semi-interested attitude towards school or life in general.

Children with a 4 often need to feel safe and secure, and it may help to give them constructive tasks every day to make them feel like they are contributing towards their security: helping to make family meals, or earning pocket money to put towards buying their own toys or clothes, and so on.

WELL-BEING

With a 4 influencing your health you may be prone to melancholia, or agoraphobia, hip or knee problems, or have trouble with your legs.

CAREER CHOICE

With a 4 influencing your career, you may enjoy doing work where you can build things: helping a company to grow, as a builder, or working in real estate. You may also work with the land, as a farmer. You may even take up a career as a feng shui consultant, working with material things, which also incorporates using your organizational skills.

You may also take up a career as a banker, an accountant, or another profession in the field of finance. You also have a creative side to your Personality so working as a fashion designer, writer or artist, may also appeal. Whichever career you choose, you are likely to commit to it long term.

FAMOUS CHARACTER ANALYSIS
Percy Bysshe Shelley Born 4 August 1792

Shelly is a famous English romantic poet who was renowned for writing extremely long poems, which covered topics such as the political and spiritual problems of the age in which he lived. They were anything but 'ordinary', and he was not respected by his contemporaries for his radical views.

Shelley often found reality hard, and he escaped by venturing into the world of visions and delusions, and was generally unsettled and disturbed. He would often sleepwalk, and he found walking in the gardens helped bring him back down to earth.

He found some security in his wife Mary, who often looked after and protected him, and took responsibility for him, as if he was a child. She often brought him back to 'safety' when she found him sleepwalking, or in a trance. Indeed marriage was one the few 'ordinary' things Shelley did. He and Mary loved to visit art galleries, theatres, museums, and they also wrote together in the same journal.

Percy Shelley died on 8 July 1822, at the age of 29; he drowned at sea. The whole date adds up to a 28 or 1, so perhaps he was searching for something new in his life. The day was an 8, which also indicates that he was cutting the ties with his past, so fulfilling his karma.

NUMBER
5
PERSONALITY

GENERAL TRENDS FOR NUMBER 5 PERSONALITY

With a 5 influencing your Personality you have the gift of clarity, and a deepest yearning to be able to communicate with others. When you communicate it helps you to feel connected to people, particularly when it concerns something important to you, or some things which you can all relate to. Communicating is what helps to make the 'world go round', and you may like to connect with different people from all over the world. You love to travel, and this brings you in contact with many different cultures and lifestyles. You may also work for a company where you meet all kinds of different people. Or you may simply like to feel in touch with the world by listening to news bulletins on the television or radio.

You may like to communicate verbally with people. However, most communication takes place through your 'body language'; even when you are with people who do not speak 'your language', you can still communicate clearly with each other, without needing to be masters in sign language. You may also communicate through telepathy, because you usually have crystal-clear thoughts which you are able to project out for others to pick up. When people are thinking about you, or sending you a message, you may be able to clearly 'pick up' their thoughts too. However, you may also like to communicate with others by using your computer to send and receive information from all around the world.

With a 5 you are a fun- and party-loving individual, and you seek mental stimulation in particular. You may do this by listening to lectures on interesting subjects, or by studying books, or taking courses in further education, or learning from your travel experiences. You have a bright mind and you are a quick thinker; you may often flit from one subject to another whilst talking with others. You may jump from one thing to the next in your life, too, in order to experience as much as you possibly can.

You may have a scientific mind, in that you like to seek out the concrete facts. For example, when somebody tells you that you have just won a competition, you may not believe them until the prize is actually in your hand. You are someone who likes to have scientific 'proof' that things work. Perhaps you may not take a painkiller until you have read in a medical journal that it has been proven to be effective. With a 5, you may also like to 'pull things apart' to see exactly how they operate; in all aspects of your life you like to find out what makes people 'tick'. You like to experiment, and you leave 'no stone unturned' in your pursuit of knowledge and information about how exactly life works.

You radiate magnetism, and others are often mesmerized by your charms. Many different types of people are attracted to you because you are so vivacious. People find your company exciting, with your bright conversation, your raunchy sense of humour, and the fascinating stories from your journeys around the world. However, you too are fascinated by people, and feel that life is simply one big and wonderful adventure, to be fully explored.

You may be a spontaneous person, with a natural curiosity that takes you out into the world of experience. You may love shopping, your curiosity takes you from one shop to the next, and you never know what you might see or buy on your trips; it's a real adventure. You may like to investigate old curiosity shops in search of unusual gifts for your friends.

With a 5 influencing your Personality, you are committed to living your life to the full. You may be very clear about what it is that you want. You are also a positive thinker, with a 'get up and go' attitude that helps you to materialize your goals.

You love exercise, and may take up sports that can boost your adrenalin and give you a 'thrill': riding, paragliding, white-water rafting, rock climbing, or sailing. You may even enjoy bungee jumping, For relaxation, you prabably prefer tennis, hiking or walking.

CHALLENGES

With a 5 influencing your Personality you may be prone to restlessness at times, as you flit from one thing to the next without fully experiencing the delights of anything you do. You may feel that there are so many things you want to explore in life that you are unable to rest anywhere. However, you can use your great clarity of thought, and your positive mind, to help you decide on what things you may like and need to spend your time on, so that you can get the most out of your life.

Sometimes you may dislike getting too deeply involved with anything, and you may struggle to escape from your commitments. For example, you may have taken on a long-term project at work, which seems to be going on for ever. You may feel intense frustration at being tied down because it is preventing you from doing other things. You may get bored, lose your concentration, and transgress easily in your communications with others. Perhaps you may even try to run away, by suddenly leaving your job (in an extreme case). However, by committing to one person, or thing, you actually learn more about life, because you are experiencing each thing to the full. When you are complete with one thing, you can feel fulfilled and then move on to the next experience.

Sometimes, it can be a challenge for you to wrench yourself away from something you have become involved with, whether it is a positive situation or not. For example, you may have got too deeply caught up in a situation at work, and you may feel that you have very little energy left for anything else. You may not even be aware that the situation is taking so much out of your energy and your life. However, life has a way of moving things along, and sometimes throws up unexpected events to bring in positive change. For example, you may suddenly get made redundant, or need to move home, which may mean moving jobs too.

At times you may restrict yourself, and back yourself into a corner, because you fear change or are scared to really 'live'. Perhaps you are frightened by your freedom of choice; there are so many things you 'should' do with your life. When you restrict yourself to one thing you may be missing many other wonderful opportunities. Sometimes, by taking risks and trying new things, no matter how 'small' they are, you are actually saying you are open to life, and you can let more energy in. By being open you attract more positive people and situations as your natural magnetism begins to shine through.

You may be very changeable at times, and you may be unable to make up your mind about anything. You may switch from liking broccoli to hating it and back again all in a day. This can make you unreliable, particularly when people are trying to make arrangements with you. For example, trying to pin you down to a time to meet may be almost impossible, and even when you do make a time, you may alter it. You may change your clothes often too. Perhaps even your friends are rotated, so that you get to see different people, instead of getting stuck with one crowd, and you prefer spontaneity. For example, you may actually get more done by making plans on the spur of the moment than by making arrangements which might fall through.

With a 5 influencing your Personality you can be unable to communicate with others at times. Perhaps this is because you feel so confused that you simply don't know what to think, let alone talk about, or because you are a thinker and have merely got 'lost' in your mind. However, out of confusion comes clarity, and with that an ability to know what and how you wish to communicate with others.

Sometimes you may desperately seek new stimulation to help relieve your boredom. You may be attracted or get addicted to outer 'remedies' to help you through, like sex, alcohol, chocolate and food. You may even get addicted to keep fit, vitamins or complementary therapies. These may pacify you for a while, but you may need to go 'inside your mind' and become clear about what it is you really need in your life. Perhaps then you can learn to break through your negative beliefs about how life 'should' be.

ROMANCE AND SEX

With a 5 influencing your relationships, finding a partner with whom you can communicate may be very important, and you will probably want to know that they can communicate openly with you too. For example, when you come home at the end of a day's adventure in life, you may be excited to let your partner know exactly what you have been doing, and to find out about their day too. So a partner who can listen to you and who has something interesting to say may be essential.

You may be attracted to a partner who has really 'lived' and who can share their experiences with you. Sometimes, you may even choose to study a subject which your partner is interested in, so that you can have lengthy discussions about it. Perhaps you may seek a partner who is intelligent, or who can stimulate your mind with facts and figures and who can help you to work life out too.

With a 5 influencing your Personality, you love adventure and you may seek a partner who also shares your zest for life; someone who loves to go skiing down steep slippery slopes, or wants to travel around the world with you, or who loves to 'dance the night away'.

You are also a 'people person', and you love arranging outings and parties with your friends and your partner. You may have such a diversity of interests that you need to organize lots of events for different types of friends. For example, soirées for your music friends, lunches for your work friends, educational trips for your study group friends, and all kinds of things for your partner's friends. You are such a highly magnetic and vivacious person that you attract many admirers, and your parties may be full of respondents all waiting for you!

Sometimes you can be very restless, so you may need a partner who is down to earth and who can ground some of your unexpressed energy. Perhaps you even need someone who can 'pin you down' and keep you stimulated enough to stay around. However, you love to be a bit risqué, and even when you are in a committed relationship you enjoy having fun and flirting with whoever's around.

With a 5 influencing your love life you can be 'tricky' in relationships because you are so changeable, and so your partner may never actually know what you are thinking, what you are going to do next, or never really know who you are. However, this may only add to the excitement of the relationship for some people, because he or she likes life to be unpredictable and spontaneous.

With a 5 influencing your sex life you may be fascinated by a partner who can get your adrenalin going in hot, steamy and adventurous sex, whilst you add to the foreplay by slipping in as many 'dirty' jokes as possible. You are a pleasure seeker, and sex is one of the most wonderful ways in which you indulge yourself (and your partner).

PHYSICAL APPEARANCE

With a 5 influencing your looks, you may have prominent and high cheekbones, large bulging eyes, a small upturned nose, curvaceous lips, a long neck, and speak with a high-pitched or husky voice. Your outstanding feature may be your 'rugged' appearance as you tend to look weather-worn from being in the open air so much.

CHILDHOOD EXPERIENCES

With a 5 influencing your childhood you may have experienced situations in your youth where your commitment to carry on with your life was tested. For example, you may have experienced losing a parent, or other unexpected and difficult events that tested you.

With a 5, your love of life and your positive attitude probably helped to see you through. It may have encouraged you to dig even deeper into your life and get on with things, rather than bury yourself or run away. Your childhood commitments may have meant: keeping on with your school work, doing chores at home, keeping your friends (instead of replacing them with new ones every five minutes), or fetching groceries, and so on.

Perhaps you were a restless child who was always diverting your attentions from one subject (or person) to another. You were probably always trying out new adventures, like climbing trees, or riding your bicycle without hands, or daring yourself and your friends to do unmentionable things. You probably had some accidents in your quest for adventure; perhaps life was a 'nightmare' for your family. Adventure may also have meant travelling into your mind and exploring your thoughts; perhaps you preferred to live your life this way.

Children with a 5 often ask, 'How?', 'Where?', 'What?' and 'Why?', so providing them with as much factual information as possible can really help to satisfy their curiosity, and also teach them about life; for example, by providing them with books, videos or cassettes, or by stimulating them by passing on facts you have learned from your own experiences.

WELL-BEING

With a 5 influencing your health you may be prone to problems arising from all types of addictions. As a result you may be more susceptible to catching colds and infections. You may also be prone to throat problems or imbalances with your metabolism.

CAREER CHOICE

With a 5 influencing your career, you may choose something in the communications field, and work in public relations as a salesperson, marketing or advertising executive, journalist, travel representative, or with computers. You may also use your clarity to instruct others, as an information officer or teacher.

You may also work as a detective, where you can stimulate your mind by working out the facts about 'Who dunnit'! You may go freelance and enjoy the freedom to work your own hours and take on temporary assignments in your chosen field. With a 5, you may also work as a scientist, psychologist, sign language or body language expert – or you may be a numerologist!

FAMOUS CHARACTER ANALYSIS
Freddie Mercury Born 5 September 1946

Freddie Mercury was the famous songwriter and singer with the rock group Queen, and he was also one of the most dynamic popular entertainers of the 20th century. He had an extrovert and extremely magnetic persona, which worked well with Queen's music, and attracted great attention from all over the world.

He was renowned for his body language, or the unusual positions he often stood in whilst performing. It must have been a thrill to have been on stage and been able to communicate with people in that way. Freddie was a brilliant communicator, and part of the group's huge success was accredited to his lyrics which often accurately identified the spirit of the masses. A large proportion of the band's music was dance music, and movement and dance were typical qualities of the 5, which Freddie explored to the fullest extent.

With a 5, Freddie had a zest for life, and no doubt did see life as one great adventure. He lived his life to the full, travelling all over the world, and being stimulated by many different types of people along the way.

Freddie Mercury died on 24 November 1991, having led an action-packed and full life. The whole date adds up to a 1, so perhaps Freddie was seeking a new direction at the time. The day was a 24 or 6, so perhaps his commitment and service to planet earth was complete on the day he died.

NUMBER
6
PERSONALITY

GENERAL TRENDS FOR NUMBER 6 PERSONALITY

With a 6 influencing your Personality you have a gift of perception and the deepest yearning to feel a part of the 'whole': you like to feel that you belong, and that you know your place within the group. For example, you may be playing the part of the mother in your family group, and like to know that your husband – the father – and your children are all playing their parts too: everyone has an equally important role. You may be part of many groups: work groups, social groups, extended family groups, a group member of your local town or village, country group and, indeed, a part of the whole world group on planet earth. You may more identify yourself as part of a group rather than as an individual (although you obviously have your own identity too).

You may be very good at 'seeing' what the whole group needs – you are very perceptive, and you have a 'sixth sense' which you can use to great advantage. You also have a gift to be able to see the whole picture, and can put everyone else 'in the picture' too. For example, you may instinctively feel that your departmental group at work needs to be more aware of the needs of another group within the company. You may call for a meeting to make everyone aware of the situation, and to see what your group can do. Similarly, if you feel that one family member is not contributing towards the well-being of your whole family, or neglecting their family responsibilities, then the family group may sit down together to try to find a resolution.

You also have a keen sense of justice and you want to make sure that everyone is 'heard', and that everyone's needs are met. You are generally very good at listening to people, and you have a compassionate attitude. You are usually not someone who blames others, but you are usually willing to look at the part you have played within the group to create a situation, too.

With a 6 you may be happiest when you are working things out with others rather than on your own. You may have a high awareness for family values, and when you have personal problems you may be more likely to turn to your family for help and support, rather than to your partner or friends. However, you are also aware of learning to sort our your own problems and how to look after yourself, and you realize that you won't be able to assist others if you can't handle yourself.

With a 6 influencing your Personality you are a communitarian, and you may even take up a career where you can help and serve your local community or, on a larger scale, be a communitarian for the world. You are one of life's 'little helpers', and you often show great devotion to 'your' causes, in whatever area of your life.

Perhaps you are a person who has a keen sense of responsibility and who takes your commitments seriously. You are not someone who will back out of your commitments when the going gets tough, and indeed, whether they be relationships, health or career commitments, you often like to experience them fully.

With a 6 you may be a natural home-maker and you like people to feel welcome when they come to visit you. You are a generous person, with a big open heart and enough love for everyone, and the ability to feed the world with warmth. You love and need harmonious surroundings to live in; you love beauty, and you enjoy the good things in life. Perhaps you like to consume exquisite foods and expensive wines, to buy or view sensual or erotic art, and you may play beautiful music which caresses your mind and opens your heart. You may also like to dress in sensual or perhaps figure-hugging clothes, in the latest fabrics and designs. Indeed, you may lead a glamorous lifestyle.

With a 6 you may be interested in culture, and if you are an artist, for example, this richness of life may flow through your creative designs. You are also very sensitive, and there may be a depth of feeling which is expressed through your creativity, which others feel too.

You are usually a team-orientated person and you enjoy many team sports, and you also love participating in more gentle exercises like meditation (particularly Buddhist) or yoga.

CHALLENGES

With a 6 in its negative guise influencing your Personality you may be someone who wants your needs to be met, exclusively, before anyone else's, and you do your best to make sure that this happens. For example, you may share your home with three other people, but *you* must use the bathroom first in the morning, and be served first at dinner. If anyone goes without, it isn't you – you are not sacrificing yourself for anyone. In business, you may be the person who wants to get the most pay for doing the same job, or who gets the most attention for the work you have done. Although you have an ability to discern situations clearly, you may be unwilling or unable to see the 'whole' picture or think that there are more people in the world than just you. But for how long will people put up with such selfish behaviour? The answer is not for very long! However, it may help to remind you that life goes on with or without you, and that no one is irreplaceable; there are plenty of human beings in the world, and usually plenty of choices.

Sometimes you may only listen to people when it is convenient for you to do so, or when there is some benefit to you. For example, your sister may ask you to pick up your uncle after visiting the dentist, but you pretend not to hear, so that the responsibility is delegated to someone else. However, if you keep 'not listening' to people, eventually they may do the same in return and ignore your requests. Learning to listen and respond to the whole group's needs can help others as well as help yourself.

Life may sometimes work out in the opposite way; that is, you may be always thinking of others' needs – the needs of the group – and forget your own. Giving to others is wonderful. But if you neglect working out your own problems, or dealing with your life, you may become so worn down that you are not able to fully give to others anyway. You may be burdened down by these responsibilities at times. However, by finding time to devote to yourself you can help everyone, particularly if you become a happier person as a result.

With a 6 influencing your Personality, you are very good at taking on responsibilities for others, but you probably tend to take on too much and end up being 'walked all over' and taken for granted. It is one thing learning to give, but giving *too* much can be detrimental to your health and to your whole life. You may even end up feeling resentful and self-pitying. Perhaps you feel ashamed, or blame yourself when you sometimes turn down cries for help, or when you do not feel you have done enough to help sort people's problems out. However, by learning to just say 'No' – without feeling guilty – you are actually learning to serve yourself first, so that you can then serve others.

With a 6, you can be an interfering person and stick your nose in to other people's affairs, or be an unwelcome guest in people's lives. For example, you may constantly drop in on a neighbour who has recently suffered some kind of trauma just to find out the latest news, rather than helping by giving them space. Perhaps you interfere by giving people unwanted advice. You may even upset people with your opinions by being critical or blaming them for their actions. By learning to remember the whole group's needs in such situations, rather than your own, you may learn to be more caring and responsible with your actions, and in the way you communicate.

You can sometimes be over-sensitive, and when you feel that others have offended or hurt you, you may try to take revenge. You may even be pernicious in your counter-attack and, like an elephant, you never forget. You may battle on with old 'wars' for years; you may even get obsessed by revenge, but you will end up hurting yourself as much, if not more than, your enemy, because everything comes back to you eventually. So you may find the wisdom to simply let things go, and let life sort out karma, as it always does in the end.

With a 6, you tend to get carried away and obsessed with things. For example, you may be completely devoted to your work, to a religion, to a belief or a cause. However, remembering that you are part of a group may help you to respect everyone's beliefs and needs, including your own. This can help you to take a holistic view of life.

ROMANCE AND SEX

With a 6 influencing your relationships, you have the ability to be one of the world's greatest romantics, and you may enjoy every moment of being in love. Roses, candlelit dinners, being swept off your feet and carried through your front door … you love it all. You love to love, totally and fully, with your whole heart, and in relationship you are prepared to give everything. You are totally committed, and you may seek a long-term relationship, with marriage and children high on your agenda; indeed, with family life taking priority over everything else.

Your extended family may be very important to you, and you may spend much time in their company. However, if your partner likes to devote all his attentions to you, he or she may feel smothered by the presence of all the in-laws, or feel invaded by their company. It might help to reassure your partner that he or she is very important to you, or to invite his or her family over to see you, to create good relations with them too.

With a 6, you invest all your emotions into your relationship, so when the slightest thing goes wrong you naturally feel it deeply. When you are in love you may also find yourself crying hopelessly with happiness and joy at the wonder of it all. You may seek a partner who is willing to devote attention to your emotional needs and happiness – someone who can make you feel really good. Perhaps you may also enjoy going out 'on the town' feeling good and looking good with your partner. Sometimes you may even get obsessed with the way you both appear. Perhaps you will find a partner whom you idolize, or he or she may idolize you too.

However, you may come to realize that you can't feel or look good all the time. You may get so carried away with the glamour of being in a relationship and fulfilling your desires, that you find the reality of life a real challenge. At the end of the day roses die, the music fades, and the candle flame burns out. With a 6, when the honeymoon period fades, your romance may develop into a deep friendship, a mutual understanding of responsibilities, and a lasting relationship. However, if the 'light of day' is too stark you may find your heart gets broken as the romance ends. Eventually you learn to let go, and learn to live and love another day. You may bear deep grudges against your ex-partner, but you generally like to do all you can to remain friends.

Sometimes you may become very jealous of the attention he or she receives from other admirers, or perhaps get jealous of your ex-partner's lovers. At such times learning to love yourself may really help.

With a 6 influencing your sex life, affection and emotional connection with your partner may be an essential ingredient for you to feel secure and fulfilled. You may seek sex as part of the wholeness of a relationship, not as a means to an end, even though you enjoy sex and the sensual pleasure.

PHYSICAL APPEARANCE

With a 6 influencing your looks you may have a heart-shaped face with low cheekbones (you probably look 'bonny'), large, full lips with an enormous 'toothy' smile, and a warm voice. You may have a large chest or breasts, and your outstanding feature may be your fullness or roundness.

CHILDHOOD EXPERIENCES

With a 6 influencing your childhood you may have been a child who loved to have lots of soft toys or teddy bears to cuddle on your bed, and story books full of happy and homely tales by your side. Your childhood probably revolved around your family life, with lots of relations who loved coming to visit. Perhaps you lived in a generally harmonious environment, surrounded by love and affection.

You may have loved animals – particularly dogs – and perhaps you spent lots of your time caring for your pets. These animals helped to calm you down when you were feeling emotional, gave you love and affection when you were sad, and generally brought you happiness. You may have loved the responsibility of owning your own pet, and made sure it was treated with respect like one of the family.

With a 6 you may have found yourself needing to take on a lot of family responsibilities even when you were young. For example, having to look after younger family members, or perhaps helping to nurse an older family member too. You may have appeared to be a very wise child, with an early instinct for what people needed. Perhaps you may have felt that you took on a little too many chores around the house at times, and resented having to pander to everybody.

Children with a 6 may need emotional support, particularly when they feel excluded from their family's affections, or at times when they are lost in their emotions, and have gone in too deep. Perhaps by offering to comfort them they will be able to feel 'whole' and part of the family again.

WELL-BEING

With a 6 influencing your health you may suffer emotional stress. You may be prone to problems with your hormonal system or experience reproductive complaints, and you may also be prone to emotional fatigue and exhaustion.

CAREER CHOICE

With a 6 influencing your career you may work as a poet, writer, singer or artist – occupations where your sensitivity can shine through; you may work in the beauty field as a make-up artist or beautician, or as a photographer or graphic designer.

You may also take up a career as a social or voluntary worker, vet, doctor or nurse, chairperson or coordinator of an organization, management consultant, politician or supervisor within any field. Perhaps you might also become a monk!

FAMOUS CHARACTER ANALYSIS
Sigmund Freud Born 6 May 1856

Sigmund Freud was a famous psychiatrist who wrote masses of books on his theories of understanding human behaviour. He believed that there were subconscious reasons for doing things, and that these were often revealed through actions, and communication. Freud was a popular psychologist during his time; indeed he still remains an icon of this age. The popular term 'a Freudian slip', meaning you have said what your subconscious wanted you to say, and that it is no mistake, originates from his name.

One could say Freud was selfish, in that although his work was about others, it focused on the 'self' (the personality). However, Freud spent his lifetime trying to see the whole picture of the psyche. He went in deeper and deeper until he almost became obsessed with his ideas.

With a 6, Freud worked on his commitments, and had an apparently loving and contented marriage, although it was probably beset with emotion at times. He also led the 'good life' with financial security, and he possessed a wonderful sense of humour too.

Freud died on 23 September 1939 having completed a lifetime of study. The whole date adds up to a 9, which he may have felt was 'judgement day' because apparently on his deathbed he denounced some of his life's works. The day was a 23 or 5, so he may have been wanting to run away from his responsibilities which had already made him famous; or perhaps he was just ready for a change.

NUMBER
7

PERSONALITY

GENERAL TRENDS FOR NUMBER 7 PERSONALITY

With a 7 influencing your Personality you have the gift of intuition, and a deepest yearning to feel safe living in the real world. You are an extremely sensitive and perceptive person, and you easily apply these qualities to help your family, friends and work colleagues. Your intuition can help you through all kinds of situations: for example, if you work as a party organizer, you will intuitively know what kind of people to 'mix and match', and what kind of entertainment to lay on. You may also have acute awareness about yourself. For example you may intuitively know when there is something wrong with your health, and make an appointment with your doctor. You like to follow your gut feelings, and when you do your life seems to really flow.

You like to be true to yourself, and to consult your own feelings and intuition rather than blindly following others' actions or advice. You like to rely on your own inner wisdom to help you through life. Indeed, you may often appear like some ancient sage or mystic whose wisdom helps to guide others too. You trust yourself; you may have learned by experience that by doing this your life becomes enriched by many positive and rewarding experiences. Because when you trust yourself, you can trust others, and trust life.

You may be aware that the process of life is made up of cycles of growth, development and learning. You may also realize that when you are faced with some challenging situations this is a necessary process for your growth or personal development. Therefore you may think that whatever happens to you is *meant* to happen. You love nature and you believe in the process of nature, and that nature, like life, works itself out in its own way and in its own time.

With a 7, you are an introspective person and a deep thinker, and you need space; you may even become hermit-like at times. You like to take your experiences and internalize them, so that you can improve both yourself and your life. For example, you may have had a row with your partner, and you retreat into a peaceful corner of your home to think about it. You may try to work out in your head exactly what you have learned about yourself, and to analyze the situation, and you will listen to your intuition too. Then you may try to see what positive changes you can make to improve life with your partner.

You need solitude to analyze things, and also so that you can contemplate the meaning of life – you can be a philosophical person at times. You may also be interested in spirituality, and a lot of your inner contemplation and time may be devoted towards thoughts about your spiritual connection with life and others. You may retreat into yourself to explore your vivid imagination, and you can be a bit of a dreamer.

With a 7 influencing your Personality you are also an instigator, and you are able to make things happen; life does not stay still for very long when you are around! You have a strong mind, and when you apply your positive thoughts and energy towards your goals or dreams, you are often able to make them real. Sometimes it seems almost like magic as you instantly materialize your umpteenth goal! You may also be able to create 'magic' for others, by helping them to realize their dreams too. You love to help make everything prosper and grow, and everyone can be touched by your magic at times.

Even when you do not have great material richness in your life, you may appear 'rich'. Sometimes this is because of your air of wisdom, or because you appear aloof, distant and detached, with your mind occupied elsewhere. People may often think you are 'special', even though you may not think that you are at all.

With a 7, you are a very organized person and a perfectionist in both your working and home environments. You may also be fussy about your appearance, and you may like people around to comply with your high standards. For example, you may like your partner to pay attention to his or her dress, or for your work colleagues to be tidy, and so on.

You may love to meditate, which allows you space to be with yourself and delve into your mind. You may also enjoy tai chi, chi kung, ballet, tennis, swimming, and walking in the park.

CHALLENGES

With a 7 influencing your Personality you may be an anxious person who is always anxious about life. You may worry even when things are going 'right', and you may not be happy until you have something to be concerned about. Sometimes you worry about 'things which are actually happening, and at other times you are preoccupied with 'What if ...' scenarios which go around and around in your head. Anxieties preoccupy your mind, and can be an excuse for not facing reality and getting on with your life. However, worrying has a tendency to make things worse, because you are focusing all your negative thoughts onto a real or perceived situation. By learning to keep your mind positive, even in challenging times, you may actually help towards creating more positive situations in your life.

You may be over-analytical about life at times. Sometimes you lose all track of reality. For example, you may analyze your work situation so much that you start to invent problems that don't exist. You may become too introspective, and so withdrawn that you become isolated and unable to 'contact' the real world. However, although analyzing life can help you to achieve clarity, it is much more helpful to simply face the facts and deal with them.

With a 7 you may prefer your dreams to reality, and keep yourself isolated to prevent you from getting hurt by people and life. However, by accepting pain as an everyday fact of life, and by learning to materialize some of your dreams, instead of simply dreaming about them, you should find that life is fun and worth the challenging times. You may also learn from the knocks you receive, so instead of burying yourself away you can go out into the world knowing that you can face what life has to offer you again.

At times you can be evasive, and you may avoid dealing with uncomfortable situations. For example, perhaps you are about to be made redundant from your job; you may cut off from your feelings or reality to avoid facing this truth. However, the more you resist, the worse it gets: life will be so much more painful when you eventually face the chop than if you'd accepted it at the time and found another job.

Sometimes you may opt out of a society altogether, and become a New Age traveller, or live in a commune or ashram, 'sheltered' from the harsh realities of life. You may drift through life with no real aims, and lose yourself to your illusions and your dreams. You may live with like-minded people. Perhaps you have no material possessions, or have denounced them in search of your spirituality; in fact life is spiritual whether you have material possessions or not. Eventually living off 'thin air' may bring you to your senses, and help you to learn to live in the real world.

With a 7 influencing your Personality you may at times lose your sense of connection to life and to your spirituality. You may be so busy materializing things and having fun that you forget that your inner self needs nurturing too. Alternatively you may feel cut off from your emotions and prefer not to go in too deep. However, life has a way of turning you inwards unexpectedly, and getting you to examine yourself.

You may have a fear of success, and you may panic when things start to go right in your life, especially when situations materialize quickly. You need to be 'real', and so accept everything that comes your way, and that may be a little scary at first. However, if you persist, you may eventually learn to enjoy success.

With a 7 influencing your Personality, you may be preoccupied and overly concerned with how you feel, and be unaware of others' feelings around you. Or you may be self-centred and refuse to acknowledge that anyone else has feelings as strong as yours, or could be feeling as vulnerable as you, or even that they have feelings at all! However, by being aware of others, and by helping them, it can divert some of the attention away from you, and can help you to feel good too.

You may be naïve at times, and easily taken in, such as by taking what everybody says at face value. However, by learning to trust your intuition, and being realistic about the facts, you may learn to get a grip on life.

ROMANCE AND SEX

With a 7 influencing your relationships you can be naïve, and you may blunder into relationships knowing very little about the person involved, and so find yourself in at the deep end. However, your strong intuition sometimes helps you out of sticky situations, and helps you to face reality. It may be sensible to protect yourself by finding out as many facts as you can about a partner before you embark on a new relationship.

You may be a 'crowned princess' who likes to believe in fairy tales. For example, after a night of passion with someone you met at a party, you may be gullible and believe them when they say that they are going to telephone you the next day. Sometimes they do call, of course, but you may feel betrayed if the call doesn't happen, and on time. You are very impatient and you are often trying to be one step ahead within your relationships.

You are a sensitive person and you may seek a partner who can be respectful towards your feelings. You also need your space, and you may prefer to be in a relationship with someone who does not depend on you for 'your' time. If you live together you may need your own room to retreat to, or you may find a partner who lives in his or her own house. With a 7 you may even prefer to be in relationship with someone who lives at a distance from you, perhaps in another town, so that you can see them at weekends or only for restricted amounts of time.

With a 7 influencing your Personality, you may be dreamy and unrealistic about your partner. For example, you may think that they are ready to move in with you, when they aren't. You may get taken in by your own illusions. You may also be looking for that 'perfect' partner, and when he or she does come your way, you may play hard to get because you are afraid of success; you may prefer to dream about them rather than take them up on their offer.

You are sensitive and you are able to intuitively feel what your partner needs. However, your sensitivity and vulnerability may make your partner feel scared, because you act as a catalyst which causes them to get in touch with their own emotions and vulnerability. Sometimes you may be attracted to a partner with whom you feel a deep spiritual connection, and this may be a very important aspect in your relationship, which helps you to feel safe.

Sometimes you may look for a partner who is protective towards you, or someone who treats that naïve child-like part of you with care. You may also attract a partner who is down to earth and practical so that when you go floating off into the clouds, he or she can 'catch you' and help bring you back to reality.

With a 7 influencing your sex life, you may seek the perfect partner with whom to fuse mind, body and spirit, and if he or she can't be found then you may prefer celibacy than making do with second best! You may also watch stimulating DVDs. However, you are also a detached person and you may enjoy quick and non-emotional encounters with others instead.

PHYSICAL APPEARANCE

With a 7 influencing your looks you may have a moon-like face, translucent skin, sensitive eyes, a sharp nose, and small lips which curve down at the edges. You may have grey hair (or go grey early), and the most outstanding feature may be your fine and delicate looks.

CHILDHOOD EXPERIENCES

With a 7 influencing your childhood you may have been a loner at times, and preferred the company of a book or your imagination to the noise and bustle of everyday life. You may also have been a highly intuitive child, and perhaps you had nightmares or sleep walked, or even had uncanny psychic dreams. You may have even felt disturbed by your dreams, particularly when they came true.

You may have been fanciful and good at making up stories to make life more interesting or even to protect yourself at times. Your vivid imagination may have helped you when writing school essays, where you described things in vivid detail. Perhaps you used your imagination to make interesting cakes or clothes, or you were inventive in the way you dressed. You may also have been fussy about your clothes, and about your friends, and perhaps picky about what you ate.

Perhaps you were also shy, withdrawn and isolated, and although you may have loved parties you may have only trusted your 'best' friend. Because you were vulnerable you may have felt unable to protect yourself at times, and you may have been a scapegoat for others' misdemeanours.

With a 7 influencing your childhood you may have used your strong mind negatively to create psychosomatic illnesses, becoming a 'sickly' child who was able to avoid going to school, or to avoid people or avoid doing certain things. However, if you possessed a positive frame of mind, it is likely you were robust.

Children with a 7 may isolate themselves because they are scared of their intuition, or even more scared of reality. However, by encouraging them to participate fully in life, and to take some exercise, it may help them to stay 'grounded', and make living in reality a little easier

WELL-BEING

With a 7 influencing your health you may be prone to gloomy moods, depression or panic attacks . You may also suffer from fatigue, eating disorders such as anorexia, or from problems with your teeth.

CAREER CHOICE

With a 7 influencing your career you may work in a field where you pay great attention to detail: as a market researcher, engineer, analyst, personal assistant, midwife or surgeon, or you may work for a financial institution.

You like to bring people together, so you may work as a professional party planner or as an organizer of some kind. You may also work as a homoeopath, a healer, or as an astrologer or numerologist, where you can use your intuition and wisdom to help people.

FAMOUS CHARACTER ANALYSIS
Madame Marie Tussaud Born 7 December 1760

Madame Tussaud was a talented Swiss wax modeller. She ingeniously invented and created her own form of magic by moulding wax models of famous people and then displaying them as permanent fixtures in theatres around the world. Celebrities were committed to wax, and kept 'standing' until the time of their decline in social popularity, when they were melted down and reformed into a new model. Her marvellous creations brought magic to people's lives, and millions of people still visit her 'shrines' today.

Tussaud, was obviously a sensitive soul with a vivid imagination, and was like a child dreaming and fantasizing about all these famous people who were 'larger than life'. She dreamt about them, met them, and then materialized them in her own life by creating them in wax.

With a 7 Tussaud was surely a perfectionist who agonized over every tiny detail about her models, right up to the completion of each one. She no doubt scrutinized every mould she made, and even today if a celebrity is not happy with their 'shadow' it is revamped or remade.

Madame Tussaud died on 15 April 1850 having realized her dream. The whole date adds up to a 6, so her love affair with art and beauty was obviously complete. The day is another 6 (or 15), which emphasizes that her duty had been fulfilled.

NUMBER
8
PERSONALITY

GENERAL TRENDS FOR NUMBER 8 PERSONALITY

With an 8 influencing your Personality you have the gift of patience and the deepest yearning to succeed in every area of your life. Indeed you may well be a high achiever and very successful, and receive great rewards for what you do. For example, you may receive fame or recognition, or financial rewards for work well done, or a new car from your employer, and so on. You may congratulate yourself for some 'milestone' that you have reached, or feel self-satisfaction from knowing that you have achieved a worthwhile goal. You may not need rewards from others, but you may often attract them.

You are a successful person, and you enjoy an abundance of material wealth and possessions. However, success may mean little to you unless the spiritual side to your Personality is satisfied too. For example, you may crave inner peace sometimes and take some quiet time to boost your creative energies and give you a break from the world of money and fast living. You may also feel a deep spiritual connection to people around you, and to humanity in general. For example, you may read international magazines to keep you in touch with news from around the world, and view it as equally important to your own. Indeed, you are successful because you are in contact with your own spirituality; you have materialized success because you are in tune with your inner self.

Often you come across as a powerful person who can handle success easily, and you do not get phased by being in positions of authority or by being in the public eye. This is because you are using your natural talents; you are simply doing what you are meant to be doing. It may not occur to you that you are any different

66

from anyone else – everyone has their own gifts. You may feel comfortable with power, but you may also realize that it is a responsibility. However, you can empower others to use their gifts; you are patient, and bring out the best in people; you make an excellent leader. You love to encourage responsibility and, as you enjoy the success of being able to stand on your own two feet, you also encourage this in others.

With an 8 influencing your Personality you may exude wealth, status and power, and as a highly magnetic, charming and attractive human being you may attract to you people of similar standing. For example, if you are the head of a large international corporation then you may attract to you heads of similarly large companies from all around the world, and you may empower each other with your leadership. With an 8 you have an enormous amount of stamina and drive. You may have a burning ambition to achieve your aims in every field: relationships, good health, work, money, status, responsibility, and so on. You may also have a great interest in becoming a leading light or an authority within the business world.

You are like a magnet and even when you do not work in big business you still exude great strength and have respect for yourself and others around you. Indeed you are a self-possessed person, and you may also exude confidence. You are not afraid to speak your mind, and you are often highly assertive. You may also be extremely organized and efficient, and you may inspire people with your strength and vitality.

Generally, you are a shrewd person and you may enjoy healthy competition with others. For example, you may be competing for promotion at work, or you may be competing with someone in order to purchase a property, and so on. You love the excitement of competition and it keeps you on your toes … by showing you that you are not the only successful person around!

With an 8 you may be someone who re-evaluates constantly; hardly a day goes by without you rethinking what you are doing and where you are with your life. You may be very aware of your actions, or your karma too, and you probably realize that you truly 'get what you give'. For example, if you mistrust someone in a business negotiation, even if they are actually trustworthy, they may start to be untrustworthy because they begin to distrust you. Or, perhaps you charged a client too much money, and soon after you were overcharged by a similar amount. However, in general you have learned to only 'take what you need'.

With an 8 you may enjoy playing all competitive sports like squash, tennis, rugby, rowing and long-distance running, or you may enjoy riding, polo, sailing, aerobics, and pilates (the popular form of stretch exercise).

CHALLENGES

With an 8 influencing your Personality you may live in a world where material possessions and the clothes you wear are the most important things in your life, along with how much money you earn or your work or power 'status'. For example, you may drive around in a showy car or wear clothes with obvious designer labels, or have the most sophisticated hi-fi system in the land. Perhaps you own a successful company with millions of dollars of turnover, or hire thousands of people throughout the world. Or perhaps, no matter how much you have, you are greedy and you always want more. It is wonderful to be able to enjoy all the material comforts of life, but when your focus is purely on money, then life can become 'dry' in other areas. However, by turning to your spirituality at times, and by connecting with people and other aspects of life, it may help you to lead a more balanced and harmonious life.

You may be brash and loud, and you make sure that you are 'high profile' within your group of friends, or to the world in general. You may show off your successes, and boast and brag to the point of boredom. However, you can actually empower people with your success by encouraging them to be successful too, and realize that their success is also your success, because it can empower you in return.

With an 8 you may be a competitive person but you can also be manipulative to get your own way. For example, by 'paying someone off' to get the company you want, or by lying; you may not play fair, and instead like people to play life your way. However, you may use your powers of manipulation because you don't respect others, or in fact respect yourself by accepting what life deals out to you instead. For example, if you were meant to win a certain work contract then you would have, and perhaps it was destined for someone else.

Sometimes you try to control life, and to assert authority over others to give you what you want. You may even bully people, or be aggressive and bolshy to intimidate them into doing something for you. Perhaps you like to 'win over' others because it makes you feel powerful. However, with an 8 you have the influence of an extremely karmic number, and you may find that you always get what you give to others – twofold! Also, by being on the receiving end of your own behaviour, you may decide it's time to stop playing games.

With an 8 influencing your Personality negatively you may, indeed, feel like a failure because you have not been able to find your perfect job, or create great wealth or answer your material needs in life – all of which are so important to you. Perhaps you are impractical and do not enjoy working hard for your money, but expect others to provide these things for you. It is great to be looked after, but you may gain more satisfaction and self-respect from providing things for yourself.

At times you may like to feel that people owe you something: a favour, or money, and so on. Alternatively you may always feel like you owe people something, when you have paid all your debts or, for example, given back the books you had borrowed. However, karma is at work here, and in some ways it is out of your control. For example, you can learn to take positive actions, but in the end life alone sorts out what you owe, and what you need to gain.

You may sometimes feel a lack of strength and support. Perhaps you feel powerless and simply give your power away, by behaving as though others had control over your life, or how you are meant to feel or act each day. However, by being assertive and standing up for who you are, and counting yourself as an equal counterpart, you can inspire others with your inner strength. This can also encourage others to 'take their power' back and to do the same.

With an 8 in its challenging guise influencing your Personality you may be someone who fears losing control, so perhaps you like to carry on each day in the same old routine with your life perfectly in tact to try to avoid change. You may even actively shy away from re-evaluating your life, or going 'inside' to think about ways in which you can change your life for the better, preferring instead to keep on with things as they are. However, sometimes when you fear something it may contribute towards creating that very thing; perhaps an unavoidable situation occurs in your life which forces you to rethink. The greater the resistance, the greater the release, so re-evaluating your life regularly may help you to adapt to life, which is constantly changing.

ROMANCE AND SEX

With an 8 influencing your Personality you may be a strong, powerful and successful person, who likes to look good, and you are able to earn your own way in life. Perhaps you are even modest about your achievements too. Therefore you may seek a partner with an equally strong character, who is not bowled over by your 'big Personality' (or ego!) and your ambitious nature.

Ideally, you may be someone who is seeking a relationship that is like a partnership, where the business world plays a large part in your life; perhaps where you socialize or travel together, or own a company together. However, you may also seek a relationship where you are able to empower your partner to be themselves, or to be successful, and for him or her to do the same for you. Perhaps you become a powerful couple together, where you take on joint responsibilities to help bring success to others, and to enrich their lives.

Sometimes you may find yourself preoccupied with material wealth to the exclusion of other things in your life. For example, if your brain is thinking 'money, money, money' then there is little time for the 'love' word (except when it is related to money). You may find yourself with all the things that money can buy, but it can't buy you love. Yes, somebody may be impressed with your worldly possessions, but at the end of the day there may need to be something else to keep the spark alight. Therefore perhaps you need a strongly spiritual or a very sexual partner who can draw your attentions to the other-worldly wonders of life.

With an 8 influencing your relationships you may be always taking control in your work situation, and you may seek a partner to take control of your life sometimes. For example, if you have been busy organizing meetings or negotiating deals, you may love your partner to arrange your social life for you both. Perhaps you may also be used to telling people what to do, and enjoy your partner (at times) giving you direction. Alternatively you may enjoy being in control of your partner, and even get possessive about him or her, and angry when he or she doesn't 'toe the line'. Perhaps you feel your partner should appreciate that you are such a catch!

You may be a bright and intellectual person who seeks mental stimulation from your partner. Perhaps you are seeking someone with whom you can share intelligent conversations about worldly matters, instead of just discussing how much money you have both made, or how successful you have been that day.

With an 8 influencing your sex life you may attract a strong karmic partner to you, and you instantly know how to satisfy each other's desires and sexual fantasies. You may at times enjoy a very high sex drive and want to deliver a successful performance in between the sheets. Perhaps you love to play power games with each other, tying each other up, or play domination games, with you 'on top' and in control, or vice versa. Perhaps tattoos also turn you on – either your own or your partner's!

PHYSICAL APPEARANCE

With an 8 influencing your looks you may have a sallow or 'rough' complexion, strong and coarse hair, eyes set wide apart, cat's eyes, straight large lips and a strong jaw line. You may be tall and slim, and your outstanding feature may be your distinctive voice, which often sounds sexy and alluring.

CHILDHOOD EXPERIENCES

With an 8 influencing your childhood you may have been brought up in a wealthy household with all the material possessions that money could buy. You may have also prized your own things, and perhaps showed off about them to your friends. For example, by having gold pens to write with instead of ordinary ball-point pens, or your parents driving you to school in a Rolls Royce or something equally luxurious. Your parents may have also been famous, or infamous, or recognized in your local society, which may have brought you a lot of attention.

You may have been a bossy child, or you may even have been a bully, at times, who picked on or was aggressive to other children. Perhaps this is because you were bullied, or because you needed to feel in control and important.

With an 8, you were particularly at the hands of karma during your childhood, from encounters in previous lives and as a result of your childhood behaviour too. Perhaps you received good karma, or the karma of reward for the things you may have done in the past, and generally led a happy childhood whether you had material possessions or not. Maybe you received the karma of retribution, where your actions in the past returned painful or difficult experiences to you, but that turned your life around for the better in the long run.

Children with an 8 may be very stubborn, and wilful, and they may need to learn to respect others for who they are, rather than what they are or what they own. Therefore it may help to show them how to respect themselves first, perhaps by treating them with respect, and being a good example to them.

WELL-BEING

With an 8 influencing your health you may be prone to problems with your knees and your joints, your spine or your bones. You may also suffer from haemorrhoids or constipation sometimes.

CAREER CHOICE

With an 8 influencing your career you may work in the business field as an accountant, a finance director, or in the financial sector in general. You may be a managing director of any company, or own your own company and be actively involved in making it a success. You may also be a manager, or a leader in any field where you display responsibility, power and authority, or work in the business world, or you may be a teacher.

You may also take up a career as an organizer in any field. You may work with the spine or back by becoming an osteopath, chiropractor or physiotherapist, or you may work as a health-care professional.

FAMOUS CHARACTER ANALYSIS
Elvis Presley Born 8 January 1935

Elvis Presley was an incredibly talented and popular composer, singer and dancer, who used his talents to light up and inspire the world with his inner creativity and joy. Elvis was a powerful and charismatic leader; he was also a sex symbol. He had a strong spirit, and he had a spiritual side to his Personality too.

Elvis couldn't always handle the pressures and responsibilities of his fabulous wealth and fame. He would sometimes go out on spending sprees and buy things in dozens instead of one by one. Indeed, he did possibly lose a little of his self-respect, and for someone in his position it would have been difficult at times for it all not to have gone to his head. He enjoyed eating and drinking, and he apparently needed pills at times to help control his life – to allow him to rest.

With an 8, Elvis obviously received the karma of reward by marrying a beautiful woman, having a healthy child, working in the field he loved best, and with as much material happiness that his money could buy for his family and his friends.

Elvis Presley died on 16 August 1977 having inspired the

world with his gifts. The whole date adds up to a 3, so perhaps he was looking to expand his life at that time. The day is a 16 or 7, so perhaps he was introspective, and was searching for the 'meaning of life' at the time of his death.

NUMBER

9

PERSONALITY

GENERAL TRENDS FOR NUMBER 9 PERSONALITY

With a 9 influencing your Personality you have the gift of knowledge and the deepest yearning to accept yourself the way you are – to accept both your 'good' bits and your imperfections, and to realize that everyone is made up of both. However, you may be more accepting of others 'faults' than your own, and you are a forgiving person who does not hold onto resentments for long. With a 9, you are a perfectionist and you are always seeking ways of improving yourself and your life. You may take a personal development class to help improve your behaviour, or a college course to improve your cooking, or further education so that you can improve your career and perhaps your finances too. Indeed you are keen on education and you probably received straight As at school. However, even if you didn't pass your exams with flying colours you may still find yourself in a career where you can be educated, perhaps by working for a boss who you think is very knowledgeable and far superior to you, from whom you can learn.

You are also a very knowledgeable person but sometimes this comes from your mind, rather than from books you may have read, or courses you have taken. Of course you may be well read too, but you can call on this 'inner' knowledge, or a sense of knowing, to help you through life. You may be an intellectual person, and enjoy discussing and debating the topic of the day; you like to keep yourself well informed with what is happening in the outside world. You also think of yourself as an intelligent person, and you join in discussions only when you know exactly what you are talking about, or when you have something interesting to say. However, you generally form your own strong opinions, and will not waver once you have set your mind upon a particular point of view.

With a 9 you set your own high standards and you may like to have people around you who conform to these. You do not suffer fools gladly, and you will verify someone's qualifications before you employ them, or check out a potential partner's background before you enter into a relationship. Indeed you can be frightfully choosy at times, in your quest to surround yourself with the 'best' in life. You usually like to dress exceedingly well too; perhaps you have been profession-ally 'colour-coordinated' or had make-up or tailoring lessons, to project your best possible image to the world.

You are a natural leader, and you are able to impress your ways of doing things upon others. Indeed you may be a teacher, or people may simply follow your example. For example, you are generally somebody who sees all people as equal, and you have high ethics, and perhaps people can learn from your opinions, actions and behaviour. You believe in justice, and you like people to be treated fairly. You may have strong morals and values, but you are open-minded, and relaxed in your views much of the time.

Generally you are a giver, and someone who devotes your attention and time to others' needs before your own, and you are generally observant and can see and feel what they need. You may be a selfless carer, and you may often help your community or work as a human-itarian in some way. You may also be respectful of people, and you have a great understanding (from your inner knowledge) which helps you to help people too. You usually possess strong psychic instincts, and you may feel or sense what you can do to help people by using this gift.

With a 9 influencing your Personality you may be a spiritual and religious person, and these qualities may play a large part in the life you lead. For example, perhaps you meditate, or go to church or to a temple regularly, or simply study spirituality or religion from books of ancient teachings. You may have a strong belief in 'goodness' and because of your liberal attitude you may believe all faiths are of equal importance in the world.

You may possess a strong discriminating mind, and you like to be sensible about life. For example, it is a fact that you will burn yourself if you lift a hot cake tin out of the oven with your bare hands; but your discriminating mind tells you to use oven gloves next time. Sometimes, you live life by your emotions, but applying your mind and logic can help you to make rational decisions, and take appropriate actions, about your health, your career and your relationships.

With a 9 you may have a creative flair for art and music, and you may well play musical instruments, or sing frequently. Perhaps these are your main forms of relaxation; but you may prefer doing a full work out at the gym, or marching through the woods, or taking up some type of dare devil sport which gets your adrenalin pumping.

CHALLENGES

With a 9 influencing your Personality you may be a narrow-minded and intolerant person at times. Perhaps you are too rigid about your beliefs, or feel threatened by people who are different from you. For example, you may have your own circle of friends and everyone outside may seem alien to you. Perhaps you are also intolerant to uneducated people, or people who have a different lifestyle. You may at times set unrealistic expectations, and feel frustrated and angry when life doesn't work out the way you think it should, or when people don't behave in an acceptable way. However, by being tolerant to others' beliefs and ways you are opening up to life and learning to accept life as it is. You may also become more educated and knowledgeable by interacting in all different types of circumstances and situations.

You may at times judge people and make ignorant comments about them behind their backs. Perhaps you are scathing of others, and become superior in your remarks, or talk to people as if they are beneath you. You may constantly criticize people and upset them with your cutting remarks. However, you often criticize yourself just as much, and it is because you have such high standards and nothing or no one can ever be good enough. Perhaps deep down inside you feel imperfect, and try to prove to yourself you are OK by making out that you are superior to the rest of mankind.

Sometimes you can be snobbish about your looks, the way you dress, and particularly about your education or your family background. In life you may also feel that these standards have to be maintained, and you may feel great humiliation if for some reason you have to downgrade: for example, if you lose your job, downgrade your house or car, or become demoted in others' eyes. However, although it's great to have the good things in life, the need to feel superior indicates that you are not feeling good enough inside. Perhaps you desperately need the approval of society and your family and friends. By being laid back and adopting an open view you may realize that what you thought of as downgrading was actually fun and interesting, and has led you to many pastures new.

With a 9 influencing your Personality you may be so busy looking for flaws in people that you fail to see their positive qualities. For example, your partner cooks you the most wonderful meal, but you simply go on about the wine which was not, in your eyes, appropriate or good enough. Perhaps you self-righteously suggest two or three other wines which would have been better. It should come as no surprise if your partner says, 'You make dinner next time!' All things in life may seem simply right or wrong to you, but there are large grey areas, known as compromise.

You may have 'Victorian' values, and you may be prudish in your views and behaviour. You may even be uptight and easily shocked by the realities of life. For example, a friend suddenly starts talking to you about her problems with PMT and it may be enough to make you blush and walk away. However, when you avoid reality it tends to seek you out, and fast, and facing it may help you to learn to be more liberal in your understanding.

With a 9 you are generally a capable person and you may feel pathetic or stupid if you can't do things sometimes. Perhaps you put yourself down because you have been ill, and haven't managed to do every daily chore, or because you couldn't do ten things at once! It may help you to learn to be more easy on yourself, and congratulate yourself for the things you do manage to achieve.

With a 9 influencing your Personality you often go out of your way to help people and you selflessly give your time and patience to others in any way you can. However, sometimes you give and give until it hurts, and you still give, and occasionally when life doesn't seem to return in the same measures, you feel disappointed. For you learning to give with an open heart, and to enjoy giving, can help you to receive, too, because you are open to life.

With a 9 you are a caring person, but you may prefer to look after yourself because you may find it difficult to receive. This is perhaps because you feel you are not worthy to accept the love, possessions and time from others, and think that your duty is solely to give. However, by learning to accept a hug, present or a treat, you are opening up to life, and giving someone the pleasure of your happiness.

ROMANCE AND SEX

With a 9 influencing your relationships you are a passionate person: about love, life and about everything you do. Therefore finding the love of your life with whom you can share your passion and joy may be essential, and perhaps your partner is passionate about you too.

You may attract a partner with spiritual interests who can teach you to connect with yourself and with the 'bigger picture' in life. You may be spiritual and religious, and this may be of great importance when seeking a long-term relationship. Perhaps you spend hours debating your beliefs and faiths together, and if you share different views, you can learn to be tolerant of each other. This applies in all areas of life; for example, you may need to be tolerant about the aftershave or perfume your partner uses! You have great faith in yourself and in your beliefs, and at times you may give your partner sermons about his or her behaviour, and about life and the way things 'should' be. Perhaps your partner likes to be preached to at times, but may resent you if you spend all your time complaining and being self-righteous about life.

With a 9 influencing your relationships you may seek a partner who is knowledgeable about life, and who is intelligent or has intellectual or creative or artistic interests. Perhaps you go to a lecture on the rainforests of Brazil together, or help campaign in an election for your local candidate, because politics interests you too. Maybe you visit an art gallery to view modern art by painters like Piccasso or Miro.

You may find that you attract to you a musician (like yourself?),or someone who can dance and who is good at expressing himself or herself. Perhaps you may sometimes be drawn to someone who does not conform to the greater beliefs that society 'puts' upon you. You may also like to be tidy and like to look your best, but you can also be slovenly and lazy about what you wear, particularly at weekends or during holidays. However, you may feel that it doesn't always matter how your dress with your partner because he or she loves you unconditionally.

With a 9 influencing your Personality you like to give, and you may try to please your partner so that you get his or her approval, and so that you feel loved. For example, you may wait on him or her 'hand and foot', or you may always make yourself available instead of thinking of your own needs sometimes. Perhaps you can find a partner who gives back to you too, and it may not all be one-sided when he or she enjoys doing things for you.

With a 9 influencing your sex life, your religious and spiritual beliefs may have some influence. Perhaps you may also believe there are certain things which you feel are 'wrong' or 'right' to do in bed, and you operate within these boundaries. However, the other side of your Personality is liberated and free and you enjoy expressing your sexuality and your body openly, with someone of equal passion and who is also relaxed about sex.

PHYSICAL APPEARANCE

With a 9 influencing your looks you may be tall, with a square face, a bulbous nose and clear skin, and you may have a lopsided mouth with medium to thin lips. You may be rugged in your appearance and your most outstanding feature is that you may look very muscular.

CHILDHOOD EXPERIENCES

With a 9 influencing your childhood you may have been brought up with a lot of discipline and with a regimented routine, with everything in its 'proper' place. Perhaps your parents ran a tight schedule with their lives and you were allocated slots to fit in; perhaps they had experienced a strict upbringing themselves. Therefore you knew that one way of getting your parents' attention was to 'slip up' and be lazy or rebellious at times.

You may have liked to win the approval of your parents, teachers and your mates. Therefore you may have been a 'goody two shoes' who was always receiving praise, and you liked to behave like a 'good girl' or a 'good boy' because you worked out that this was the best way to get attention. Perhaps you did well at sports or at academic subjects in school, and often found yourself at the top of the class.

With a 9 there may have been an emphasis on learning or education in your home, and perhaps you were surrounded with sophisticated games or lots of books. Perhaps you were encouraged to play 'serious' games which stimulated your mind, right from an early age. Perhaps you loved to play 'grown ups' too, and imitated your parents by dressing up in their clothes. You might have enjoyed a creative atmosphere at home, with music and art high on the agenda.

Children with a 9 often feel guilty if they can't perform to their own (or their parents') high standards, or requirements of achievement. It may help to encourage them to love themselves for who they are, and to show them that they are loved without needing to be perfect in their behaviour or output in life.

WELL-BEING

With a 9 influencing your health you may be prone to problems with your eyesight, or you may suffer from blocked sinus and migraines. You may also be prone to muscular aches and pains from keeping your body in shape.

CAREER CHOICE

With a 9 influencing your career you may work in the field of education, as a teacher, researcher, careers advisor or secretary. Perhaps you also devote your time to charity work, or fundraising projects to help the underprivileged and the sick, or you work as a nurse, doctor or healer.

With a 9 you may be a leader in any field, or work in the military or navy or in the services, or work as a judge, diplomat or politician. You are also good with your hands, and you may work as a musician, artist, sculptor, reflexologist, massage therapist, or as a cook or gardener.

FAMOUS CHARACTER ANALYSIS
John Lennon Born 9 October 1940

John Lennon was the extremely successful pop star, singer and musician with the group the Beatles, who found themselves the focus of mass hysteria and popularity in the 1960s. He also became an icon for the masses (particularly when he went solo in his career) because of his amazing talents.

Lennon had keen interests in politics, sex, religion and social issues, and was deeply spiritual too. He felt free to express his views through his songwriting skills. He felt liberated about his sexuality too; he posed completely nude in promotional material. He was certainly non-conformist and not seeking approval, but felt free to 'be himself'.

With a 9 John Lennon's second marriage was to Yoko Ono an extremely creative and artistic person, and it appears that they truly inspired each other. John was apparently indulgent in his desire for passion and humanitarian interests, and was also interested in the bigger picture – not just himself.

John Lennon died on the 9 December 1980; he was shot,

having inspired the world with his musical and artistic creations. The whole date adds up to a 3, so perhaps he was seeking other ways of expressing himself in his life at that time. The day was a 9, which is also the same as his Personality Number, so perhaps he really was reviewing and discriminating about 'life and politics' on the day he died.

NUMBER
10/1
PERSONALITY

GENERAL TRENDS FOR NUMBER 10/1 PERSONALITY

With the 10/1 influencing your Personality you have the gift of leadership and the deepest yearning to follow your goals in life. With the strength of two 1s you may also feel the need to assert your leadership skills and share your knowledge. People look to you to show them the way because you are a born leader.

In the 10/1 you also have the zero influencing your Personality. Zero has an unusual mission here because it emphasizes your gifts and intensifies the qualities of the 1, and therefore the work which you need to do. For example, if you are displaying the dependency aspect of your Personality, the zero will intensify your need to work on strengthening your independence. The zero can also offer protection: physically, emotionally, mentally or spiritually. Sometimes you may feel this protection when you go through a period with this number influencing your Personality. It may feel that facing challenging situations is somehow made easier by the zero's 'cushioning effect'.

With a 10/1, you like to get really involved in your work or life, and you enjoy the challenge of your goals. Like all 1s, you like to set your goals regularly, so that there are always creative challenges to stimulate you.

As with all 1s you share the incredible ability to be able to conceptualize, and come up with an abundance of ideas. Then you are able to apply your creativity, and use your ability to focus and follow them through. You may also be steely-eyed in your focus because there are two 1s influencing your Personality, which intensifies this quality. This energy can be directed towards work, a relationship, or towards any project – everything you do is handled in this very creative, focused and energetic way.

With a 1 influencing your Personality you may be naïve at times because you have no sense of 'self' or individuality, and you may withdraw from the world by retreating into your mind of ideas and thoughts.

At times you may give off an air of superiority or seem aloof which can put people off because you appear inaccessible. However, sometimes you may do this to keep people away, because you may not like to get too close or intimate with them. You may also like to feel 'exclusive' and different, and this may also show in the way you dress – with original creative flair and style – or the way in which you do things. You may like to feel your individuality shining through so that you can sparkle. You generally love yourself, and feel comfortable with who you are.

Often, you like to be noticed and you may do this through your creativity, in the way that you dress, or in your bright and stimulating conversation. You love to develop your intellect, and you may want people to know that there is more to you than simply your outward appearance.

As with all 1s, you have vitality and energy which really shines through. You go through life with a great sense of purpose and direction. You may often show great wisdom, and courage, and you may possess a real understanding and caring of people, and know how to help them. You are also charitable, and you understand people's suffering. For example, you may take food to the poor on the streets, and give it with love, or you may help to break down people's opinions about the underprivileged to show that they have importance too. You may be a pioneer in your attitude towards life; this may be literally pioneering paths or mountains, or in politics, or with your concepts and ideas. You like to break down barriers between people and lead the way ahead.

With the influence of two 1s in your Personality this intensifies your need for independence, and to learn to do things for yourself and on your own. You may dislike relying on others for anything, which can be a problem sometimes, particularly when your car breaks down. You may prefer to walk to work rather than accept help from a willing neighbour. However, being able to rely on, and care for, yourself brings you self-esteem. Knowing how to look after yourself means that you also know how to look after others, if and when you choose.

With a 10/1 you love to exercise in the gym, do aerobics and go cycling; you tend to enjoy any physically demanding exercise, and also that which requires your mental focus.

CHALLENGES

With a 10/1 influencing your Personality you may lack the courage to pursue your goals in life; perhaps you may be fearful that you cannot achieve them. You may be extremely creative, but you may be lazy and lack the drive to go for what you want. This can result in frustration, and you may have low self-esteem. Sometimes, taking some exercise may help refocus your energy and help to revitalize you.

Sometimes, you can get rigidly stuck focusing on one goal and lose track of everything else in your life. However, as with the influence of all 1s, your goals *are* your life, and your need for creativity is great. By getting 'stuck' your energy can stagnate, until your realize that there are other goals to be achieved and other things to focus on in life.

However, you may not know exactly what it is that you want. This is challenging, but often your goals in life are simply based on expanding your gifts. For example, you may be good at listening to others' problems and coming up with ideas of ways in which you can help people to solve them. You may like to expand on this by taking some professional training, or setting up your own company to offer people professional advice, and so on.

With a 10/1 influencing your Personality you may be forceful in your opinions, and expect others to follow through on them, and agree with you. This is because you have a strong vision of your goals and like to ensure that they get carried out.

At the other extreme of a 10/1 challenging influence, you may be lacking in opinions. You may also lack drive and simply get stuck in a rut (like all 1s) at times, and not care about achieving your goals or channelling your creativity. Sometimes you may also be a victim to others' opinions and ideas about how you 'should' live your life, and be intimidated by their superiority. You may lack the ability to stand up to others when they are flaunting their self-importance and being arrogant. For example, your sister may tell you that she thinks you ought to take your elderly aunt out for the day because she has much more important things than you to do. You may feel obliged to do as she says. However, you have the choice to either look after your aunt because you would like to, or to refuse your sister's commands if you also have something important to do.

With a 10/1 influencing your Personality you may expect people to look up to you, and perhaps you would like them to think that you are important. This is simply another way of expressing your outer need to impress people as a result of your inner lack of self-esteem. For example, you may be a successful model, leading a jet-set lifestyle and breaking the frontiers of exhibitionism. You may need all the world telling you how important and successful you are, because if they tell you that you are wonderful, then you must be! However, when you feel happy within yourself, and love yourself, you do not need to feel 'better than' anybody, but you can accept your own (and others') individuality. Once you have found this quality inside yourself, you will no longer need to go searching for confirmation from others.

With the 10/1, you may have an urge to seek out and go for new opportunities. However, you can be single-minded and sometimes ruthless in your pursuit of these, and you may use everything that comes your way simply for your own ends. For example, it may be that you own a company and you see an opportunity for development and expansion by teaming up with another company, who are normally competitors. However, when it comes to the contract you may want to take larger shares than they do in the project, because you may want as much as possible for yourself. This is because you are self-centred, and sometimes only think of the world by the way it can offer and give you things. With a 10/1, eventually, you may realize that sharing the finances may also mean sharing the rewards in this situation, and could lead to more joint projects in the future.

You love doing new things, which means that you may not stick to one project, idea, or with one person for too long. That is, until you learn ways of finding 'freshness' each day, even if you are working with or on one thing for a lifetime!

ROMANCE AND SEX

With a 10/1 influencing your relationships you are usually a caring and giving, self-sufficient individual, who seeks only to give to your partner. You may even be too giving and need to learn to think of yourself and your own needs. Paradoxically, you can, of course, be self-centred and stubborn at times, and you may like to get your own way by shouting and arguing – your behaviour veering between the extremes of giving and taking.

In order for you to learn about independence, which is a key issue for all 1s, you may attract a partner who does relatively little for you practically, so that you learn to do things for yourself. 'Can you do the weekly shopping for me?' you ask, 'Can you pick up a package for me on the way back from work?' The reply may be, 'No, sorry, too busy!' and so you learn to do it for yourself.

You may seek an extrovert, bubbly partner who can help to bring you out of your shell if you are displaying much of the introverted, withdrawn aspects of this influence. However, an intellectual partner to whom you can relate about literature, art and current affairs may also appeal. You like mind-stimulating chat, particularly when it is with someone you love, because it helps to bring you close.

With the influence of the 1, you may revel in intimacy, and you may be able to handle your emotions wonderfully. However, you may attract a partner who can 'open you up' emotionally to allow you to express yourself even more.

Sometimes you may stay 'stuck' in one relationship because you cannot express what you want to say or do directly. There may be lots of arguments, and if you are unhappy within the relationship you may even have an affair to try to end it, perhaps because you are simply unable to confront the situation. This may be the only way you can handle the pain of your feelings, and instead of saying 'Can we talk about …?' you handle the situation in a non-direct way.

Eventually you may learn that being direct is a lot less exhausting than arguing, and can often help you avoid, for example, walking out of a relationship. It may help you to try to resolve the situation by direct communication instead. Once you are able to do this you may thrive off emotional intimacy, and feel safe to be 'open' within a relationship.

With a 10/1 influencing your Personality you can be very focused in your mind, and you may also have an interest in spirituality too. The key issue of independence means that you may attract either a strong, independent partner or, alternatively, an emotionally dependent partner who can benefit from your warmth, wisdom and caring personality, and someone with whom you feel spiritually connected.

With a 10/1 influence you generally have a dynamic and high sex drive. Sex for you may simply be a physical release of all your unused creative energy. But you enjoy the physical warmth, the focus of a job well done, and the ability for you to achieve yet another goal: satisfaction.

PHYSICAL APPEARANCE

With a 10/1 influencing your physical appearance you may be tall and slim, with clear, shining skin (and possibly a ruddy complexion), and an attractive face with a protruding jaw. You may have a large mouth, thin lips, and one of your most prominent features is your distinctive tone of voice, which is usually high but alluring.

CHILDHOOD EXPERIENCES

With a 10/1 influencing your childhood you were probably a wise child with an ability to care for any brothers and sisters, and with a real understanding of their needs. For example, you were the first to make sure that they got dressed in the morning when your parents were busy, and you may have read them books at night. You were an independent child, and you liked to do your own thing.

Sometimes you were independent out of necessity, because your parents were too busy, or not around very often. Perhaps you may even have been an only child, so that you had to learn to do things for yourself. You may also have been spoiled because of this, and felt extra-special because you were the centre of attention, and perhaps you had a lot of self-worth.

You may have been an isolated, withdrawn and angry child, who was always pushing others around; you may have been quite destructive at times. You may have sometimes felt abused by others – particularly mentally– because you were unable to stick up for yourself.

Children with a 10/1 may often need a caring, loving environment in which to grow up, to help them learn to express their individuality. They may be sporty, and letting these children indulge in physical activity can help them to disperse any pent-up emotions and unfocused creative energy.

WELL-BEING

With a 10/1 influencing your health you may find that you are prone to diabetes or hypoglycaemia, and blood sugar imbalances. You may also be susceptible to infections, and you may get athlete's foot. Like all 1s, you may be prone to mental and physical stress or exhaustion.

CAREER CHOICES

With a 10/1 influencing your career you are equally happy working either with a group of people or independently. You may like to embark on a career which will stimulate your mind and your creativity, but whatever career path you follow, setting goals for yourself is usually essential.

You may also be wealthy, and not need to work for a living. You may simply fill your diary with fund-raising activities or charity events, or enjoy voluntary work of any kind.

With a 10/1 you may also be a banker, advisor or, like all 1s, you may be a leader or pioneer of some sort. Perhaps you work as a model, an architect, or as a town planner.

FAMOUS CHARACTER ANALYSIS
Joyce Grenfell   Born 10 February 1910

Joyce Grenfell was a wonderfully spirited and humorous human being, who took a leading role in the immensely popular British *St Trinian's* film comedies, which were at the forefront of British entertainment for many years in the late 1950s.

With a 10/1 influencing her life she took on the role as a naïve and gullible physical education teacher at St Trinian's school. She was often portrayed as a victim of physical abuse by the pupils, and mental abuse from the other teachers. Her character was unassuming and quite fearless. Joyce may or may not have displayed these characteristics in her real life, but they are all aspects of the 10/1 influence.

With a 10/1 Joyce strived fearlessly for her goals with wonderful warmth and sense of humour.

Joyce died on 30 November 1979, having explored many of her Personality traits in her career as an actress. This date adds up to 13 or 4, which brings the influence of change and transformation. Perhaps she was planning a change of some sort. The day of death was the 30th or 3, bringing the influence of expansion, the kind of which 'expanded' her soul into another realm.

NUMBER
11/2
PERSONALITY

GENERAL TRENDS FOR NUMBER 11/2 PERSONALITY

With an 11/2 influencing your Personality you have the gift of intuition and the deepest yearning to inspire others. You also want to be inspired by life, and you will attract inspirational people to stimulate you; you believe that all people are your teachers. You may have a great interest in spirituality, and you may look for a guru or spiritual teacher who can help you to discover your inner truth and help you on your spiritual path.

You are a charming and charismatic character, and you attract many interesting individuals who may seek you out, perhaps as their spiritual teacher or guru too. You have an incredible ability to uplift people, and to help them to 'see the light at the end of the tunnel'. You are a natural healer and a carer, and you are always thinking of ways in which you can help others.

You are a born leader, and as there are two 1s this quality is strong. Your need to drive forward with your ambitions, and your need to make and take opportunities, is also great. You are a perfectionist, and you set your sights high, and focus strongly on your goals; you may particularly enjoy focusing all your creative energies into goals which can help others too. For example, you may set up a healing centre, a retreat, or a yoga and meditation centre. However, you can use your creativity and leadership to inspire others in any chosen field, and in your own original way.

You can be an intensely sensitive person, with a lot of 'get up and go' which keeps you active all day (and night) long, because of the finely-tuned nervous energy which passes through you. When you channel all this creative energy into your work you may achieve fame as you radiate inspiration to the world.

With an 11/2 influencing your Personality you can be more of a calm, placid and peace-loving person. Perhaps you enjoy quietness for contemplation, so that you can contact your intuition and get clarity about your life. You may also possess a great need for harmony, particularly in your home, which is your sanctuary. You may be very choosy about who you let inside, and you may be intolerant of people shouting or of too much noise in your environment.

You may be an intellectual person, and you may feel the need to educate yourself constantly, to keep your mind stimulated with new ideas. You are a good listener, and you really absorb all kinds of information, from whatever source. You are very observant, and you pick up fine details about what is being communicated.

With an 11/2, you can easily relate to others, and you often use your intuition and your instincts here; you may even use telepathy with those close to you. You are an open person, and people find you an easy 'ear' because they know you are also open to what they say. You are usually able to see both sides when people seek your opinion, but you can be tactful and diplomatic in your replies. In fact, sometimes you prefer to listen rather than to give any advice. You have a caring, warm and considerate side to your Personality too.

Sometimes you run around too much, and get tired. However, you know how to look after and nurture yourself, and you may schedule extra rest into your day, eat nourishing foods, or book a massage to help relax you and make you feel good again.

With an 11/2 influencing your Personality you like to make all the decisions, because you are good at it; you use your logic to work out the facts and your instincts to find out your gut reaction. However, you may also enjoy co-operative decisions, for example with a group of people at work. Here you enjoy negotiating ideas and concepts and listening to the different needs for the whole group, and working together to find a solution to issues which may arise.

You may enjoy sports which require you to work hard for the goals, like hockey, cricket, badminton or squash. However, you also enjoy passive and gentle exercise, and relaxation such as yoga, meditation or tai chi.

CHALLENGES

With an 11/2 influencing your Personality you are a self-centred person, who may only be interested in helping people when there is something in it for you. For example, you may help a friend to set up a printing shop, but that is only because you want free printing and services for the rest of your life. In one way this tendency can actually help to teach you to receive, which is a major challenge with 1s (or with 11s). So, being selfish may be a positive thing for a while. However, if you are only out for yourself your friends will eventually lose patience with you until you learn to give and to think of them sometimes. You are learning to find balance in your life, which means give and take.

At times you may be prone to temperamental outbursts, due to your sparky, nervous energy. You can be volatile; you may also bite your nails, or exhibit nervous habits such as wringing your hands or pacing up and down. These outbursts can, however, be directed in a positive way into your creativity. At these times you may need calmness and emotional stability to help soothe your mind.

You can be dreamy and become lost in your spirituality. With this lack of concentration you may be accident-prone; perhaps dropping or knocking things over, or even forgetting things. Having accidents may be a way of telling you that you are not grounded. It may also be a way of bringing some issue to your attention, and by using your intuition it may help you to get clarity about what it is. However, on an earthly note, it may also help you to bring your awareness to what you are doing and to focus on the matters at hand.

With an 11/2 you may at times neglect your spirituality and only focus on outer achievements in your life. This may bring you 'hollow' success. For example, have you ever heard of people winning the Lottery but continuing with their 'old' jobs, or the same lifestyle? Winning money may have been the original goal, but perhaps they soon realize that it is an empty achievement, and that spiritually they may be rich in their lives already. There are of course many reasons for their actions. With the influence of two 1s, you may be typical in that you love to work, but may not be overtly concerned with monetary gain. Sometimes your inner self needs goals too, which may be to grow rich with knowledge or wisdom, or loving and caring and sharing.

With an 11/2 influencing your Personality you are manipulative in many ways, playing on people's emotions to get what you want, or to get sympathy for yourself. You can be very self-indulgent in your emotions, and you may enjoy moaning about your emotional pain. You are intensely sensitive to others' pain too, but at times you tend to ignore their feelings, because how you feel is infinitely more important. When you play with others' emotions you may eventually attract someone who plays around with you. By experiencing this form of manipulation it may help you to let go of hurting others.

You may be confrontational at times, and challenge others with your opinions. You may try to force your opinions onto others, and be reluctant to listen to what they have to say. You may also deplore negotiating with people, whether for a table at a restaurant or in a business deal. Indeed, you can be full of your own self-importance, and as far as you are concerned, what you say goes. Part of you always likes to make the final decision on your own because you are a leader.

Sometimes you can be very stubborn, and wilful and rebellious in your actions and attitude. However, when not influenced by the challenging qualities of an 11/2, you are likely to go about life in a gentle, caring manner. You are fundamentally a sharer, and you may even like to share the decision-making, share the workload, share a relationship and share your life with everybody around you. You are also your own strong individual.

With an 11/2 influencing your Personality you may often have very high expectations from your own input into your life. This is great because it is teaching you to go for what you want, and to achieve things. However, when you start to demand and expect the same from others, you may experience disappointments when you realize that life cannot always be lived out in its ideal.

ROMANCE AND SEX

With an 11/2 influencing your love life you may feel that you have to give up your individuality in order to share yourself in a relationship. This may particularly apply if you are female, and getting married, in which case you may be giving up your 'single' name, and you may feel this loss of individuality strongly. However, with the 2, you are learning to share, and you may enjoy establishing a new identity for yourself within a committed relationship.

Finding a partner who is down-to-earth may also help you to ground your nervous energy and allow any access friction to melt away. A steady relationship or a stable partner may also be in harmony with the more placid side of your nature, and help you to stay calm. For example, when you are having a temperamental outburst it may help you to have someone close who understands you. You may also be an anchor for your partner during times of emotion, because you know how to stay calm in a storm too.

You can be exhausting at times because your energy is so focused and concentrated. Your partner may back off for a while when you are too intense. Or, if he or she has a great sense of humour, he or she may encourage you to lighten up and laugh, or give you a different focus of attention.

Spirituality is an important issue with an 11/2 and sometimes your spirituality can take up the largest amount of space within your relationships. For example, discovering your inner self may sometimes be more essential to you than sex, or meditating may be more relevant to you than carrying out some household chore. If this aspect is strong, then you may look for a partner who can be your spiritual teacher. This may come in the form of a soul mate with whom you have deep connections and with whom you can share a life of spiritual evolvement.

You may have a magnetic, attractive and vibrant Personality, and you may look for a partner who can match these qualities. You bestow care, love, warmth and nurturing on your intimate partner, so you expect more than simply superficial charms in return. You may also possess a fine mind, and you may require someone with whom you can discuss intellectual matters. You have high expectations about what you want from your partner, and from any relationship, and you may feel angry or bitter when things don't go like a dream.

With an 11/2 influencing your sex life, you may prefer to satisfy your emotional needs for intimacy and sharing, love and affection, than expressing your love through steamy sex. However, you may also find a lover with whom you can burn out your intense feelings of passion. Having a spiritual connection may be very important to you, even if you do feel detached from your partner emotionally; spiritual ecstasy can also get you 'high'.

PHYSICAL APPEARANCE

With an 11/2 influencing your looks you may have a wiry or weak appearance, with a troubled expression. You may look hard if you are influenced by the 11, or soft and round if the 2 energy is stronger. You may have high-arched eyebrows and a high-pitched voice. Your outstanding feature may be your eyes, which are clear, deep, intense and vibrant.

CHILDHOOD EXPERIENCES

With an 11/2 influencing your childhood you may have been dreamy, passive and quiet at home or in school. You were probably a highly sensitive and intuitive child, with an awareness of spirituality and other energies apart from your own. You may have also been a very caring child.

You may have been sensitive to others' opinions, and with your high expectations, may have taken criticism to heart. At times you dismissed your – less than perfect – achievements by being rebellious and refusing to co-operate with your family, teachers or friends. However, you were an achiever, and your determination to make the grade at school usually meant that you did achieve a glowing school report at the end of term.

With an 11/2 you may have been an independent child who liked to sort out and do things on your own. You may have also been a leader, and with your energy and vitality probably had a regular number of friends and new recruits to your gang.

Children with an 11/2 may sometimes be hyperactive or unable to sit still, with a short span of concentration. Therefore encouraging them to work on a number of different creative projects may channel their energies and help to keep them occupied. Also, encouraging a child's passion – cooking, painting, writing or playing musical instruments – may help to focus their energies and calm them down. These children may also need a lot of physical affection.

WELL-BEING

With an 11/2 influencing your health you may be prone to nervousness, stomach upsets, insomnia, tension headaches or depression. You may also suffer from nervous or emotional exhaustion, asthma and eczema sometimes.

CAREER CHOICE

With an 11/2 influencing your career, you may take on work as a counsellor, carer or complementary therapist – particularly as an acupuncturist – which stimulates your mind. You may also work as a spiritual healer. Any of these careers may inspire you to use your knowledge and your intuition to help others.

You may also work as a writer, chef, artist or musician, and inspire people with your creativity. Perhaps you may take up a career as a diplomat, mediator or lawyer, and use your creativity as an actress or actor. Whatever career you choose, you may achieve recognition or fame.

FAMOUS CHARACTER ANALYSIS
Salvador Dali Born 11 May 1904

Salavador Dali was a living work of art; not only was he original in his creations but he often dressed with great individuality and spark too. He was known for his surrealist paintings, which he captured from deep within his spirituality and imagination. For these he received great fame and recognition, and he stood strong as a leader within society.

With an 11/2, Dali was inspired by life, and his work continues to fascinate the masses. He was typical of Personality Number 11 in that he was notorious for his temperamental outbursts, through which he often verbally expressed his intense feelings and moods. He often lacked tact in his communication, and he was blunt, direct and spared no polite graces.

Dali, it would appear, found the love of his life, his soul mate, whom he married and shared his life with. It is said that she was his 'muse', who inspired his life and his greatest works of art.

Dali died on 23 January 1989, having inspired others with his concepts and ideas. The whole date adds up to a 6, so perhaps he had completed his service for one lifetime. The day was a 23 or 5, which encompasses the heavenly gifts of art and beauty, so as an artist he no doubt died with these visions circling his mind.

NUMBER
12/3
PERSONALITY

GENERAL TRENDS FOR NUMBER 12/3 PERSONALITY

With a 12/3 influencing your Personality you have a gift of abundance and a deepest yearning to be able to create. You are very family-orientated and you may find that a lot of your social time is spent with them; for example, getting the family around the table for meals, visiting other relatives, family holidays together, and so on. You may also have a strong desire to create your own family; if not, then the question of whether or not to have children may be an issue for you. However, with such a strong family around you, there are usually plenty of children in your extended circle to nurture and play with.

You may possess a wonderful, light and joyous sense of humour and you really love to play – you seem to find all kinds of things to amuse yourself. You have a mischievous child-like quality, and you may spend hours playing with children and entertaining each other. You are easily excited because, like a child, you get stimulated by the simple things in life and you can usually find something to giggle about. However, you are also fiercely protective of others, and you may feel very protective towards (your own) children.

With a 12/3 you are abundantly creative and love to express yourself in whatever way you can: pottering around in the garden, cooking, writing, painting, communicating, talking, and so on. You are usually an extrovert and bubbly person and your enthusiasm and enjoyment of life really shine through. You are also a 'doer' and you don't know how to stop: for example, you may be working, then you'll read, then you'll smooch with your partner, then you'll go shopping. Sleeping may be the only way for you to curb your activities, but you may find that you do not need long hours of sleep either. This may be because you have so much to do in your life, and you focus on living so intensely, that you just take the minimum you need. You usually seem to have boundless amounts of energy to keep you going.

You may have a strong mind, and you are usually bright and witty too. You may be an intellectual person who prefers a more sartorial sense of humour in your more serious moods, and indeed, you can be deadly serious at times. You may like to develop your mind by studying, reading, attending lectures or involving yourself in discussions with your friends, about literature, art, politics or social issues. You may also have a keen interest in spirituality and religion. However, whatever you are discussing, you usually find your topic of conversation ends with one of your favourite subjects – your family.

You are generally a warm and generous person, and you love to give. People are often mesmerized by your ability to look after others and by the depth of affection that you show them. You are a tactile person, and you like and need to feel connected with others physically.

With a 12/3 you are a social animal who likes to get out and about to meet others. You may find talking to new people easy, and you are able to adapt to all kinds of situations and conversations. Indeed, you are an easy-going person and you seem to get along with everyone. You are also a likeable person and people find themselves drawn towards your bright mind and your lightness, joy and humour.

Perhaps you are also socially aware, and you may set great store by good manners. For example, you may be very aware to say 'thank you' to the host for a party, or you may ask permission to bring a guest with you to a dinner party. However, such social niceties are important for you to be happy with yourself, your family, and with the company you keep.

You can be a very focused person and you may like to set goals in your life which give you an outlet for your abundant creativity. These may be work or personal goals, but family goals are important too. You have many original ideas, which once materialized may bring you great happiness and success. You are usually direct in your communications, and you are firm with others when going for what you want. You are an ambitious person and little can deter you once you have set your sights on your goals.

You enjoy all kinds of sports, but you may get plenty of exercise running around all day because you are an active person anyway.

CHALLENGES

With a 12/3 influencing your Personality you may be a fussy person who is always finding fault with people. You pay great attention to detail, and you can be very hard on yourself, but you may also pull people apart at times to try to get them to fit your high standards. However, there are always things which you like about some people and things which you dislike about others, but it is impossible to change the whole world to suit yourself. Learning to relax and accept life's little idiosyncrasies can help release a lot of the stress that may have gone into unnecessarily reprimanding others, and it may make you a more popular person too.

However, you may also be too relaxed and laid back at times to bother to pick on others. You may have a carefree attitude towards life and let things go, even when it may be to your disadvantage. For example, an engineer comes to mend your washing machine and it seemed to work better before than after, but you just can't be bothered to ring up the plumber and say anything about it. Sometimes when you do make the effort to do things you may 'mess them up' because you don't concentrate or are unfocused, or do not know enough facts. Indeed, you may be unable to keep your attention on things for any time at all. It may help you to try to find a balance between being relaxed and casual, or over-concerned and fussy about things, and between 'being' and 'doing'.

You may be an untidy person and make a mess wherever you go – your home, your office, in the car. However, being untidy is an expression of your energy, which is all dissipating out. Sometimes drawing your energy in, and tidying up your mess, can help you to feel more centred and clear, and enable you to get on with your life.

With a 12/3 influencing your Personality you may have the uncanny ability to create confusion and chaos in your life. This may be because you have so many things to do that you run around 'like a headless chicken'. You may also feel inner conflict about your life, because there are so many outer demands on your time that you just cannot ever seem to do enough. However, looking at all the different aspects of your life may help you to make decisions about any changes that may need to be made to simplify your life.

Sometimes you may find that adapting to changes in your life is a challenge for you. This may be because you may feel unable to cope with yet one more thing demanding your attention. Sometimes you may also dissipate your energy or become exhausted from spreading your energies too thinly around, particularly during times of great change. You may realize that changes are often for the better. By giving in and being adaptable to life, your energies can simply flow with these changes, instead of using up your energy to fight them.

With a 12/3 you can be stubborn, wilful and destructive. You possess a sharp temper, which may not arise often, but when it does it may explode into a fury of anger and aggression. You may even be vindictive at times, particularly when you feel hurt, abandoned or let down. However, feelings need to come out, and they usually tend to explode when you have been bottling them up for some time. By being more laid back and expressing your feelings in a constructive way it may help you to heal your hurts, and to resolve situations in a positive way.

You may feel frustrated when your goals don't materialize the way you planned, and you may feel like giving up sometimes. However, you usually have so much going on that as soon as one little thing goes right it helps to spur you on to your next goal. With a 12/3 your sense of humour and your lightness and joy are never too far away, and by going out to play and having some fun socially it may help you to cheerily look forward to each new day.

With a 12/3 influencing your Personality you may be prone to fits of jealousy and be very possessive at times. This may be because you can be so full of your own self-importance or – the flip side of this – because you sometimes just don't feel good enough. But everyone is special and important in their own way. However, you may enjoy your freedom, and learning to allow others their freedom, and so to be the best they possibly can with their individuality, may encourage you to do the same.

ROMANCE AND SEX

With a 12/3 influencing your love life you may be someone who loves and needs to be involved in a strong family life. So attracting a partner who also relishes family activities may be of utmost importance. Perhaps your partner was an 'only child' and would love to get stuck into family life with you, or perhaps he or she has a good family life already, and you can feel even happier knowing that there are more people to add to your family group. You love socializing as part of any group, and like all 3s, you may seek a partner who can join in with the fun of the group too.

You may have a bright mind and possess a good head for business, but you may also like to be able to turn to your partner for some good advice too. You love to communicate your ideas and to share them with others, and you are a leader, but sometimes you may like to feel that someone else can take the lead. Therefore you may seek a partner whom you can rely on to give his or her own strong opinion when it is needed.

It is likely that you are fussy about your appearance and as you may not get out of bed without applying perfect make-up and coordinating your 'dress', you may also expect this from your partner. However, you have an easy-going side to your nature, and sloppy jeans on Sundays may be ideal.

With a 12/3 influencing your Personality you are a kind, considerate and generous person, and you may do your best to give your partner what he or she needs. For example, you may make sure you buy his or her favourite chocolate ice-cream, or may offer a lingering and relaxing massage at the end of a hard day. You also love to be pampered, and showering you with attention and affection may be just what your partner needs to do.

You have a happy outlook on life and you are a born optimist, which you also like to project towards your relationship. So that even when you do have arguments with your partner you still end up laughing or as friends. However, when you break up from a relationship, you may get emotional for a short while, but it doesn't take you long before your thirst for fun and excitement makes you go back for more.

There may be so many things for you to do that you may not put enough energy into your relationships to make them work. For example, you may have many business and social projects on the go at once, which all require your attention. However, by attracting a strong partner who is able to express to you when he or she is feeling neglected, you may be helped to bring your focus back to the relationship. Finding a partner who likes routine, may also help you because, no matter how busy you are, if you eat at 8pm – that's it! These boundaries may help you to commit to your relationship in many different ways.

With a 12/3 influencing your sex life, you love to play with your partner, and foreplay may be just as delicious fun as the thrusting sex which you also enjoy. You aim to please, but you can be critical about your partner. You are easily able to express yourself about what exactly it is that turns you on.

PHYSICAL APPEARANCE

With a 12/3 influencing your looks you may be tall, with a long neck and a long face. You may be slim-built, with narrow hips and sloping shoulders, and a wide straight nose. You generally have small but 'open' eyes, which may look watery. Your outstanding feature is your high forehead.

CHILDHOOD EXPERIENCES

With a 12/3 influencing your childhood you may have experienced a lot of care from your family, and your grandparents may have been greatly influential over your upbringing. Life may have revolved around your family, and as a result you may have felt that you needed very few friends, because you usually had someone to play with and everything you needed at home.

You may have been brought up in academic surroundings, with perhaps a library of books for you to choose from. Your family may often have been involved in intellectual discussions, and right from an early age, where you could, you liked to contribute your opinion to the conversation. You may have enjoyed learning, and been focused on achieving good grades at school, particularly to please your parents.

Perhaps you were a happy-go-lucky child who was always in tune with life. You may have also been an active child who, when not reading, took time off to join in any kind of sporting activities. You may have loved sports days, because you loved to compete.

There may also have been an artistic leaning in your household, and arranging flowers, sketching portraits of your family or making things with your hands may have been popular pastimes.

Children with a 12/3 often want to do everything at once: they want to play, they want to study, they want to talk. It may help them to set clear boundaries on when they can do what, and where, so that they can get the most out of their day.

WELL-BEING

With a 12/3 influencing your health you may be prone to digestive problems such as stomach upsets, and you may suffer from poor circulation. You may also sometimes have problems with your skin or have skin sensitivities.

CAREER CHOICE

With a 12/3 influencing your career you may take up work where you are able to communicate to others, for example as an entertainer, or a television or radio presenter where you can sometimes use your lightness and joy to uplift others.

You may also take up work as a landscape gardener, cook, nutritionist, masseur or writer. However, you have a bright mind and a head for success, so you may embark upon a career as a business executive of any kind, a teacher, an academic, leader or politician, or in any field where you can work hard channelling your creativity to achieve your goals.

FAMOUS CHARACTER ANALYSIS
Grace Kelly Born 12 November 1928

Grace Kelly was, as her name suggests, full of beauty and grace. She had a serene and often pristine look, and an elegant bearing which made her stand out from the crowd. Grace often appeared cool, calm and collected in the public eye. She also possessed all the additional attributes needed for her career as a model; she was tall and slim built, with a well-proportioned figure.

Grace explored her creativity and her need for expression by becoming an actress, where she sometimes played society roles. She was also in real life a member of high society, and with a successful career, money and looks, she found herself a leading role by marrying a prince – and so became Princess Grace.

With a 12/3 Grace focused on what it was she wanted from her life. She was apparently freedom-loving, and she was stimulated by travel and meeting new people. Grace liked to explore the opportunities available to her. She appeared happy-go-lucky, and some would say, a 'lucky' woman who led a rich and abundant lifestyle.

Grace died in a car crash on the 13 September 1982, having led a full and successful life. The whole date adds up to a 6, so perhaps Grace was looking for a way out of her 'duties' or responsibilities on that day. The day was the 13th which represents change, so Grace went for that opportunity.

NUMBER
13/4
PERSONALITY

GENERAL TRENDS FOR NUMBER 13/4 PERSONALITY

With a 13/4 influencing your Personality you have the gift of adaptability and you also have the deepest yearning to feel secure. Feeling secure means that you also feel safe, and when you feel both of these you are able to handle whatever comes your way. For example, you may be so secure within yourself that even when you lose your job suddenly, it has no major effect upon you, and straightaway you may start looking for another one. That is not to say that you don't feel things, because you are sensitive at times, but you can cope.

You may really thrive off change, because it challenges you to be adaptable, and you love that. Perhaps you find life boring when it simply settles into a daily routine. Sometimes, however, there seems to be constant change in your life, or you may find that there are frequent dramas for you to sort out. However, you are a laid-back and relaxed person, and you generally take things in your stride. You may even enjoy focusing on inventing practical solutions to challenges in your life, because you are a natural problem-solver, and like to use your mind.

At times, you may also enjoy risk-taking, because it takes you away from the monotony of everyday survival into the unknown, and gives you the chance to improve your life. For example, you could risk money on the stock exchange, cash in your savings and start up your own company on a whim, or move to another country, just for a change. However, you are usually a down-to-earth person, and sometimes you only take risks after cautiously assessing the facts, and how your physical security may be affected.

With a 13/4 influencing your Personality you may always be on the look-out for new opportunities and new goals. You are also a leader, and by being the first to take a risk, or to attempt to change, others may follow you, and you may influence positive change too. For example, you may be the first banker to bill your accounts to your customer in a new and more practical way; other banks may then follow your lead and implement your new structure. To you, opportunities mean change, change means growth and growth means that you get to learn more about life in a practical way.

You may thrive on responsibilities, because they allow you to feel like you are actively participating in your life. You are also a 'doer' and an active person, and you may not be the type to sit around whilst everyone else does all the work for you. You probably even enjoy working hard at times, and you may put a lot of effort into making your life work.

Generally you are an ambitious person, and you may address all your dynamic energy and vitality towards your goals, and really go for what you want. Then you may use your down-to-earth qualities to materialize them. You may often be brilliantly creative in your own original way.

With a 13/4 you are a strong individual, with a bubbly sense of humour and an ability to really uplift and inspire others with your lightness and joy. You may also be outgoing and extrovert, and you often like and need the company of lots of different people. Whether at work or in the social environment, you love to chat and to communicate your own individuality through this wonderful form of self-expression.

Perhaps you also have an interest in mysticism, or spirituality and religion. However, you are realistic and you do not let your interests or your beliefs carry you away. You may also enjoy art, literature and politics, and find yourself deeply involved in conversations about any of these fascinating subjects. However, you are strongly opinionated and you may not be swayed easily by others' beliefs; you can also be quite serious.

With a 13/4 you are a home-maker, and you help to build up your security by having a strong and solid foundation, as your base. You are a warm and caring person and often generous with your hospitality, and you instinctively know how to make your guests feel comfortable. Perhaps you love to entertain and have lots of family parties, and many guests at your home. However, you also need solitude at times, and you may withdraw into your home away from your busy life and create some space for yourself.

You may love chess, bridge and playing board games for relaxation. You may also love walking and aerobics, and enjoy many sports activities.

CHALLENGES

With a 13/4 influencing your Personality you may be very insecure at times and lack the confidence to go out into the world and express your individuality. Sometimes you may get wonderful opportunities coming your way, but you simply withdraw into a 'corner' and refuse to budge. However, at these times it may help you to take a deep breath and take the plunge by trying something new, no matter how small. Little by little you can then learn to 'stand up' and be happy to express who you are.

You may prefer life to go on as it is, with your own steady routine, uninterrupted by change. You may also resist change to the extent that your life gets stuck 'in a rut', from doing the same old things every day. Deep down you may fear change, and cling on to your lifestyle in order to survive, but the firmer you stand, the greater you may fall. Sometimes when you cling onto things life has a habit of eventually forcing you to let go. However, resisting life for a while may also mean that when you do move forward, changes may occur much faster and in a more forceful and dynamic way.

With a 13/4 influencing your Personality life may throw up dramas for you, and at times life may even seem like one big drama. Sometimes these occur because you are very emotional, or because you are avoiding dealing with conflicts in your life. There may also be a side to your Personality which thrives on drama, and you may prefer the excitement of dealing with these challenges, rather than settling into a dull routine. However, by learning to constantly adapt to change, and to ride the challenges that come your way, you can stay 'grounded' and handle the dramas in a positive way.

Generally you are a practical person, but you may find yourself in a mess at times because you are unable to accept responsibility for yourself or to deal with problems in a practical way. For example, you may have had a knock in your car whilst out shopping, but because you avoided filling in your insurance papers at the time, you may not now be able to claim any compensation. Learning to be efficient and handling life as it comes may save you more problems later on.

Sometimes you can be an 'all or nothing' person. For example, you either love or hate chocolate, rather than thinking that chocolate is just OK. However, there are always the grey areas, and when you make such 'black-or-white' decisions about things, you may miss out on a particular experience. For example, you may want to go to the cinema with your partner, but your partner wants you to go to the football with him, but you make a decision not to go out with him at all. However, the grey area may be to make a compromise, by spending an hour at the football and then going off to the cinema as well. Finding the grey areas may help you to lead a more fulfilled life.

With a 13/4 influencing your Personality you may take unnecessary risks, which may be destructive or harmful towards the people around you. For example, you may half-cook food in the microwave for the whole family, because you are really hungry, which may result in them getting food poisoning. Or you might put your house up as security with the bank for some vague business venture, with very little practical proof that it can succeed. However, sometimes the only way to learn is by your mistakes, which may teach you to be more down-to-earth later on.

You may at times find yourself addicted to aspects of your life: food, sex, coffee, alcohol, gambling, vitamin pills, exercise, worrying, or people. You may also resist these things by being celibate, restricting your diet, avoiding alcohol, or by not getting involved in relationships. However, when you feel secure in yourself, you may not feel the need to be extreme about anything in your life. You can simply get on with it calmly.

With a 13/4 you may be over-opinionated or argumentative, and cause dramas and disagreements. Your radical viewpoints or behaviour may annoy people. However, sometimes people may need to be stirred up to encourage them to change when they have become too stuck in their outlook or in their ways. But you can also learn from listening to a variety of opinions which may help you be flexible in your views, and with your life too.

ROMANCE AND SEX

With a 13/4 influencing your love life, you may be a person who relishes your security, and therefore finding a partner with whom you can form a stable and steady relationship may be essential to you. You are persistent and determined, and once you have found your partner then you are prepared to give it all you have got to make it work.

You are a loving, warm and caring person and you may seek a partner who is affectionate, like you, and also someone who is unafraid to express how much they love you. However, you are also a practical person, and you may take into consideration your partner's love by how much they do for you. For example, putting up shelves for you, or driving you to work every morning. You may also need to know that you and your partner can provide financial and material security for yourselves, which is an important issue.

If you are bringing up children alone you may seek a partner to help give physical security to your children, and you may enter into a committed relationship to fulfil their practical needs. You may not be in love with your partner, but building a strong relationship with him or her may satisfy your basic needs.

Intimacy may be scary for you, and particularly at the start of a new relationship you may find it challenging to express your innermost self to your partner. However, as you get to know that person more, and you persevere, you may eventually feel safe to let go a little and feel relaxed and at ease within your relationship. Sometimes you are the one to be intimate and carefree, and you may even be over-expressive at times, when your partner isn't. Again, it may help to persevere until both of you feel more comfortable and can relax with each other.

With a 13/4 influencing your Personality you may enjoy challenges in your relationship, and you may prefer a partner who is going to make you work hard for him or her. For example, he or she may be someone who never quite commits themselves to the relationship in some way, so you may put even more effort into your relationship to win their attentions and to help make it work. You like and need to feel secure, but the free spirit inside you may still like to feel 'free' even when you are in a committed relationship, which may throw up challenges for your partner at times.

You may be a dynamic and energetic person who focuses much of your attention on inspiring your partner with your wicked sense of humour and playfulness. You are also a deep thinker, and you may enjoy discussing current affairs with your partner too.

With a 13/4 influencing your sex life you may seek a romantic partner who can whisk you off into the setting sun for a sultry weekend of sex and passion. You may be turned on by 'risky' sex – by having sex when you may get caught out, such as in crowded public places or with other people about. However, friendship is often the essential ingredient in a happy and exciting sex life.

PHYSICAL APPEARANCE

With a 13/4 influencing your Personality you may be small to medium height, with dark skin. You may have high arched eyebrows, almond-shaped, heavy-lidded eyes, and chunky hands and legs. Your most outstanding feature may be your long and prominent eyelashes.

CHILDHOOD EXPERIENCES

With a 13/4 influencing your childhood, you may have been a bright and energetic child who was always being stimulated by new ideas and things to do. For example, you may have invented your own games, or built your own play-house, and you were probably very good at making things with your hands. Perhaps you were also stimulated by learning about new things, by studying an encyclopaedia, for example.

You may have felt happy and secure as a child, perhaps with a solid structure and a creative environment at home, and with discipline from your parents. You may have enjoyed entertaining your friends at home, going to parties, or chatting away merrily – you were usually a very popular child. It may have taken you a while to make friends, but once you did, you were very loyal. However, you may have held grudges against them if you felt that they had let you down.

With a 13/4 you may have loved to take risks at times: for example, by leaving on a later bus to get to school and hoping you would be on time. When you didn't have an outlet for your creativity you may have been over-expressive, emotional or aggressive, and even got yourself into all kinds of dramas. For example, you may have had an accident as a result of climbing a tree. Then, ironically, perhaps you lapped up the attention you received and loved the excitement which relieved the boredom of your daily routine.

Children with a 13/4, are usually very creative, but they may need plenty of encouragement, particularly if they are lacking in self-confidence, to express themselves in whatever way they can. For example, by encouraging them to talk, to paint, to play, and to stimulate their minds generally.

WELL-BEING

With a 13/4 influencing your health, you may be prone to injuries from accidents when you are not concentrating, or from taking irresponsible risks. You may also be prone to stomach problems (such as ulcers), urinary problems, or blood-pressure imbalances.

CAREER CHOICE

With a 13/4 influencing your career you may work in a business where there is a lot of action and change, for example on the stock exchange, in the Investment sector, as a politician, environmentalist or social worker, or in the media.

You may also be a leader of some kind, a public relations person, party organizer or entertainer, or you may be a painter or even a blacksmith. You may also work as a mystic, massage therapist, artist or writer, or work in any field which involves taking risks.

FAMOUS CHARACTER ANALYSIS
Sir Alfred Hitchcock Born 13 August 1899

Sir Alfred Hitchcock was the king of drama, who spent most of his life expressing his abundant creativity by directing many, many films, some of which brought him various Oscar nominations. His films were often so dramatic, full of intrigue and suspense that people were left literally hanging onto the edge of their seats! Hitchcock was also something of an exhibitionist and full of his own self-importance, and always insisted on playing himself in a 'walk on, walk off' role in his films. For example, he might be seen sitting in a cafe in the background, or walking past the main character.

Hitchcock was a brilliant director and a leader in his field; you always knew that if it was a Hitchcock film you would get your money's worth! For Hitchcock, the challenge of making these movies must have been awe-inspiring and exciting, and he directed his dynamic drive and ambition towards his goals in a disciplined and practical way. Certainly his rigorous work routines required a lot of stamina. He was certainly a 'doer', with no time to sit around and get bored.

Sir Alfred Hitchcock died on 29 April 1980, having enjoyed the freedom to express his creativity in his celebrated life. The whole date adds up to a 6, which indicates that he may have felt complete with his service to humanity on that day. The day is a 29 or 2, so perhaps he had given up trying, and felt that there were no other challenges left for him.

14/5

PERSONALITY

GENERAL TREND FOR NUMBER 14/5 PERSONALITY

With a 14/5 influencing your Personality you have a gift of adaptability and an intense yearning to feel deeply connected to life. You thrive on change because change keeps things moving, and it keeps you on your toes. Change also means that you face many different experiences, and even when things get tough you appreciate that there are still important lessons to learn from these experiences. Change means new stimulation, new ideas, new situations, and new things to do.

Sometimes when there are too many things going on externally you may find yourself turning to your intuition to get clarity about your life. For example, you may have been running around all week, and take time off at the weekend, to withdraw and to be on your own for a time. You may meditate, listen to music, read, or potter around your home. Taking time off, to be 'with' yourself, can help to bring you down to earth, and give you space to delve into your mind to find the knowledge which you seek about life. Therefore your need to explore the depths of your mind may be great, and you may be inspired to do so as often as you can.

You may sometimes turn towards spirituality or religion for inspiration, and to help you examine 'the meaning of life'. You may love to study and find out about different cultures and philosophies, and this may help you to feel closer to 'all' people and more connected to life.

With a 14/5 influencing your Personality you are a practical and sensible person with a realistic attitude towards life. You can act impulsively at times, but generally you like to ascertain all the facts about a situation before you jump in. You may also take a while to commit to people or things, and you may seek guidance from your intuition to help you make decisions. However, once you have made commitments you do not 'budge,' and you devote your whole being to following them through.

You are a highly ambitious and creative person. Your intuition can provide you with many innovative ideas which you can methodically work towards materializing. You are dynamic and a hard worker, and you possess a determination to accomplish your goals, in a totally focused way. Usually you are a positive thinker, who likes to make the best out of your life.

You may be very independent and responsible, and like to rely on yourself to get things done. You are often brilliant at organizing others and your daily routine. For example, you may be a public relations executive who launches a major product all around the world, with great organization and flair. Perhaps you also incorporate your leadership skills by pioneering the launch in a special way. You are a strong individual with your own unique style, which shines through everything you do.

You are a highly magnetic person and you draw a variety of people and situations to you, which ensures you don't get bored. You live life in the fast lane at times. You are quick-witted, a fast thinker, and often a fast talker too. You are often fascinated by life and by people. There is so much to do and learn; you like to feel free to explore as many opportunities as you can. Sometimes you enjoy being spontaneous and going along for a while without plans.

With a 14/5 you love to communicate with others, and you may often be aware of and understand the power and responsibility of communication via words and speech. For example, if you are a media representative you may be very conscious of your responsibilities in delivering your messages to the world via your speech. You may also be acutely aware of delivering clear and positive communication to your partner, friends and family, and think before you speak. Perhaps you are also fascinated by communication through symbols (logo and design, for example), or through the power of numbers.

You may enjoy walking, tennis and working out in the gym, or perhaps you go for fast adrenalin-pumping sports too.

CHALLENGES

With a 14/5 influencing your Personality you may be lazy at times, and resist life, because you are too fearful that making a move means changes in your life. For example, if you find a fantastic new night school course, but you are very set in your routine, then you may drop the idea of the course. You may also resist doing new things because change makes you feel insecure. However, by handling change in a practical way, and by just plodding on and doing the best you can each day, it can help you to cope with change in a positive and more comfortable way.

Sometimes, you may restrict yourself by staying in the same old relationship or job, rather than facing the change. However, there is a part of your Personality which is open and adaptable to change. By allowing a little movement to 'free up' your resistance you can learn to enjoy many new experiences.

Sometimes you may create great problems in your mind by finding reasons why you can't move forward. For example, you may passionately want to start your own company, but you come up with every possible excuse as to why it cannot work. This means that your goals and ideas sometimes remain 'stuck' in your head. Alternatively, you may procrastinate for a long time before taking any concrete actions towards materializing them. However, the power of your logical brain may eventually help you to sort out these doubts and enable you to move on with your life.

You may sometimes find yourself facing (unexpected) traumatic situations, or realize that you have helped to materialize problems with your strong powerful mind. You may feel like running away, and even compulsively walk out of a situation, just to get away from facing life or your responsibilities. However, 'you can run but you can't hide', and you may find yourself facing similar situations later on if you don't deal with them at the time. By delving into your intuition and your mind you may find ways of handling challenges in a more constructive and practical way. For example, perhaps your partner suddenly wants a divorce, after you have been working so hard to keep the relationship together. Instead of literally running away you may be able to go inside and think about your situation calmly; you can then communicate your clarity to your partner in a positive and constructive way.

With a 14/5 influencing your Personality you may at times prefer to live your life in your mind rather than in the material world. This may be because life in your imagination is much more exciting than the reality of your life. Sometimes you may even try to 'escape' physical reality by taking alcohol, cigarettes or drugs, and you may sometimes find yourself addicted to one or more of these things. However, addictions are a way of taking you deeply into your inner self, so whilst it may seem like you are running away from life, you are actually going deeper in. Addictions can be dangerous and destructive, and can take over your life. Sometimes seeking professional help may be the only way for you to get through. Putting as much effort into your life to make it exciting and full – love, friends, work, travel – can also stimulate you.

You feel free to communicate, but sometimes with your quick mind you may say things without thinking, and hurt others. Sometimes these words are 'truthful' because they come straight from your intuition, and you may be as surprised as the recipient at what comes out. Whether or not you say what you mean, you get back what you give, and you may not always enjoy the consequences. Perhaps it may help to take responsibility for what you say, and learn to treat others in a respectful way.

At times, you may find it difficult to communicate with people, or perhaps you are too lazy to be bothered, particularly if you are out in the world having a good time. This may land you on the spot, for example, by forgetting to instruct your bank to pay your direct debits for household bills on a certain date. Sometimes making an effort to communicate, even if you find it a challenge, can help you to avoid unnecessary unexpected events.

ROMANCE AND SEX

With a 14/5 influencing your relationships you may sometimes feel like you are blessed with good karma, as life always seems to bring good and wonderful things your way. Or perhaps it is your positive attitude which takes everything in life – even the challenging times – as a blessing and a gift. You may have a loving partner, interesting friends, and stimulating and rewarding work. Your relationships are the highlights of your life because you are a 'people person', and with your magnetic charms you are popular too.

You are an independent person and do not rely solely on your partner for entertainment or fun. Indeed you may love to go out to parties and social gatherings, and go travelling into the big wide world, all on your own. You may also love to go out with the crowd and meet up regularly with different groups of people – and it may be important for your partner to fit in with that too.

A partner who you think is more intelligent than you, or who has lots of experience of life, and knowledge to share, may be very attractive to you. You may like a worldly partner who can tell you stories from around the world. You are also a deep thinker, and you may find a partner who can help to stimulate you, by discussing art, literature or public affairs. You can at times be a deeply spiritual person and you may need to feel spiritually connected with your partner, as much as physically and mentally too.

With a 14/5 influencing your relationships you love to communicate with your partner, and you sometimes welcome practical feedback too. For example, your partner may make suggestions about what you can wear, or what to cook for a dinner party, or how to sort out a problem at work or with your children. You respect your partner's opinions, which can help you to work life out. However, you can also be stubborn and wilful, and you do not always like to be told what to do. You may follow your own opinions, and do your own thing too. You have a strong intuition and logic, and you may turn to your mind to help you sort life out.

You may seek a partner who can be spontaneous; for example, someone who enjoys doing silly things, or who loves to turn up 'out of the blue' with flowers for you, or who suddenly forgets dinner on a Friday night and takes you off into the horizon for a weekend of adventure and passion. You may thrive off the thrill of change, and you may like life and your partner to be exciting and a little unpredictable at times.

With a 14/5 influencing your sex life you feel free to express pleasure, and you are uninhibited about just how much noise you make on the road to satisfaction. You can be a tough cookie to please because you may have a persistent sex drive, and you want to experiment with your partner too. However, if you are someone who lives your life out in your head and you are not very physical, then talking about your sexual fantasies may be as far as you choose to go.

PHYSICAL APPEARANCE

With a 14/5 influencing your looks you may have large bulging eyes, clear skin, an upturned nose, a high forehead, and eyebrows that meet in the middle. You may have a large face, with high cheekbones and a prominent chin. You may also be of medium height, and your outstanding feature is your slim build.

CHILDHOOD EXPERIENCES

With a 14/5 influencing your childhood you may have been an intuitive and spiritual child, who was often coming out with 'truths' which would shock others. For example, you may have told your aunt that she was a terrible cook, or your teacher that he was too bossy. This may have made you unpopular, even though you came out with good things too.

Perhaps you enjoyed studying science, religion and history, and anything which could educate you about life. You may have been a bookworm, reading many books at once. You may have liked to withdraw into your mind when you read, and escaped physical reality for a while.

With a 14/5 you probably enjoyed school because there were lots of interesting children and many things to do and learn. You had a bright and inquisitive mind and picked things up quickly, but you were probably restless and sometimes found it hard to keep your attention focused. However, you probably worked hard, as you were ambitious too.

You may have loved taking part in sports, and probably happily skipped around and played games. Perhaps you enjoyed hide and seek, dancing, narrating or acting in plays. With your curious mind you may have loved jigsaw puzzles, or taking toys apart and putting them together again to see how they worked.

Children with a 14/5 may find changes challenging. For example, the move from junior to senior school, or even something simple like a change in the time they need to get up in the mornings. However, children seem to know naturally how to survive – by just getting on with life – and by being patient with them, they can adjust to changes in their own time.

WELL-BEING

With a 14/5 influencing your health you may be prone to problems with your intestines and your immune system. You may also be prone to throat and thyroid problems (connected to your self-expression) or arthritis.

CAREER CHOICE

With a 14/5 influencing your career, you may take up work in public relations, marketing, sales or advertising, or work in the travel, computer or electronics industry. You may also excel as a writer, journalist or researcher, or take up a career as a singer, model, actor or actress.

You may take up work as an administrator, information officer, librarian, accountant, linguist or translator, speech therapist, philanthropist or private detective.

FAMOUS CHARACTER ANALYSIS
Albert Einstein *Born 14 March 1879*

Albert Einstein was the German-Swiss scientist who won the 1921 Nobel Prize for physics with his Theories of Relativity. Einstein was extremely ambitious and used his energy and drive to pioneer his original theories; with hard work and determination he used his scientific mind to prove them.

With a 14/5 influencing mind and matter, Einstein's relativity theory was applicable to both; during his inspiring life he explored these qualities to the full. His life must have been full of excitement and adventure from experimenting with ideas and concepts.

Einstein was a strong individual who was fascinated and curious about the facts of life, and he probably had great clarity about what he was meant to do with his own life; he may also have taken direction from his intuition.

Albert Einstein died on 18 April 1955, having explored his mind and experimented with life. The whole date adds up to a 6, which is a number for 'service', so like many others who died on the same day, he must have completed his responsibilities of service to the world. The day is an 18 or 9, so having inspired the world with his knowledge, he was happy to close the book, and seek inspiration elsewhere.

NUMBER
15/6
PERSONALITY

GENERAL TRENDS FOR NUMBER 15/6 PERSONALITY

With a 15/6 influencing your Personality you have the gift of beauty and a deepest yearning to find the wisdom in (your) life. Wisdom describes the knowledge that you may acquire from different experiences, from a sense of knowing about them, or from having accumulated that knowledge. You may have heard the saying, 'I need to find the wisdom in this', whether it be describing an event, someone's actions or something deeper, like philosophical or spiritual matters. Learning from any situation means that *you* grow wiser, and that with this knowledge you can then help others with their lives. Sometimes people may see you as some kind of 'wise person' or 'sage' because you always seem to have an answer. Perhaps you have accumulated this knowledge from many lifetimes before, or from experiences with many different types of people and situations throughout your life.

You often have really strong gut feelings about things, and much of your wisdom comes from your inner self, and this sense of 'knowing'. You also possess a quick, active and perceptive mind, and you are very intuitive. For example, you may 'pick up' from listening to your best friend that he may need to be careful when signing a contract for his new house; your good advice of caution may help him to be more thoughtful in his negotiations.

With a 15/6 you are a communicator, and you love to communicate your wisdom to others, perhaps by being a doctor, and helping people with your wisdom about medicine, or by being a fashion designer and reflecting social changes through your clothes. You may also communicate by making speeches; you can explain things with great clarity and are really able to see the whole picture; you can make your audience feel really involved with what you are saying. You may also communicate your wisdom simply by talking to the people you meet every day, and increase your knowledge by listening to them in turn.

You are a bright, witty and intelligent human being, and you often like to communicate with others about things which are stimulating and important to you, such as your relationships, health issues, your career or social life, or about homely matters such as cooking, gardening and creative design. You may be passionate about animals too.

Perhaps you can be described as a 'people person', and you are stimulated by talking to many different types of people, of all ages. You are also adventurous and like new things to do, such as travelling to unusual destinations, so that you can meet new people, see beautiful things and enhance your wisdom. You may love to go on safari to Africa or to the Amazonian rainforest. Some people describe you as a 'beautiful person', perhaps because of your magnetism; however, this often emanates from your inner beauty, because you love life, you cherish being human, and you often see beauty and goodness in everything and everyone.

With a 15/6 you are a sensual person who loves silks, velvets and tactile fabrics. For example, you may love to lounge on your leather chair and feel this texture close to your skin, or on another occasion prefer to languish against silk or linen. Because you are such a sensitive person, the colours in your home and in what you wear can easily influence your mood. You may need to find out what the best colours are for you, perhaps by consulting your instincts or by being colour-coordinated by a professional. You are a touchy-feely person and you are really affected by the moods of people around you. Therefore you may be choosy about who you mix with.

You are an ambitious person, with a strong will. You like to set your goal, focus on it intensely and then speed through it with great steam so that you can then move quickly on to the next one. You are ultra-creative, and you make the most of the abilities.

Generally you are fun-loving and energetic, benevolent, caring and warm. You like everyone to feel happy – your family, your work colleagues and your social group – and you actively take some responsibility for making this happen.

You may enjoy aerobics, tennis, swimming and adventure sports, or like fun physical exercise such as sex and dancing.

CHALLENGES

With a 15/6 influencing your Personality your life may swing from high to low from one minute to the next. This may be because your sensitivity causes you to suffer emotional imbalances, or because you have a quick mind which reacts instantaneously in either a positive or negative way to situations around you. You have such a strong mind that you can easily influence situations with your thoughts and will. And if you really think hard enough then you contribute towards making things happen too. By learning to use your positive mind to help calm your emotions, you can learn to be mindful towards the actions you take and in the way you communicate, and so create more settled situations in your life.

Sometimes you find yourself in extreme circumstances, but by working through these situations and by going deeply into things which you either like or dislike, you can turn your life around and find new meanings. For example, being in the depths of poverty may help you to discover new values in your life, and may also turn you towards your spirituality, enabling you to get strength from inside.

You may sometimes be extremely self-centred, and this may actually contribute towards creating extreme or negative situations in your life. For example, your whole family may want to go on holiday abroad for a week, but you are so busy working that you may refuse to go, or to pay for them to go. They may get very resentful towards you and as a result may 'send you to Coventry' because they feel so hurt. Similarly, in a business situation you may think only about maximizing your profits, and make great savings by paying your workers so little that eventually they walk out on you. However, there is a part of you which is good at taking responsibility for the whole group, and by looking at the group's needs above your own you may avoid shocking and unexpected circumstances in your life.

With a 15/6 influencing your Personality you may get carried away with your desires and become obsessional and addictive in your pursuit of them at times: your work, your goals, a person, or even about the way you dress. You may get addicted to food, alcohol, drugs, sex or shopping, or to your mind-sets. You may also get obsessional about providing money for your family, or get addicted to health foods or keep fit. However, you are adventurous and you like to experience life to the full, which is why you can get so intense. The lessons learned from life can eventually help bring you back to 'wholeness' within yourself.

You may be a perfectionist and have high ideals about how you want people and the world to be. This may apply to your work, your goals and ambitions, or you may try to create a 'perfect' relationship. Of course, when life doesn't turn out the way your desires tell you it should, you can get very angry and rebellious and take it out on people; you may be vindictive or even vengeful or spiteful at not getting your own way. By getting angry with people you are creating your own karma, which will certainly come back to you in some way. Eventually you may learn that even when life doesn't seem to work out for you, it is actually working itself out in its own perfect way.

With a 15/6 you are very ambitious and headstrong, and you may become very pushy in pursuit of your desires. For example, you may push your partner into going to the movies when he or she wanted to stay at home and rest, but the whole evening turns out to be a disaster as he or she sulks in protest. Or you may push it so that you get selected as head of a team at work. But then you find that you don't like the job when you get into it, and realize that you should have applied for another one instead. Your ambitions often give you focus and a direction in which to go, but even ambitions come and go and by letting life flow, rather than trying to push it, it can show you which opportunities to aim for.

With a 15/6 influencing your Personality you may be a person who likes to take on group responsibilities and to look after people in any way you can. However, you may feel trapped and want to escape when you have taken on too much at times. But by using your logical mind, and your instincts, you can learn to take on realistic commitments in your life.

ROMANCE AND SEX

With a 15/6 influencing your relationships you may be someone who likes to experiment with lots of different partners, because you get bored easily. You may attract the most intelligent, affluent and interesting people, but you still keep looking around for more. You love to be stimulated by change, and you have an insatiable desire to experience life in all corners of the world, and sometimes with as many different types of people as possible.

You love to dance the whole night through, and to party until dawn with your romantic partner. You are flirtatious, spontaneous and fun, and people are drawn in by your animal magnetism. You are also a tactile person, and you feel free to express yourself physically within your relationships; you enjoy holding hands, linking arms, or rubbing your partner with sensual oils. You may like to tease people, or play practical jokes on them too. Sometimes you can go almost too far in your quest for sheer amusement; finding a partner who doesn't take your jokes 'personally' and who can also laugh at him- or herself may be essential for the compatibility stakes, particularly if you are seeking a long-term relationship.

Sex may play a large part in determining the length of your relationships, because you are a sensual and a sexual person, and you love to express your sexuality with your partner. For example, if you are in a long-term relationship and your sex life blows out, you may stay together for 'the sake of the children', but you may seek outside sexual stimulation as well. Your urge to satisfy your sexual instincts is great, and it is possible to find a partner who shares the same needs.

With a 15/6 influencing your relationships you like to explore your mind as much as your emotions and therefore finding a partner with whom you can exchange ideas, and who can stimulate you mentally, is important too. You like to be able to communicate with your partner. However, you may also be drawn to a partner with whom you feel a strong spiritual connection.

Often your instincts draw you to a karmic relationship, with someone you feel you have known for a long time, or whom you instantly recognize. You may quickly form strong bonds, and influence each other's lives greatly, and you may want to make a commitment with this partner or settle down. You are a generous person; once you have made a commitment you may fall deeply in love. You can be very romantic, and you may love to walk along the moonlit beach hand-in-hand or go for romantic drives through the country or for picnics in the warm sunshine.

With a 15/6 influencing your sex life you like a lover who can locate all your erogenous zones, or who can experiment with aphrodisiacs to turn you both on. You may love to be led around the garden at midnight, blindfolded, for a sensual delight, or you may enjoy the element of surprise in your animal lust for a good sex life. You may also be open to romantic love, at times.

PHYSICAL APPEARANCE

With a 15/6 influencing your looks you may have a broad, wide face, straight eyebrows, chubby cheeks, a wide nose, large voluptuous lips and a long neck. You may be of medium height, and your most outstanding feature may be your round tummy.

CHILDHOOD EXPERIENCES

With a 15/6 influencing your childhood then you may have been a 'wild child' who was always getting into trouble from an early age. Perhaps you were always showing off, or fighting, or perhaps you got expelled from school for doing something especially naughty.

You may have been exposed to people with food or alcohol addictions, or perhaps you were addicted to chocolate and sugary drinks. You may have been a highly emotional child who experienced extreme mood swings.

You may also have been a precocious child who was very aware of yourself, your body and your sexuality. Perhaps this was influenced by the behaviour of older brothers and sisters. However, you may have grown up in a warm and loving environment, which may have meant you felt comfortable being you.

With a 15/6 you may have been a caring child who loved to nurture younger members of the family, and to help your parents with chores around the home. You may have particularly liked cooking, taking the dog for a walk or shopping for clothes (for everyone), which may have been one of your favourite pastimes.

Children with a 15/6 often feel restless; when they are doing very well at something at school they may suddenly give up and want to try something new. It may help to encourage these children to think about the long-term results if they keep up with the good work, by explaining to them the potential rewards from using their talents.

WELL-BEING

With a 15/6 influencing your health, you may be prone to problems with your digestive system. You may also suffer from arthritis, from blood-sugar imbalances, and you may be prone to emotional and mental stress sometimes.

CAREER CHOICE

With a 15/6 influencing your career, you may work in the communications field: in public relations, advertising, marketing or sales, or in the travel or computer industries. You may also work as a lawyer or representative.

You can be a highly charged and magnetic person, so you may be a popular singer or musician, dancer, artist, writer, journalistic editor or detective. You may also work in the field of glamour, as a beautician or make-up artist, or as a chiropodist. You may take up work in one of the caring professions, as a doctor, nurse, massage therapist or counsellor.

FAMOUS CHARACTER ANALYSIS

Dame Agatha Christie Born 15 September 1890

Dame Agatha Christie was a successful crime writer whose books were often made into popular films, such as *Murder on the Orient Express* and *Death on the Nile*. With a 15/6 Agatha loved seeking adventure through her travels, and many of her themes were drawn from all over the world. Dame Agatha obviously had a wonderfully creative mind as well.

Her books were full of intrigue; the reader had to try to work out the facts and solve the mystery whilst cleverly being thrown off the scent. Sometimes her characters talked about their 'hunches'; she obviously had an awareness of instincts in her life.

Agatha, with a 15/6, must have been fascinated by life, and was always in need of new stimulation. She may also have been committed to family life, because her murder scenes were often set around family situations.

Dame Agatha Christie died on 12 January 1976, having enjoyed a long and adventurous life. The whole date adds up to a 9, so perhaps she was discriminating about her life at that time. The day is a 12 or 3, so perhaps she felt complete with her writing and was seeking some kind of expansion that day.

NUMBER
16/7

PERSONALITY

GENERAL TRENDS FOR NUMBER 16/7 PERSONALITY

With a 16/7 influencing your Personality you have a gift of being at ease with people and life, and you have the deepest yearning to find wholeness within yourself. In order to find wholeness, you need to be prepared to experience every aspect of yourself – including your weaknesses – and to be able to accept who you are. For example, you may be hopeless at cooking, but by saying 'OK, I'm useless at cooking, I accept that, and what can I do about it?' you are helping to heal your 'shadow' and are working towards wholeness. You can also help bring others to wholeness by encouraging them to feel safe to accept themselves the way they are.

You may be extremely intuitive, and you have strong emotional instincts centred around those you love. However, you may get premonitions, or psychic dreams, some of which may be centred around events taking place in the outside world. For example, before the death of Diana, Princess of Wales, many people had 'hunches' that something untoward was going to happen to her, and some even 'saw' the crash in a flash of emotion. With a 16/7 you have the ability to tune into positive and challenging collective feelings. For example, if you are a successful fashion designer, you are likely to be able to pick up from the collective exactly what to design next. You can be a creative outlet, and use this gift to give the world what it needs.

You may be blessed with the ability to understand both yourself and other people, and to give them what they need. You are a natural healer; you seek happiness and fulfilment through helping others, and your healing energies are often called upon. You may be drawn to work as a healer, or to use your animal instincts as an animal healer, because you have a passion for all creatures great and small. However, you are also working to heal yourself, and you are able to nurture and look after yourself, and gain more wisdom about life (and yourself) from helping others.

With a 16/7 influencing your Personality you are a compassionate person, and you always have time for others. You are a good listener; you pay great attention to detail and you are clearly able to see the overall picture; you can 'read between the lines', and do not go just by what people tell you.

Often you are close to, or influenced strongly by, your family group; perhaps you spend a lot of time with your family or live with your extended family. You are also a community-orientated person who loves to be a part of a larger group. Indeed, you may socialize in groups, or you may be a collaborative 'team' member who loves to work with your colleagues towards a goal or aim. Within your group or family you may believe that everyone is important and that all have an equal role to play and their own responsibilities, as part of the whole. You may be good at taking responsibility or thrive off responsibilities at times. You may also encourage people within your group to use their gifts too.

With a 16/7 you can be introspective, with a need to find solitude within your environment and within your mind. Here you delve into your imagination and allow your intuition to give you information which may help you with life. You also have an analytical brain, and like to think things through in a logical way. You like space, away from the crowd, at times.

At times you are soft and gentle and you love to be inspired by beauty, and, you may be devoted to nature too. You may love to look at beautiful landscapes, and perhaps you see beauty in life wherever you go.

You generally have a deep sense of trust in life and you may be easy-going and like to go with the flow. You are a strong individual and a natural leader and you listen to your intuition and your 'truth' to help guide you, particularly with your goals. With a 16/7 you are an ambitious person with dynamic creativity, and you use your energy and your strong will to help you achieve your goals.

You may be a 'water baby', and you may love to swim or jog for relaxation. You may also enjoy aerobics, working out in the gym, or a simple meditation.

CHALLENGES

With a 16/7 influencing your Personality you may get too introspective, with no grip on reality, at times. You may also find it difficult to
'get things together' or to materialize things because you may be too
laid back and casual about life. For example, you may be so dreamy that
you put the buns in the oven but forget to turn it on, and this can
reflect your attitude to the rest of life. Although it's great to walk
around singing, laughing and dreaming about life all day, you may miss
out on the opportunities for growth that may come your way. By
using your will-power to push you on, you can jump into life instead
of dallying with it.

You may have lots of work, a wonderful partner, a lovely home,
money, a good social life and your health, but you may take all these
things for granted. You may even think that this isn't enough and
that you've got to have more, and feel sorry for yourself at times.
Perhaps you start to get lazy about life, by turning up late for work,
neglecting your partner, or exercising less and less. You may even use
people at times. However, often when you take things for granted
they eventually slip through your fingers, and you end up with less, not
more. By learning to appreciate what you have *now* in your life, and to
count your blessings one by one each day, your love for yourself and
life can grow, and more life and appreciation can come your way.

With a 16/7 influencing your Personality you can be over-
emotional and influence people around you so that even if they were
calm initially they end up getting angry, sad or ecstatically happy in
your company. You may also have a habit of making people react, by
just being who you are, but particularly when you are in an emotional
'state'. However, it's wonderful for you to be able to feel your emotions
so deeply, and express them at appropriate times. But it may help you
to use your will-power to focus on something 'concrete', or to get up
and do a little exercise to help centre yourself if you are too emotional
or out of balance on these occasions.

You may also become obsessional about your creativity, your
work or your relationships. You may also be a perfectionist, or an
obsessive worrier sometimes. You may even become obsessional about
your spirituality or mysticism, or about your psychic instincts. Perhaps
you may even get hooked into a religion, and get obsessed with your
devotion towards religious beliefs, rituals and philosophies, or with a
particular cause. All this implies that something is out of balance in
your life. But sometimes, by going into things deeply, you learn to
experience those aspects of your Personality which may later be

integrated, and which then may help you to find wholeness in your life (again).

At the other extreme, with a 16/7 you may be completely cut off from your emotions, and you may even be cold and calculating at times. You may mistrust people and life, and always be waiting to catch someone out; perhaps out of revenge or spite, because you have been emotionally hurt or betrayed in the past. Perhaps you think that by being calculating it can somehow protect. However, you may only ever achieve wholeness by allowing yourself to accept all the things that life brings your way, including the joy, the hurt and the pain. When you push life away it has a habit of returning to you with stronger lessons until you learn that you can't ever run away.

You may be an intellectual person with a bright mind, and forthright and provocative in your opinions. You may also be self-centred, and unwilling to see anyone else's point of view. Even when friends approach you for your help, you may not listen to them properly, but only consider your opinion to be of importance, and find great satisfaction in telling them what to do. At times you may try to become too involved in and interfere in people's lives. However, when you don't listen you are missing out on life and all the things that you may learn; you can learn a lot from keeping quiet and listening to others' opinions.

With a 16/7 life may seem like an illusion as you seek but fail to fully comprehend the 'meaning of life'. However, this belief is a part of life and is another important experience.

ROMANCE AND SEX

With a 16/7 influencing your Personality you may be an observer of life and prefer living out your relationships 'in your head' rather than experiencing them for real. This may feel safe, and it may give you a thrill for a while, but it cannot provide you with the practical experiences of being in a relationship. For example, you may be loosely involved with a partner who travels a lot, and whom you seldom see. You may daydream and use your strong imagination to make up aspects of the relationship which don't even exist.

Sometimes even when you do see your partner you may misinterpret his or her actions. For example, you may think that he or she is ready to marry you when all that has been said is 'I'll see you tonight for dinner'. Sometimes you live in a world of illusion with no grasp on reality, and so finding a partner who is very clear with his or her communications and actions may help ground you into reality.

With a 16/7 you are an affectionate person who loves to kiss and cuddle and to hold hands; you are one of life's romantics. You may need to go deeply into a relationship with one partner and you may enjoy the responsibility that comes with intimacy and commitment. For you, sex is a part of the relationship which helps to bring you into wholeness, and to help you grow closer to your partner. Indeed you may not feel 'whole' until you are loved by your partner.

With a 16/7 influencing your relationship it may take you a while to learn to trust a partner, and whilst you are getting to know him or her you may enjoy 'safety in numbers' and go out to parties and the cinema together but in a crowd. You may fear intimacy too, and even when you have met the 'right' partner you may be detached from them for a while.

However, there is a part of you which may enjoy casual relationships and use them as a way of exploring your sexual identity. You may even get obsessed with your sexuality and with trying to find out 'who you are'. Indeed, you may be unsure of your sexuality or prefer to make friends with people who do not make any demands on you sexually.

Often you have lots of original and creative ideas and you like to dress in your own stylish and individual way. You love aesthetics too, so finding a partner who has a nice touch, smell and feel may be essential to keep you happy in a relationship. However, you can be jealous if your partner is very good looking, and you may get emotional when he or she attracts a lot of attention from other people.

With a 16/7 influencing your sex life you have strong animal instincts and a high sex drive at times, which needs to be fulfilled. You may experiment sexually with different partners, or have group sex; you like to feel that you have choice. However, you may prefer romantic love and get involved with a friend to explore love and sex instead.

PHYSICAL APPEARANCE

With a 16/7 influencing your looks you may be of medium height, with sensual, cat-like eyes, large, bonny cheeks and large but thin lips. You may have wide hips and shoulders, with small breasts or chest. Your sultry looks are your most outstanding feature.

CHILDHOOD EXPERIENCES

With a 16/7 influencing your childhood you may have experienced lots of love and lived with a touchy-feely family who physically wrapped you in warmth and affection. You may have loved caring for your little friends and family. Perhaps your life at home was full of animals, and you enjoyed the responsibility of looking after your own pets.

You may have been an emotional and destructive child who was always getting into fights, or perhaps you were hypersensitive and got 'picked on' as the brunt of people's abusive arguments. At times of sensitivity you may have retreated into your mind to escape physical reality, and you may have been a dreamy child too.

You probably loved to play with your imaginary friends, like ghosts or dolls, who you treated as if they were real. You may have loved playing magic games, or made up your own games with your creative imagination. Perhaps you liked ballet or, with your musical talents, playing the violin, or loved to paint beautiful pictures or design clothes for your dollies.

With a 16/7 perhaps you were brought up in a family in which your understanding of sexual identity was clouded or confused. Perhaps you didn't have strong 'role models' in either of your parents or the other adults who were around you.

Children with a 16/7 can be very picky about what they eat. Sometimes this may be because they feel the emotions of the people around them and, if there is a lot of tension, they may develop tummy aches. However, they may stop picking at food when they feel emotionally secure and safe within their environment.

WELL-BEING

With a 16/7 influencing your health you may be prone to hormonal imbalances, or to allergies. You may also develop eating disorders, like being picky with your food, or in extreme cases develop anorexia nervosa or bulimia

CAREER CHOICE

With a 16/7 influencing your career you may work as a healer, animal healer or veterinary surgeon, surgeon, pathologist, doctor or nurse, or you may work in one of the caring professions. You may also take up a career as an alchemist, city analyst or researcher, or work as a problem-solver or leader in any field.

Perhaps you may also work as a model, artist, writer or designer, or work in the navy. You may make an excellent manager, or work as a make-up artist or in the theatre.

FAMOUS CHARACTER ANALYSIS
Oscar Wilde Born 16 October 1854

Oscar Wilde was a flamboyant Irish writer who possessed a bright mind, and who was intellectual and witty. He was famous (or infamous) for his daring prose, through which he expressed his provocative feelings and observant opinions about life.

With a 16/7 Oscar married and had children and was contented for a short while, but he never really committed himself because in truth he was homosexual. He experimented with his sexuality and it took courage to look at his feelings and to leave his wife eventually. However, Oscar created such a reaction with his overt behaviour and with his writing, that he was imprisoned, particularly for his homosexuality. He certainly tried to break down the barriers of people's prejudices and exposed his vulnerability by being open about who he was.

Wilde originally lived the 'good life' with his wife and she was wealthy in her own right, but she later provided financial support for him, even though it was said that he did not appreciate her great acts of selfless kindness.

Oscar Wilde died, in dirt and squalor, on 30 November 1900, having enjoyed his sexuality to the very end. The whole date adds up to a 6, so perhaps his obsession with the sensual life was complete. The day is a 30 or 3, a number for self-expression, so perhaps he felt there was nothing left for him to express, at least in this lifetime.

NUMBER

17/8

PERSONALITY

GENERAL TRENDS FOR NUMBER 17/8 PERSONALITY

With a 17/8 influencing your Personality you have the gift of precision and the deepest yearning to find out the 'meaning of life'. You may be a deeply spiritual person, and spend time reading books about philosophy, psychology, religion and different types of healing. Perhaps you travel to different countries to visit churches, temples, religious sites or holy men and women to find out more about others' spiritual beliefs. Or, you may study the history books from throughout the ages so that you can feel connected to humanity that way. You may even go on archaeological digs to discover ancient ruins and artefacts so that you may feel connected to past civilizations too.

However, you are naturally introspective, and you may not travel physically but simply journey inside to discover 'who you are'. Perhaps you may meditate, or do yoga, or sit in a peaceful room; or you may switch off when you are watching television, going for a jog or swimming; all these can be ways of meditating too. You may go into your mind to connect with your own spirituality, which may then help you to feel connected to others. With a 17/8 you may also attract to you like-minded people with whom you feel a deep spiritual connection. You may also attract spiritual people to you in all areas of your life, without realizing that you have this ability. It is also possible that you may not be aware of your spirituality at all because it is so deeply ingrained, so therefore it is not necessarily a topic of conversation for you.

You have a strong intuition, which may help you with your life, and you are often guided by your 'truth'. For example, it may help you to find a suitable job, assist with your relationships and with decisions that you need to make. However, most of all your intuition helps you to help others. You may also have strong feelings or instincts about people, and perhaps you have psychic dreams about your friends and family which may give you important information about how you can help them too. You do have a practical side to your nature and you do not get carried away with your instincts. You are able to use your logical brain to help you sort out fact from fiction, and you are not easily taken in by illusion.

With a 17/8 influencing your Personality you have a deep sense of trust in yourself and in life. Therefore you do not panic when things go wrong or when you have challenges, but you keep going courageously, knowing that all will be resolved it its own time and way. You may find that when you trust life things go more smoothly, because you are thinking positive thoughts, which can only serve to benefit you.

You may be a perfectionist and have high ideals, and you are very precise about what you want. You pay great attention to detail, and you can be a fussy dresser, or like the dinner table to be set 'just so', and so on. You are a deep thinker and a hard worker.

You may be very ambitious, and you possess dynamic creative energy and the ability to go for your goals in a direct and purposeful way. You go for life 'full on', and you may materialize your goals through sheer determination and courage. You receive kindness or material wealth as a result of your achievements, but you do not need them because your reward is your inner happiness.

With a 17/8 influencing your Personality you have great strength of character, and you stand firmly on your own two feet. Others are often inspired to follow your lead, since you are a powerful person who commands authority and respect. You may enjoy taking on many responsibilities and you use them wisely. You may also be clever with money, and know where best to invest it, or where to find a real bargain. You have the ability to instigate people, and you are a natural at bringing people together and empowering them to take responsibility for themselves.

With a 17/8 influencing your Personality you like to re-evaluate your life regularly, which helps to keep your intellectual mind stimulated with new ideas and to give you clarity about situations you are in, or which direction to take. You are well aware of the role karma plays in your life, and when you re-evaluate you may analyze how you have contributed to creating the situations around you.

With a 17/8 you may love competitive sports and rigorous work-out routines, or relax with yoga, meditation or the stretching exercises of pilates.

CHALLENGES

With a 17/8 influencing your Personality you may be an incredibly pushy and aggressive person who sometimes manipulates situations to your advantage. This may be because you think of yourself all the time and what life can give you, rather than what you can give to life, and you always want things to go your way. You may be spoiled both materially and for attention because you are such a magnetic person, and you may use your sometimes lethal charms to get what you want. You may also be inclined to kick up a fuss when people don't rally round to your way of thinking, or to your demands. However, life may not always bring you what you want, but can teach you a lot about yourself even when it doesn't go your way. Sometimes when you try to manipulate people and life you find that it will backfire on you sooner or later because 'what you give is what you get'.

Sometimes you may be bossy and like to throw your weight around, and you are stubborn and you don't let people tell you what to do. You may like to keep yourself in control of life and in control of others too. Perhaps you are fearful of letting go because then you may panic and not know what to do. However, by letting go of control at times you allow space for change, which may bring fruitful things into your life.

As questions of control are probably important for you, with a 17/8 you may also feel disempowered by others and even occasionally let *them* control *you*, perhaps by allowing somebody to bully you at work, or by tolerating someone who tells you that you are useless and that they are better than you. By being assertive and taking the courage to stand on your own two feet you can learn to take responsibility for the part you have played to create the situation, and may teach others to do the same.

You may do all you can to avoid 'failure' in your life. For example, you may not go in for your driving test unless you are sure that you have a good chance of success, or start a new relationship until you feel certain it can work. This may be because you have low self-esteem, or because you want to be the best at everything you do. Sometimes your fear of failure means that you don't even try, and you may simply retreat into your imagination and live out there for a while. However, sometimes your intuition can come up with ways in which you can move ahead without feeling scared of rejection or of 'losing' in life again. By simply dreaming about your life and your ambitions you may never know if you can materialize them; by taking some actions, you can find out.

With a 17/8 you may be very materialistic and base your sense of achievement on your salary or on your possessions. You may be pre-occupied with success, or get greedy for more even when life is dealing you an ace. Sometimes you may push yourself too far, by working too hard to get more and more, and perhaps become too serious about life. You may end up with exhaustion from not taking a break. Perhaps you even get really depressed at these times, and you may feel like you don't know how you are ever going to get back on your feet again. However, by going 'inside' your mind to think, and by taking time to re-evaluate, ideas may spring up which can help you through a crisis. Perhaps you can turn to spirituality to find inner strength, where you may be led to the answers you are seeking; and these may not just be connected to money, but to equally important things in life.

Sometimes you may have delusions of grandeur, and you may feel like, or be, the owner of a country estate. You may be full of your own self-importance and be very egotistic, and you may be some sort of exhibitionist too. Sometimes you may be pig-headed because you are used to getting what you want, or because you are multi-talented and are successful in so many areas of your life, or because of the riches you have acquired. However, by learning to respect and appreciate others' gifts you can learn that everyone is important. Your reward may be that you feel good inside about yourself, instead of needing to show yourself off to the outside world.

With a 17/8 you may feel great pain and anxiety when you are not able to materialize things in your life, because you put a lot of hard work into making things right. Alternatively if you live out your life in your head you may panic when things start to physically materialize and produce success in your life. However, by finding a balance between your spiritual and your material needs you may find that your anxiety and panic disappear and you can get on with living. You may then feel at peace and satisfied with both these aspects of your Personality.

ROMANCE AND SEX

With a 17/8 influencing your relationships you may be a strong, powerful and charismatic individual who attracts many possible partners and suitors. You are also a dynamic person with a strong urge to succeed with your goals, and once you have found a partner with whom you feel a 'charge' you will go for the relationship 'full on'. Of course, you can be naïve and gullible sometimes, so you may find yourself taken in by your partner's one liners or charms, and the relationship may not lead you where you would like every time. Sometimes you may experience trauma in your relationships, but this may be a tool to take you within yourself to find your inner strength, or even take you off in search of your spirituality or your quest.

You are an idealist and you may conjure up in your mind the perfect picture of the man or woman of your dreams, and you may be surprised to find that in reality they do not match up to your expectations. However, you may be seeking a partner who is spiritual, or a partner who is daring and bold, or you may seek a partner who is independent, like you. However you may not find a Prince Charming whom you can rate 10 out of 10, but perhaps you attract a wonderful partner to whom you can give 8 or 9 out of 10 instead.

With a 17/8 you are a go-getter, independent and assertive. For example, you are happy to be financially self-sufficient and ask for a pay rise from your boss even when (or before) it is due. You may be a gutsy person in life so you may attract a partner who appreciates your pluck and recognizes your courage in standing up for yourself.

You may seek a partner who has a very successful career and who can provide money and material wealth for you. You may enjoy your partner taking you to all the best restaurants and buying you designer clothes or taking you on exotic holidays abroad. Perhaps you attract a karmic relationship to you and it is your partner's karma to provide you with these things. You may be a deeply spiritual person and you may be looking for a partner with whom you can talk to about the 'meaning of life'. Even if they can't provide you with all the material trimmings you may feel a strong love for your partner from deep inside.

With a 17/8 influencing your Personality you and your partner may both be highly successful and independent people and lead an exciting and active life. However, you may find friction if you compete with each other professionally, and you may need to let go of being better than him or her and always wanting to win. Perhaps you feel superior because you earn more money than your partner, or vice versa. This competition may keep the relationship going but it may also be destructive if there are no other, particularly spiritual, aspects involved.

With a 17/8 influencing your sex life you simply exude strong sexual magnetism, and you are also a powerful individual who may like a partner who can match you, or dominate you in bed. However, you can be demanding, and if you have a few nights with less-than-perfect sex you may withdraw into your mind and make up fantasies for yourself, or with your partner the next time you have sex.

PHYSICAL APPEARANCE

With a 17/8 influencing your looks you may have cat-like eyes which are set wide apart, a straight nose, an oblong face and a high-pitched and sometimes breathy voice. Your outstanding feature is your body, which may be strong and stout.

CHILDHOOD EXPERIENCES

With a 17/8 influencing your childhood you may have had a strong competitive streak, and you may have always been trying to prove yourself, and prove that you could be better than friends and family. For example, if your sister represented the school in tennis, then you may have represented your county or state so that you got more attention than her. Indeed with your competitive nature sports were essential for you; perhaps you particularly loved riding, cross-country, tennis and gymnastics.

With a 17/8 you were probably a typical high achiever, and got straight As at school and excelled at everything you tried to do; you were probably sporty, intellectual, bright, and popular too.

You may have sometimes felt not good enough, or that you weren't appreciated, because you may have always done so much in order for people to like you. At these times you may have been introverted and introspective and perhaps you preferred to be alone rather than with others because you may have felt little self-worth or value.

With a 17/8 you were probably a sensitive and kind-hearted child who, for example, was happy to take on responsibility for your younger brothers and sisters or for people around you.

Children with a 17/8 may find that when they are very young they often absorb the identity of people around them, rather than forming their own identity and individuality. However, by encouraging them to pursue interests that they like, and to choose their own clothes, for example, it may eventually help them to form their own identity in life.

WELL-BEING

With a 17/8 influencing your Personality you may be prone to acne, kidney and bladder problems, or problems with your adrenal glands. You may also be prone to depression, and have weaknesses in your feet or your knees.

CAREER CHOICE

With a 17/8 influencing your career you may work as a leader in any field, or as a teacher, or in any position within the field of education. You may also work as a researcher, analyst, accountant, or in finance.

Perhaps you may take up a career where you can reveal 'the truth': as a director or a producer of documentaries or as an author in the philosophical, spiritual or even business field. Perhaps you work as a psychologist, or as a healer, or take up work as a seamstress, or a fine artist, or work in an area where you need to pay great attention to detail.

FAMOUS CHARACTER ANALYSIS
Jane Austen Born 17 December 1775

Jane Austen was a famous writer whose books about romance in 19th-century society captured the imagination of the masses, and which are still extremely popular today. Some of her books have enjoyed further popularity with film and television, like *Emma* and *Pride and Prejudice*.

Jane was a pioneer because it was difficult for a woman in those days to pursue a career, and she was extremely successful. She helped to break down people's illusions, showed them that women could be just as competent as men.

With a 17/8 Jane was an extremely talented writer, with a strong character, and she was strong-willed and focused on her goals. She had been well educated and was shrewd, and she was probably eager to prove herself. Jane wrote about typical characteristics of the 17/8. Her stories were mainly about formality and social etiquette, and based around characters who were idealistic and dreamy, or rigid, aloof and detached yet well-mannered.

Jane Austen died on 18 July 1817, having inspired the world with her creativity. The whole date adds up to a 6, so perhaps her work for the community was complete. The day was an 18 or 9; perhaps she was discriminating about how else she could 'break out' of her caste and experiment with new areas of her life.

NUMBER
18/9

PERSONALITY

GENERAL TRENDS FOR NUMBER 18/9 PERSONALITY

With an 18/9 you have the gift of strength and the deepest yearning for recognition, and to recognize your own personal power. For example, you may know that you are good at leading others, and therefore you may believe that you 'should' get recognition for this, by receiving more money, status, authority or more responsibility, or you may even think that you 'should' be looked up to at times. This is because you recognize your own self-worth; you know what you are good at, you work extremely hard, therefore you deserve the recognition!

The 18/9 is a powerful karmic number, so some of the recognition you may receive in this lifetime perhaps results from things you have done in the past. So, for example, in the past you may have been a selfless leader. Perhaps helping and inspiring people in this way means that you recognize your leadership skills in this lifetime, even though you may not be consciously using them. For example, you may find that you are always being asked to lead a family, a work group or a project. Perhaps you may even find that you resist using your leadership skills in this lifetime because you have done it so much in the past. However, it is a talent that you can call upon if and when you choose.

Religion and spirituality may play an important part in your life. Perhaps you may visit a church or a temple, or you have faith in goodness, and respect all doctrines, philosophies and religions equally. You may hold strong views in these subjects and you may even study them academically, or teach others about your beliefs. Perhaps you use the power of faith to help give others strength too. Your views are defined and strong, but so is your connection to your spirituality and your inner strength, and to humanity

You have the courage to follow through with your convictions and to lead and teach others. You may be a very flexible person, who is willing to adapt and change your point of view, and you do not get stuck into thinking that life 'should' be one way or another. For example, in your teaching you may also be able to break down others' rigid and outdated thinking. You encourage people to have faith and courage during challenging times in their lives, and to believe in the positive benefit of change. However, you do sometimes impose your ideas, beliefs or opinions onto others; you also encourage others to follow their own path in life.

With an 18/9 influencing your Personality you may be emotional at times, but you are basically ruled by your head and your logical mind, and you like to work things out. You may be bright and intellectual, with interests in literature, art, music, good conversation and the good things in life.

Perhaps you have humanitarian interests and do charity work, or work for a large organization, or for your community. You are also a highly ambitious person, who will want to get to the top in whichever career or path you choose. You are an ideas person, and you set your goals, focus on them with great intent, and then use hard work and organizational skills to follow them through. You have an abundance of creativity, and with your strong will you are a real dynamo. With an 18/9 you may attract powerful people, and those who are leaders in their field; you, of course, are 'the best' at what you do, or rather, you do your best in life. You may be a successful person, and may like to provide your own material security.

With an 18/9 you may be an open and friendly person who will talk to anyone. You may be a relaxed and liberal person who likes to experiment with life: booze, sex, clothes, hair-styles, lifestyles, and so on. For example, perhaps you write your own music and sit around strumming your guitar into the early hours of the morning experimenting with your talents. Variety is the spice of life, and you may not always conform to society; you can be rebellious sometimes.

With an 18/9 you love power sports which require stamina and mental focus, such as polo, riding, sailing or windsurfing. You may also love physically demanding work-outs through aerobics, step classes, sessions at the gym, jogging or cycling.

CHALLENGES

With an 18/9 influencing your Personality you have very strong views and opinions, and no matter what, you are always 'right'. This is because you are stubborn and like to feel that your opinion is the one that 'counts'. For example, you may be rigid in your views, rigid in your taste of decoration, rigid in eating habits or rigid in your lifestyle, with little room for movement or change. You may also have rigid mind-sets which you use to 'guard' your life. However, sometimes by learning to be flexible you can accept that life will not fall apart if your opinions change. Being willing to back down instead of stubbornly pursuing your point of view can allow your mind, body and spirit to breathe in fresh air, and help you to relinquish your need always to be in control.

You may be a controlling person who pushes your weight around in an aggressive way. Perhaps you dominate others, or manipulate them, or perhaps you like people to run round you and serve you in some way. Sometimes, however, people need to have somebody to control them, for their own good. For example, your partner may have been told by the doctor that he or she needs to go for an X-ray to see if there is a broken bone, but your partner refuses to go. So you find ways of using manipulation and control to get him or her to go. You then use these qualities for selfless reasons, not to activate a goal for yourself.

With an 18/9 influencing your Personality sometimes you can be cynical and sceptical about life. This may be because you have extremely high expectations and you may be disappointed when life doesn't come up to scratch. Perhaps you withdraw by spending a lot of time on your own, or 'in your mind' so that you connect with your inner strength to help you to replenish your faith in people and in life.

Sometimes you may flaunt your wealth or power, or use your authority to make you seem better than others. Perhaps you do this by boasting about your achievements, or by using your position of authority to get people to do things for you. Sometimes it may seem that you think yourself so important that you can change and bend the rules by which society lives. However, like karma, laws are there to be respected; there are spiritual laws to be adhered to as well as physical earthly laws, and you will reap the rewards or retribution for your actions at a later date. You may need to be aware of taking responsibility for your behaviour, which can sometimes get out of hand in your quest for success.

You may be a self-centred person who likes to put yourself first. For example, if there are ten people around the dinner table all you may be concerned about is getting fed first, or having the biggest helping of food, or sitting in the 'best' place. Perhaps you do this because you feel that you may be left out unless you look after yourself. Eventually you may learn to share, and realize that by giving and receiving freely everyone can benefit. By learning to be selfless sometimes, and by learning to give, you may feel inner happiness too.

With an 18/9 influencing your Personality you may be a thinker who spends a lot of time 'in your head', but you are a sensitive person and may feel hurt by what others do or say. Although you may repress your feelings deep down inside, this anger usually wells up and explodes in a torrent of emotions from time to time. Giving yourself permission to accept your feelings, instead of thinking yourself pathetic and weak, can help you to understand that it takes courage and strength to do this at these times. Perhaps it may also help to express how you feel directly to the person concerned, or to talk openly about your feelings (regularly) with a good friend.

You may be a knowledgeable person who has an understanding of people and the world in which you live. However, you may criticize others (and yourself) at times for not knowing enough, or when you feel out of your depth. For example, you may give a speech and find that the notes you prepared didn't contain enough facts about the subject and you feel a failure, and give yourself a hard time. However, you are not perfect, and even when you think you know a lot about life or a subject, there is always more to learn.

ROMANCE AND SEX

With an 18/9 influencing your relationships you may have a very high opinion of yourself generally, and you may like to think that in a relationship you are the 'king pin'. For example, you may have a wonderful and well-paid career, or you may have the responsibility of great power in your life. Therefore you may not like to go out with a partner who you think is 'better' than you, for example, by earning more money than you, or having more status in life. Perhaps it may be essential to find a partner who builds you up by telling you how wonderful you are, or a partner who likes to feel there is an authoritative 'parent' around the place. Alternatively, you may enjoy having a partner to compete with, who inspires you to use your ambition and drive to achieve even further success in life.

You may be the type of person who is happy to organize your partner's social life and your joint activities together, but you may not like him or her doing the same for you. This may be because you often like to stay 'in control' of your life and like to take responsibility for yourself.

With an 18/9 you may possess charisma, charm and a natural magnetism, which may mean you draw many potential partners to you. Sometimes you may attract more creative and artistic people who are reflecting this side of you, or serious intellectual types who are able to stimulate your mind too. You also have an earthy sexiness about you because you have an animal, instinctual side to your personality, so you may attract a partner who loves to feel his or her way through a relationship with you. However, you are sensitive, and you may not enjoy being drawn out of yourself because you may be afraid of intimacy. Perhaps you may feel safer to connect spiritually with your partner, rather than connecting on other levels.

You have very high expectations and you may be seeking the perfect mate. However, even when you have found him or her you may not recognize it, and indeed you can get bored easily and like to experiment. You may need to pay attention to your behaviour because you can be wild and wilful sometimes in your quest to find out more about life. However, a strong, powerful or affluent partner may have the ability to keep you interested longer than you think. With an 18/9 you may be liberal, and you may attract many different types of partners with whom to experiment.

At the other extreme, you can, conversely, be prudish and fussy about whom you go out with, and you may also be rigid in your standards, sometimes judging your partner and making critical comments about him or her, or even judging others' behaviour in their own relationship. You may think there is an appropriate or 'right' way of doing things in a relationship, and you may like to conform to the nth degree.

With an 18/9 influencing your sex life you may often have a high sex drive, and therefore seek a passionate partner to keep you satisfied. You may like to experiment with your sexuality, or like a partner who is open enough to enjoy social gatherings (in bed too). Your high ideals may also mean that at times, to avoid disappointment, you may prefer self-gratification instead.

PHYSICAL APPEARANCE

With an 18/9 influencing your looks you may be tall and muscular, with a large face and deep-set 'intense' or startled eyes, which are set wide apart. You may have heavy eyebrows and a high forehead, and your outstanding feature is your nose, which is small.

CHILDHOOD EXPERIENCES

With an 18/9 influencing your childhood you may have been an independent child who liked to do things your own way. You may have enjoyed teaching your younger brothers and sisters what to do, and you were probably a leader from an early age, empowering other children to follow you. You may have also been a shrewd child, and you may have been direct, or even manipulative at times, to make sure that you got what you wanted.

Good manners may well have been instilled into you by your parents, and they may have been strict or rigid with what they considered acceptable behaviour. You may have experienced a formal and traditional upbringing. Perhaps you felt over-controlled by your parents at times, or felt pressure to be perfect, or resentful of their criticism of you. Maybe you got sick of being continually told to do the 'right' thing, and to 'be sensible', even though you probably were most of the time.

With an 18/9 you may have been a serious child who loved to study and to talk about grown-up issues, like the environment. Perhaps you loved listening to music, dancing and going out for long walks, or sitting at home quietly being creative.

Children with an 18/9 may be very strong-spirited and have enormous amounts of creative energy, which they need to express. Catching their attention in absorbing hobbies or interests may help to calm them down, or to release any pent-up frustration.

WELL-BEING

With an 18/9 influencing your Personality you may suffer from problems with your feet, your knees and your spine, or arthritis, or stiffness in your joints. You may also be prone to problems with your liver, or suffer from headaches.

CAREER CHOICE

With an 18/9 influencing your Personality you may work as a leader, teacher (particularly of religion, philosophy and spirituality), theologist, researcher, careers advisor or (social) secretary. Perhaps you take a role as a politician, judge or diplomat where you can serve your community; or perhaps you are a charity worker or humanitarian.

With an 18/9 you may be an artist, writer or musician, or you may work as a healer, and you may use your hands in your career. You may also work in any field where you can use your organizational skills, for example as a public relations executive or as an administrator. Perhaps you work with computers, or in the financial sector, for example as an accountant or a financial management consultant.

FAMOUS CHARACTER ANALYSIS
Louis Tiffany Born 18 February 1874

Louis Tiffany was the son of the founder of Tiffany & Co, one of the leading and most exclusive jewellery shops in the world. He also became renowned in his own right for designing and producing the most exquisite stained-glass windows for churches and for public and private buildings. He also produced blown-glass tableware decorations, which are collectors' items and considered an investment today.

Tiffany came from a family with great wealth, status and power, and no doubt he was driven by his ambition to be the best at what he did. He obviously had high standards to live up to, and he succeeded in producing exquisite art which became an inspiration to others.

With an 18/9 Louis incorporated his ideas and spirituality into his work, and his designs were exhibited in places of religion and worship, and were uplifting. He became the authority in his trade, for which he received great success and fame.

Louis Tiffany died on 17 July 1937, having enjoyed a life of recognition and karmic reward. The whole date adds up to a 4, so perhaps he felt that he had consolidated what he needed to do in his life. The day is a 17 or 8, so perhaps he was re-evaluating his life on the fateful (karmic) day he died.

NUMBER
19/1
PERSONALITY

GENERAL TRENDS FOR NUMBER 19/1 PERSONALITY

With a 19/1 influencing your Personality you have the gift of power, and you have a deepest yearning to be accepted by those around you and to be able to accept yourself.

With the influence of the 1s and 9 in this number you are a natural leader, who likes to show others the way. You often love to be the first to do new things. For example, the first person to climb a mountain, or the first person to own a power-generated solar home, and so on. You are also able to show people how to live their lives by setting a good example. With a 19/1 the concept of leadership is important to you, but you may sometimes prefer to follow the lead of others and be inspired by their example and leadership style.

You are a strong and powerful individual, with great faith in yourself and your beliefs; once you have made up your mind about your opinions or your goals nothing can dissuade you. You also have faith in humanity, and like to think up new ideas to help make the world a better place to live in; you have an inventive mind. Then you lead the way through practical action.

With a 19/1 you may particularly be interested in art, history, religion, politics, social issues, literature, and also spirituality. You are an intellectual, and you may love to discuss these subjects wherever you go: at dinner parties, at home, with work colleagues – in fact, with anyone who has something to say. This is because you have a strong mind and like to stimulate it as often as you can. You are in search of knowledge and you know that you can acquire this from people and life just as much as through books and courses.

With the influences of the 1s and the 9s in your Personality you are a very powerful person who can get what you want. Your energy, vitality and dynamic will help work towards and achieve your goals in a practical way. As with all 1s you do not give up easily, and will stubbornly maintain your focus no matter what events or people try to distract you.

You enjoy the creativity and the process by which you achieve your goals. For example, you may want to teach a new subject to your class of students. You are really pleased when it goes down well with them at the first lecture. However, you were passionate in your creativity when you were writing and producing the course material and you loved this as much, if not more, than the presentation. With a 19/1 you can be original in your creativity, which instils energy into your work and makes life exciting for everyone around. You often stand out and people take notice of you; your individuality really shines through.

You may be keen on maintaining your independence, and like all 1s you are self-reliant, self-sufficient and enjoy the benefits of time spent alone. You enjoy your own company and you can look after yourself. You have a warm and caring side to your Personality, and you can be selfless in the way you care and think of others, and may even have a humanitarian streak. However, sometimes you do things for people because you are desperately seeking their approval, which is an important issue for you.

With a 19/1 you can be superior, which makes you think that you have some sort of superficial self-esteem. You like to be the best at what you do, and you will like to be the authority in your chosen field. You may find that you have some 'special' status in your life, such as a royal title, or being head of a company, a supermodel, or a famous name. This can be a brilliant experience because it helps you to understand and learn to handle power. You may also find that you crave status and power, and you will work hard to achieve it, hopefully without losing your humour along the way.

With a 19/1 influencing your Personality you may enjoy watching and sometimes participating in cricket, baseball, polo or golf. You may also like to jog (around the most exclusive and expensive patch in the neighbourhood!).

CHALLENGES

With a 19/1 influencing your Personality you may be very fixed on your ideas and beliefs, and the way they 'should' be implemented. For example, you may be an artist who believes that everyone 'should' always paint like Dali, Rembrandt or Matisse, which leaves no room for the Picassos of this world. However, you have such original ideas that when you do get stuck on one way of doing things for too long, other ideas will pop up to help you change your course. You may then stop to think about new ways of applying your knowledge to the idea or situation, which helps you to learn to be adaptable.

You have extremely high standards and you like to be the best at what you do. You may be very hard on yourself when you do not match up to your own standards and beliefs in what you can achieve, or in the way you 'should' look. You can also be very critical, of yourself and others, and judge your and their performance according to your beliefs. You can be rather judgemental and 'hard work' for your friends, family and acquaintances, with a constant stream of complaints about things. It may help you to learn to relax your mind a little, and learn to enjoy being who you are, whilst remembering that life is perfectly imperfect, most of the time.

Sometimes you may show a lack of belief in yourself and repress your opinions and beliefs, and lack faith in your creativity and your abilities. You may, at times, be a timid individual who prefers to be led and told what to do, rather than instigating things yourself, and you may feel powerlessness at times. Working through this side of your Personality can help you to experience these things so that when you are ready to take a step forward with your life, you can use your leadership and power in a selfless way.

You may be over-opinionated too, and always think you are 'right', and you may not regard others' opinions as being of any worth. You may think that you are superior and, like all 1s, enjoy being 'exclusive'. For example, you love to dine only at the most expensive restaurants in town, or only live in the most 'exclusive' area. Being 'exclusive' is great because eventually it can help to teach you about your inner values and self worth. At some point you may realize that there is much more to life than trying to prove you are important. It can also help to teach you that when you exclude others, you are also excluding a part of yourself, and you are isolating yourself from life too.

With a 19/1 influencing your Personality, you may 'crawl up' to authority, and to anybody with status or power. Being around these people can help to teach you about these qualities. For example, you may marry a politician or a member of the royal family, work with the managing director of a powerful organization, and so on; you are experiencing their lifestyle and learning to handle power too.

You may also, at times, feel threatened by authority, and rebel. You can feel guilty and full of self-loathing when you don't feel good enough, and you are always trying to improve yourself and to show others that you can do better. You may give your power away to people who you feel are better than you, or in a better position than you. This can lead you to feel intense anger, which you may express indirectly towards them. For example, you are angry that your work colleague, Peter, got promoted and is now in authority over you. You may indirectly create problems for him by being lazy or refusing to carry out his commands, or generally making life difficult. By learning to feel good about your individuality, you can learn to feel safe when people of power, authority and status are around you.

With a 19/1 you may have a caring heart, but when you do help people you sometimes do it for your own gain. You like to feel that people owe you something, and you can be hard to please. For example, you lend a book to your cousin, and so you expect her to lend you her entire library in return. However, you may find that people do not always do things for you in return, and perhaps they never will, until you learn to give with a kind heart and do things for others because you want to, instead of expecting something back.

You may be self-pitying and feel really 'put upon' by others. However, it may be that you are really 'putting upon' yourself (or creating the situation that makes you feel like that). At these times making an effort to give even more to others can really help to 'break' your mood and your attitude.

ROMANCE AND SEX

With a 19/1 influencing your relationships you may be warmer and more affectionate than other 1s. You are very sure about what your are looking for in a partner, and although you are sometimes withdrawn, when you see what want you go for it, hook, line and sinker. The normally detached person disappears and you may then throw yourself passionately into the relationship 150 per cent. Of course that is not to say you will stay with that person – with a 19/1 you are often striving for 'better' and more.

However, when you have found your 'perfect' partner, and made a commitment, you may actually put a lot of energy into making it work. After all, you have let a special person get close to you and share your intimate inner self. Like all 1s, you need your goals, and your relationship may be one of them.

With a 19/1 influencing your love life you may be artistic, creative, religious or spiritual, or one of life's intellectuals. Therefore you may attract a partner who has some of these characteristics. However, like all 1s, you may not relish emotional intimacy and sharing, although there is always scope for learning. An emotional partner may send you into despair; with your strong, discriminating mind, you wonder what all the fuss is about and why people get so emotional at times. However, a partner with whom you feel safe to get emotionally intimate can help you to reach your inner feelings, and to release blocked emotions which you did not even know existed. With a 19/1 you may hold back when you first enter a relationship, and it may take you a while to open up to your partner.

Sometimes you like to bask in glory, and may attract someone who buys you diamonds and pearls. You seek the best. You may look for a powerful, strong, partner who you think is simply unique, and with whom you can be 'seen' swanning around town, illuminating the best parties, attending the best restaurants. You participate with an incredible zest, and a mind full of stimulating conversation and knowledge.

However, status to you may be someone who you look up to, and not necessarily someone with a title, or who has a flashy lifestyle. For example, you may seek someone older, a father figure, an authoritative parent, who can look after you. Sometimes you can be rebellious, and a father figure can usually handle that.

With a 19/1 influencing your sex life you can add a spark of originality to love sessions, and really be creative in turning your partner on. You like to get into your power in between the sheets, and enjoy a passionate and vibrant sex life. You like the best, to feast on caviar and champagne, and have high expectations from your partner sexually. But sometimes your mind enjoys ways of finding pleasure without your body, and sex may not always be your raison *d'être*.

PHYSICAL APPEARANCE

With a 19/1 influencing your appearance you may have a very high, prominent forehead, an upturned nose and sloping shoulders, and speak in a deliberate and serious way. Your eyes may be set wide apart, and they may turn down at the outer edges. Your outstanding feature is that your figure is usually in proportion, no matter what your size.

CHILDHOOD EXPERIENCES

With a 19/1 influencing your childhood you may have been a stubborn, wilful child, who seemed adept at getting your own way. You may also have been spoilt, and were allowed to indulge in your favourite things too often. However, having so much choice may have helped to teach you to discriminate about what you really wanted to do with your time, and your life.

Your parents may have expected you to behave like an adult even when you were very young. You probably did have fun with your friends and family, but in a serious way. Perhaps you were never allowed to really 'let your hair down', which meant you may have been really rebellious at times!

You may have excelled in art and music, and spent many happy hours entertaining yourself. You may also have been stimulated by books and by learning at school, where there may have been pressure for you to achieve. However, you probably liked to do well, and your peers' approval encouraged you to greater success, and to feel good in yourself.

Children with a 19/1 need love and warmth, and to be accepted for who they are rather than what they can achieve. They may sometimes need the guidance of authority, because they can easily 'step out of line'. But they may also need the freedom in which to develop their independence. To that end they need to be encouraged to do things and to think for themselves.

WELL-BEING

With a 19/1 you may be prone to problems with your digestive system, in particular your gall bladder or your liver, and you may suffer from candida or thrush, or migraines. As with all 1s, you are usually strong and robust much of the time.

CAREER CHOICE

With a 19/1 you may indulge yourself in an outpouring of creativity, as an artist, musician or creative writer. Sometimes you may be focused on achieving, and will like to be paid well for your work; at other times the enjoyment your work gives you may be all that matters. You are able to follow through on your new ideas, and can be original in your work.

You may also be a historian, judge, academic, politician, or religious or spiritual leader. You may be a humanitarian, a teacher or leader of any kind, who inspires others with your selflessness, caring and knowledge, and your bright mind. With a 19/1 you may also be a personal assistant, a prince or princess or royalty, a president, or a managing director of a company. You generally enjoy being in a position of power and authority.

FAMOUS CHARACTER ANALYSIS
Edgar Alan Poe Born 19 January 1809

Edgar Alan Poe was an instigator of his own unique way of writing. That is, he specialized in writing short stories and poems about the weird and fantastic, attracting a lot of attention and great respect from both inside and outside the literary world.

With the influence from the 19/1, Poe was a powerful man. He was an idealist, who was inspired to write his own wonderful words of wisdom for the world, which are still widely read today. He was also believed to be touched by mysticism, and his works often contained tales of outer-worldly experiences.

The influence of the 19/1 meant that Poe possessed the energy to help drive him forward towards his goals. It also helped him to stand out from the crowd, to be himself, and to assert his individuality. He was also passionate about his work.

Edgar Alan Poe died on 7 October 1849, having achieved status in his life, and received even greater acclaim after he died. This whole date adds up to a 3, which influences creativity and writing, so even when he died perhaps he was designing some light prose in his mind. The day was the 7th, which was influencing him with the quality of introspection. Perhaps he was pondering upon his life works and his spirituality, or wondering where to go next.

20/2

GENERAL TRENDS FOR NUMBER 20/2 PERSONALITY

With a 20/2 influencing your Personality then you have the gift of calmness and the deepest yearning for contentment. With this number there is a zero influencing the 2, which emphasizes your need to learn to find inner peace and harmony within your life.

With two 2s your need to relate to people is great, particularly through your emotions. When you open up and share how you feel with others, it helps you to feel connected to them. You also love to hear people talk and share their emotions with you too: in this way you bond with them, and you can really 'feel' them in your life. For example, when one of your friends is ill, you may get a strange feeling that something is wrong, and call her to see that everything is OK. You are often right about your hunches, and often follow through on your gut feelings. You also find that your closest friends and your family are able to 'feel' you in the same way.

You may feel that the best way to sort out life and problems is by discussing them openly with the people involved. This may often include discussing feelings too. 'Openness' is a key word for you because you like everything to be done in front of people, directly. You are usually able to take in both points of view in any situation. You are like an anchor, or a mediator, and as with all 2s you like to remain unbiased. You always take into consideration the other side, even when you are personally involved in discussions. You are good at making decisions, but you do this after carefully weighing up the pros and cons.

What you like best is for people to reach a mutual agreement. You usually like both sides to 'win', or for there to be a happy compromise.

Co-operation is another key word for you. You may feel that people get much more accomplished when they are willing to co-operate and negotiate, than by confrontation or by making demands. For example, a cheque for work you have completed is late, and as days pass by and it doesn't arrive in the post, you get more and more upset. You ring your customer, but instead of getting angry and demanding your cheque 'right away, or else ...', you simply ask why there has been a delay. Then you can both discuss ways of sorting out the issue in a co-operative way, which may result in you getting your cheque the next day. Perhaps there had just been a problem at the post depot, and there was a delay.

With a 20/2 influencing your Personality you are a tolerant person, but you will generally not put up with things which bring disharmony to your life. For example, you may not easily tolerate extreme emotions from others, or when your new next-door neighbours play loud music until three in the morning every day. You will go as far as you can to negotiate a considerate response and a compromise of actions with them. However, when all else fails, you may enter the law courts to help bring peace to the whole neighbourhood. At the end of the day you like justice and mutual respect between people in life.

You may be a person of moderation and sometimes your life may be one of limited excess; 'middle of the road', with a bit of joy and a bit of sadness. This ensures that you avoid extremes in your life and that you are able to trundle along in a contented way. You are a simple person and you like to live a peaceful life in harmony with the earth, your inner self and the people around you.

You are often a thoughtful, caring and warm person, and you (like all 2s) love to nurture and care for yourself and others. Sometimes you can be very soft with an air of gentleness about you. When people have problems and they come to you for a listening ear, they often calm down simply on hearing your voice. Often you hardly mutter a word, but your whole energy is calm. The world needs calm people, and you are placid and do not get upset easily.

Sometimes when you have lots of work you like to delegate some of it out to others, and you are receptive to their comments. You do not like to put pressure on people to do things that they can't. You also believe that life is about give and take.

With a 20/2 you enjoy listening to soothing and relaxing music, and you may be very musical too. You enjoy casual cycling, swimming, yoga, walking and gentle stretch exercises.

CHALLENGES

With a 20/2 influencing your Personality you may at times enjoy confrontation and like the emotional charge you get from 'rubbing up' against others. You may feel that life is not a case of 'we' but of 'me against you', and that you are either the hunter or the hunted. Sometimes confrontation may simply be the only way for you to have an outlet for your emotions, which you may find difficult to express in a positive way.

You may sometimes feel in the middle because everybody comes to you to discuss their feelings and problems. For example, your friend Sarah may tell you how she feels about her boyfriend John, and John may do the same. However, you may use this information to play one person off against the other. Sometimes you may do this because you cannot easily handle everybody's emotions, and you may feel angry that people can't talk to each other directly. Eventually you may find it easier to tell Sarah and John how you feel about being 'in the middle', and be honest and direct with them too.

With a 20/2 you may sometimes find that you take sides for or against people and are unable to maintain an impartial view. For you, when challenged by the influence of a 20/2, there perhaps always has to be a winner or a loser. However, by taking sides with the underdog you may be able to help them to find their strength; or by backing the winner you may help them to feel good about themselves. Eventually you may realize that people win in every situation because they are gaining more experience and learning more about life. For example, in your eyes your partner James 'won' by being selected for the rowing team and his friend Dougal 'lost' because he wasn't picked. However, Dougal did 'win' because he learned how to accept life's little setbacks gracefully. Dougal later won a place with the tennis team, which coincidentally turned out to be his best move yet.

You may be a manipulative person at times, and try to get your needs met in a covert way; you may act deceptively to push a situation in the direction you want. Perhaps you want to avoid confrontation, or are unable to express your feelings in an open way. You may also feel that in order to get what you want you must exert pressure. However, being manipulative can help to teach you something. For example, if you are trying to push an estate agent towards buying a particular property, for which there are many competitors, then it can teach you how to focus on exactly what type of property you want. However, things can backfire because people and situations cannot be manipulated to suit your needs alone.

With a 20/2 influencing your Personality you may be indecisive at times for fear of taking anybody's side or hurting someone. You may feel pressured by these decisions, or only able to reach a conclusion by being backed into a corner. For example, your partner said that he would like you to spend New Year's Eve at his family's house, but your parents have requested the same too. With the pressure on, you simply opt out at the last minute and decide to spend New Year together at your home, instead. Decision-making is a necessity of life, and by making prompt decisions you can actually cut down on the agonizing feelings that indecision causes you.

You may find in life that you are sometimes overwhelmed by your emotions. Perhaps you allow yourself to wallow in sadness, for example, instead of making a decision, or taking an action, that may help you to feel better. You can also be overwhelmed with happiness, but in a dreamy and unrealistic way at times. 'Isn't everything wonderful,' you beam, as your life falls apart at the seams! Extremes of emotions can create disharmony in your life, but at least they teach you how to feel. Your feelings change all the time, but eventually you return to your centre, or calm.

You may be over-cautious, and fearful at times. As with all 2s, you may fear getting in contact with your own emotions, or be fearful of others' strong emotions. You are naturally a carer, and have a great ability to use your love to look after people. However, you may sometimes fear using these feminine energies (whether you are male or female) and shy away from allowing them in. Perhaps you feel 'soft' or vulnerable when you nurture yourself or others. But feeling vulnerable means that you are 'open' to life, and this is a strength, not a weakness, because it allows more life in, which can only be a good thing.

ROMANCE AND SEX

With a 20/2 influencing your love life you may be someone who sees balance with your partner and with other aspects of your life as an important issue. For example, you may have a successful career and need to balance your time between that and your relationship. You may have children, and balance out time spent between them and your partner so that nobody misses out. Balance may also mean that you both take turns in doing different 'chores'. Or, if you like cooking and your partner likes driving, you can use these skills to help bring balance to the relationship.

You love to share; perhaps you and your partner make a

sumptuous supper together, lay the table together or put the children to bed together. You may both even work together – togetherness is fun! With two 2s influencing your Personality your desire to find that special person is strong. You are searching for your soul mate – someone with whom you can share your whole mind and body, heart and soul.

With a 20/2 influencing your relationships you can be an indecisive person who finds it a challenge to make up your mind about whether or not to go into a relationship. Sometimes deliberating may mean you actually lose the chance of that relationship. However, when you meet your soul mate your gut feelings will usually tell you who's the 'special one' for you!

You love affection, and hugs and kisses need to be woven into your everyday routine. Therefore finding a demonstrative partner may be essential for your inner happiness and well-being. You may also seek to find a relationship where you feel free to share your feelings and desires with your partner with tenderness and love.

You may be unable to look after yourself at times, and you may become dependent (particularly emotionally) on your partner. Sometimes your partner may like to treat you as a dependent child, yet at other times he or she may run away when there is no adult to share with. When you rely too much on somebody else keeping you happy, then you may be fearful about losing their support. Learning to nurture and care for yourself means you can then learn to share with your partner, instead of always needing to receive.

With a 20/2 you are a highly sensitive person, and you may feel very vulnerable emotionally in a relationship. If your partner upsets you in some way you may defend your vulnerability with an outpouring of emotion. Staying 'open' when you feel hurt, instead of getting over-emotional, may help you to understand what it is that is really upsetting you. Then you can share these feelings with your partner.

With a 20/2 influencing your sex life your need to please and satisfy your partner is as great as your need to be loved and showered with affection. Sex is another enjoyable way that you can relate with your partner. You may also be seeking stability through regular sex with that special 'one'.

PHYSICAL APPEARANCE

With a 20/2 influencing your looks you may have a wide face, full lips and large breasts. You may have watery eyes and a roundness about your body, even when you are slim. Your quiet, whispery voice, that draws in others, may be your outstanding feature.

CHILDHOOD EXPERIENCES

With a 20/2 influencing your childhood you may have been a vulnerable and sensitive child who enclosed yourself in a protective 'shell': your dreamy imagination or your mother, to whom you may have clung for emotional security. However, you may have also felt safe to open up to your feelings inside your shell, and it enabled you to choose when it felt safe to come out too. Sometimes these children may not emerge from their shells until they are older, or when they feel safe to be themselves.

You may have been a demanding child who would sulk for hours, or even days, when you did not get your own way. However, you gave as much as you got, and you were generally caring, wise and thoughtful. You may have enjoyed helping your parents with chores around the house.

As with all 2s you may have been a quiet or shy child, passive and gentle, or at other times you may have cried a lot and experienced deep emotions. Perhaps you sometimes felt suffocated by others' emotions around you too; for example, if you had an emotionally 'smothering' parent who was over-protective towards you.

Children with a 20/2 may sometimes feel that they are 'misunderstood'. A part of this may be because they are incredibly sensitive and dreamy. These children may need to explore all their feelings and to share them with people with whom they feel safe to connect in this way, so that they can feel 'heard'.

WELL-BEING

With a 20/2 influencing your health you may sometimes be prone to PMT mood swings, or suffer from depression. You may also be prone to asthma, eczema, sinusitis or breathing difficulties.

CAREER CHOICES

With a 20/2 influencing your career you may choose to work as a lawyer, a mediator, an agent of some kind, a diplomat or a negotiator. These are areas where you can stay focused and unbiased 'in the middle', and enjoy finding mutually beneficial decisions for both sides.

You may also use your ability to relate to others by taking up a career as a customer services representative, a personnel officer, a manager or a market researcher. Or you may enjoy work as a counsellor, carer or therapist, or anywhere in the health-care professions. You may also work as a bookkeeper.

FAMOUS CHARACTER ANALYSIS
Natalie Wood Born 20 July 1938

Natalie Wood was an incredibly sensitive actress who was best know for her legendary performance in *West Side Story*, a film about love and romance in the midst of confrontations between gangs of youths. Her outstanding features were her sensitive and at times gentle voice, and her incredibly expressive eyes.

With the 20/2 influencing her Personality Natalie radiated warmth and appeared to be a loving and 'open' person, with a deeply caring nature. When she appeared in public, she had an air of calmness and tranquillity, and her femininity really shone through. She was a popular actress, with whom people obviously felt they were able to relate.

Natalie died on 29 November 1981. With the 2 she may well have feared the very thing that killed her – drowning. The whole date adds up to a 5, which is a number for the unexpected and a number for change, so perhaps she was trying to make a change in her life that day. The day was a 29 or 2, which also resonates with Natalie's Personality number 2; perhaps she was trying to face her fears and to find balance in her life on the day she died.

NUMBER
21/3
PERSONALITY

GENERAL TRENDS FOR NUMBER 21/3 PERSONALITY

With a 21/3 influencing your Personality you have the gift of providence, and a deepest yearning to create abundance in your life – of love, joy, fun, good health, friends, work and money – and when you do have all this you love to share it with others. You are an extremely generous and giving individual, and you may believe that 'God' or someone is looking after you because there always seems to be so much in your life. You may often feel like you are 'blessed', or that you are protected in some way. You do not take your life for granted, and you may often say 'Thank you' out loud or think just how lucky you are. However, even if you have not created abundance, then it may be time to be grateful for what you do have. Perhaps you have created an abundance in one particular area of your life, so think yourself 'lucky' for that!

Spirituality and religion may play a great part in your life, and you may realize that an abundance of money is useless and empty without inner happiness. However, you may not necessarily go to church or meditate every day, but you may feel that all humans are spiritually connected, and in that way everyone is equal. You believe in treating everyone with respect; you believe in 'goodness' and kindness and you are optimistic, with a positive outlook on life. Even during challenging times you may feel that you are simply privileged to be alive.

You may be a highly sensitive person, and you often feel things deeply. You may also be psychic, and get positive or negative 'hunches' about people, particularly when you first meet them. Often you may follow your instincts, and although you may not always be right, this can also help to teach you about life. You may also get gut feelings about people you are close to, and perhaps you can always tell when the telephone is about to ring.

With a 21/3 influencing your Personality you are a cheery person, and you'd love everyone to be happy. Sometimes you are happy to sacrifice yourself to make this happen, such as by missing seeing a film with your friends so that you can look after your pregnant sister or cook your grandparents a meal. You have an incredible knack of being able to cheer people up with your vibrant energy and enthusiasm about life which leaves people feeling 'lucky' about their lives too.

You generally follow your instincts, but at the end of the day you may be a fatalist. You generally take things in your stride and accept life the way it is. You may not like it when, at times, life doesn't run smoothly, but you try to make the most out of every situation; you are a born optimist.

Family often takes up a large proportion of your life, and you may see them regularly. You may live next door to each other, or even live with different generations all sharing the same house. However, even if you do not get together that often, you may feel a deep connection to your family, and you may all share a strong influence over each other's lives. You can also be very protective towards your family, particularly your own partner and children, or even towards close friends who have become part of your extended 'family'.

With a 21/3 you love to socialize; you are generally a happy-go-lucky person, and you have a brilliant and witty sense of humour and a bright mind, which you often use to entertain others. You may be a simple and straight forward person, gentle, caring and warm, and you are often genuine and sincere in your relations with others. You love to communicate, and travelling and meeting new people inspires you.

You are generally ambitious, you like to succeed and you also love the challenge of new goals. You have a strong drive and you may be very focused on mastering many goals at once, which challenges your flexibility. Perhaps you may also negotiate your goals with integrity, honesty and co-operation, so that everyone can 'win'.

With a 21/3 you are a highly creative person with an abundance of ideas. You may also love to have fun in the gym, participate in any sport, or relax with a game of golf, or enjoy gentle yoga and meditation.

CHALLENGES

With a 21/3 influencing your Personality you may be a cautious person who tentatively follows your goals and ideas. Perhaps this is because you lack confidence in yourself at times, or because you fear failing. However, by the law of averages some of your goals and ideas will bear fruit. So by taking a deep breath you can boost your goals with positive energy and help materialize them.

Paradoxically, with a 21/3 influencing your Personality you may also have a tendency to be over-confident about achieving your goals. This can give you a feeling of superficial 'luck' which may backfire because you are trying to manipulate life to your advantage instead of letting it flow. For example, by telling everyone at work, 'Yes, of course I'm going to be promoted!' (even though life knows better!). At these times you may find your goals, your money, your possessions or your relationships 'flow' away from you instead. However, being over-confident may help to teach you what you really do want in your life, but also that sometimes you need to accept what life gives you instead.

Sometimes you may be so busy doing and giving to others that there is simply no time left for you, and you may feel drained. Perhaps you think that giving to yourself is too selfish. However, by devoting some time to yourself you will have more love, energy and vitality to give to others later on, and will help to keep yourself healthy too.

With a 21/3 you may feel superior because you are able to look after your family and friends and provide them with an abundance of material things. You may feel like you are always giving to them, and that makes you feel very important. However, it is life that is looking after them (and you), and love, wealth and possessions are all here to be shared. You may eventually realize that even when you give something you receive something too. For example, you may give someone a birthday present, and the look of pleasure on their face is a gift for you. You may drive someone to the airport in your car; they may be so grateful that it leaves you with a feeling of goodness and happiness all day long. By sharing yourself, instead of feeling like you *have* to give, or take, you can actually learn to enjoy life much more.

You may be a 'difficult' and confrontational person at times. You may also love to argue your point instead of discussing things, and you usually like to win. However, all this behaviour simply gets you noticed – because you may have the loudest voice or opinion – and you simply love the attention. Sometimes you can use these qualities to help others in a positive way, such as when you confront the council about why they want to build a car park over the children's playground.

However, co-operative discussion, rather than anger, is by far the best route for achieving successful change.

With a 21/3 you are generally a happy and outgoing person without a care in the world. However, for all that you are outgoing, you are very sensitive to people's feelings and sometimes you can also be erratically emotional and moody. One minute you're wallowing in sadness, and the next you're feeling contemplative, and so on. You may also be over-sensitive, and 'cut off' from your feelings to protect yourself from getting hurt. However, you also possess a strong mind and, generally, a positive outlook on life. So, at times of emotional unbalance, you can use this strength to let your body know who's in control, instead of letting your emotions control you. This may then help you to feel peace and harmony in your life once again.

Being successful is important to you, and you may feel frustrated when life doesn't always deliver what you want, or what you think you need. Sometimes you can be greedy and no matter how successful you are, or what you've got, you always seem to want more. Perhaps you may also grab things for fear that they'll go away. However, these actions show that you believe in scarcity, and therefore what you believe is usually what you get. So by grasping at life, love, food and money, you make these things quickly dwindle away. Eventually you may realize that simply taking what you need, instead of what you want, provides room for others' needs to be met too. It also allows other things to flow into your life.

ROMANCE AND SEX

With a 21/3 influencing your love life you have an abundance of love and joy, which you are only too happy to share with others. Therefore finding a partner who loves life, laughter, lightness and sharing may be essential. You are also a magnetic and attractive person, and you may find yourself inundated with romantic offers, some of which you simply cannot refuse. You usually love variety, and you may like to try out many of the opportunities that come your way. Perhaps you go dancing with one partner, to dinner with another, and enjoy sizzling sex with both of them (not necessarily at the same time!). You can also be petulant at times, as you are spoiled for choice; you can also be moody and demanding, and sulk when you don't get your own way.

Generally you love the freedom of being able to express yourself within your relationships. You may look for superficial liaisons, with no long-lasting commitments, and you like to feel free. You simply love change, and you can be very changeable about your current partner, as your mind wanders to the potential of greener pastures elsewhere.

You are someone who likes to be able to communicate with your partner and to talk 'openly' about your feelings and life, to him or her. You may also like a partner with intellectual interests, with whom you can talk about politics, art and literature, or who is spiritual or religious in some way.

You love socializing, and you throw your doors open to the world, by holding parties and dinners in your own home. You are a wonderful host or hostess and a brilliant entertainer, because you are very thoughtful, and you pay attention to detail. For example, the food, music, lighting and setting are always perfect, as is your choice of guests.

You may also love to travel, and there is no better way to make friends than by seeing the world. When you are feeling footloose and fancy-free you may even meet your ideal partner, who loves travelling, and with whom you may travel your whole life through.

With a 21/3 influencing your love life, you may have a strong mothering instinct (men too!) and you may like to look after your partner and feel lovingly protective towards him or her. You like this form of loving kindness, and perhaps you may find a partner who can become a part of your family and with whom you can have children.

With a 21/3 influence you may have an abundant sex life, and be inventive with your techniques – you enjoy variety. You may passionately indulge in playful foreplay; orgasm isn't the only goal. With notions of partnership being important for you, you may seek many partners to satisfy your sexual expression, or, on the other hand, simply enjoy the emotional security with one loving partner.

PHYSICAL APPEARANCE

With a 21/3 influencing your looks you may be of medium height, with high cheek bones, a large prominent forehead, a long wide face and high eyebrows. You may have small hips, and be fleshy and curvaceous if you are a woman. Your most outstanding feature is your voice, which often sounds elated.

CHILDHOOD EXPERIENCES

With a 21/3 influencing your childhood you may have been an emotional and sensitive child, who wrapped yourself away in your studies to avoid getting too close to people at times. You may have been withdrawn and shy, or even lacked the self-confidence to go out into the world by yourself. For example, you may have always liked to go to school with your best friend, or to have taken your brother with you to parties or when you went shopping. You may have felt too conspicuous alone, and needed the security and emotional support from those around you.

Perhaps you were spoiled, with the freedom to do just what you wanted, when you wanted; you may have had too much freedom at times. Perhaps there was not enough discipline or structure in your life, except at school, which may have helped you to learn something about rules and boundaries. You may have also been spoiled with money and material possessions, or smothered with love and affection too.

With a 21/3 you were usually a light-hearted and fun child, and you may have been brought up in a highly active and creative environment, with lots of laughter in the air, music playing in the background, food being prepared, work being carried out, and lots of visitors, particularly family members, who always seem to stay around.

Children with a 21/3 often need an outlet for their energy and creativity, and may need to be encouraged to express themselves in whatever positive way they can, such as by dancing, playing a musical instrument, or helping around the house. They may also have a great need to feel loved, and may often need to hear 'I love you' to help them feel safe.

WELL-BEING

With a 21/3 influencing your health you may at times be prone to skin problems, asthma, hormonal imbalances or emotional stress. You may sometimes suffer from muscular aches and pains too.

CAREER CHOICE

With a 21/3 influencing your career you may be a successful businessman or woman, diplomat, negotiator, peacemaker, religious or spiritual leader, or an agent of any kind. You may also manage an inheritance of money or property; for example, you may manage a country estate.

Perhaps you work in the creative field as an artist, writer, musician (you may be very musical), chef, singer, nanny or professional carer. You may love to use your hands in your career, by becoming a massage therapist, physiotherapist or professional wrestler.

FAMOUS CHARACTER ANALYSIS
Charlotte Brontë Born 21 April 1816

Charlotte Brontë was a successful novelist, and in her work she described life in Victorian England. There were not many ways a simple Victorian woman could express herself, and writing became an outlet for Charlotte's abundant creativity. Women of the time were meant simply to get married, and Charlotte created controversy when works published under a male pseudonym were revealed to have been written by her. Her books offered a major break-through for women of the period, and encouraged them to follow their own careers too.

Charlotte was very intellectual and bright, but held a somewhat serious and sartorial sense of humour. She liked to discuss matters with her sisters, who were also novelists, and they loved to exchange tales or gossip over afternoon tea.

With a 21/3 Charlotte was brought up with a strong religious influence because her father was the vicar at the local church, which stood at the end of their garden. There was an abundance of spirituality, love and respect in their household, but little money; clothes were recycled or made, and food was often scarce.

Charlotte died on 31 March 1855, having lived an often hard life. The whole date adds up to an 8, so perhaps she was karmically complete. The day was a 31 or 4, which is the number of the flag-bearer; she certainly waved the flag for Victorian women and their rights.

NUMBER

22/4

PERSONALITY

GENERAL TRENDS FOR NUMBER 22/4 PERSONALITY

With a 22/4 influencing your Personality you have the gift of imagination, and the deepest yearning to materialize your dreams. You have the ability to 'feel' your dreams, as though they were real, and then to work towards materializing them in a step-by-step manner. However, you may often find that you share your dreams with others, and you instinctively feel what others need. For example, if you are a property developer, it may be your dream to build a children's nursery in your local village or town, instead of a new supermarket (because there are already plenty). You may negotiate for the land and, having bought the plot, set to work to lay these new foundations for the benefit of the many parents locally who share your dream.

You may often enjoy doing things which can help everyone around you, particularly those which may help to bring material security to others. You are realistic about the goals you set, and you will often plod on unto the end to achieve them. Sometimes you may even possess an unshakeable determination to leave the world a better place than before you came in to it, by in some way providing more security for others.

Your home is very important to you, and you will naturally seek material security for yourself and your family. You may need to know that you have solid roots to work from, and your home may be the foundation for your 'success' in life, because it is somewhere you feel safe. You are also self-disciplined, and you may often work hard to provide the kind of material security for which you long.

You are a reliable and dependable person and you like to be honest in your dealings with others. You are loyal, and you tend to attract long-term friendships and relationships because of these qualities. For example, in business, if people can rely on you to provide goods which match up to their description, then they will continue to buy from you in the future. You also like to buy reliable products too.

With a 22/4 influencing your Personality you take your responsibilities seriously. For example, you are not the type to forget to lock your front door when you go out, and you would certainly remember to hand in a work report on time. You may even thrive off responsibilities and like to take on more, but you are likely to have very clear boundaries about these. For example, in your home you may agree to pay the mortgage, but this may be your limit, and so you ask your partner to pay for the heating, lighting or food.

Generally you enjoy routine, because it helps to give some structure to your life. For example, knowing that you always take the train at 8.15am, or that you do the weekly 'shop' on a Thursday, can actually help you to feel secure.

With a 22/4 you are a caring and warm human being, and you have a giving nature; you are always eager to please. You may enjoy sharing your life, your material possessions and your feelings with others. You are a good listener, and people often come to you with their problems, and you may like to be honest with others by sharing your feelings too.

You are generally a peace-loving person, and you like to feel at harmony with yourself and your surroundings. You may like to have lots of greenery and relaxing colours decorating your environment, and to have peaceful people in your home who are respectful of each other's (emotional) needs.

With a 22/4 you may be decisive and able to make practical decisions easily. However, you also have strong instincts and you may like to take these into consideration before making any final decisions. For example, you may want to buy a car and you have seen its service history, but your instincts tell you that something is wrong and it would be better to buy another one. Sometimes your gut feelings save you from making mistakes, but you are a sensible person too, and are not ruled by your emotions alone.

You may love to play golf for relaxation, or take part in any team sport like cricket or baseball, or simply to walk. You may like to practise yoga, gentle exercises, or to meditate at times.

CHALLENGES

With a 22/4 influencing your Personality you may be ungrounded and dreamy about your goals. You may also be too lazy to put in all the hours of slog and labour required to achieve your goals, or you may even leave your work for others to complete. You may set impractical goals for yourself; for example, you may think that you can finish a building project in three weeks, but it may take a week to get the bricks delivered and another few days for the builders to arrive. Perhaps you did not order the materials soon enough; maybe you unrealistically promised your client that their building would be ready on time. This scenario may be applied to your whole life, and it is unlikely to guarantee success in the long run. However, being sensible and practical about the goals you choose may be the first helpful thing to do. The next essential step is to put in some hard work to help you materialize them.

You may be materialistic at times, and your need to produce may override any other feelings. For example, you may be hungry or tired, but you simply ignore this as you carry on working. You may also be a workaholic and drive yourself into the ground to get the job done and to provide the material security that you require. Listening to your feelings may help you to stay healthy; by taking food or sleeping, when your body needs it, you will have more energy to focus on your work and your dreams.

With a 22/4 influencing your Personality you may at times fear for your survival and fear that you will not be able to materialize your basic needs. For example, you may worry about losing your job by being made redundant, or losing your home; you feel insecure. However, you may even fear these things when there is plenty of money in your bank account and when the work scene is really secure. You may realize that whatever situations you may need to face, you can do your best to work them out practically and get on with your life in a step-by-step way.

Sometimes you can be dishonest, and you may try to control and manipulate people to get your own way. This may often be because you are unable to express your feelings in a positive way, or because you fear that your request may be refused and you will get hurt anyway. For example, you may want your partner to run you to the station in the car, but you ask in a non-direct way. 'Honey, wouldn't you like to get some chocolate cookies from that shop near the station?' you ask, but your partner refuses on the grounds that there is plenty of stock in the kitchen. However, when you feel safe to express your emotions honestly and directly you are actually more liable to get your needs met, because people feel comfortable and react openly in return.

You are a very sensitive person and sometimes you can be defensive towards people in an attempt to protect your deep vulnerability. You may feel so open that you are 'touchy' even with your closest friends, who may sometimes find you difficult to be with. However, instead of defending yourself, it may help to simply say, 'Hey, I feel vulnerable at the moment – can we talk another day?', instead of putting yourself into a desperate situation and pushing people away.

With a 22/4 influencing your Personality you can be insensitive to others' needs at times, perhaps because you are cut off from your emotions, or simply because you do not want to feel their pain. Sometimes you may need to cut off from your own feelings for a while in order to survive, because otherwise you may feel too much of their (or your own) pain.

Perhaps you may retaliate against people because you are hurt, and you can even be cruel at times. You may also be prone to irrational outbursts of emotion when you are overwhelmed by the intensity of your feelings. However, the earthy, practical side of your Personality can help bring you back to reality, to face your feelings and situation calmly.

With a 22/4 you may be a warm and giving person, but find it more difficult to receive. On the other hand, you may find it hard to give to others, but easier to receive. However, by learning to both give and receive, you are helping to make the world go around.

ROMANCE AND SEX

With a 22/4 influencing your relationships you are a loving, nurturing and warm person, and you particularly like to be able to exchange your loving energies with a similarly giving and receptive partner. You may be quite placid and calm too, and gentle and 'soft to the touch' when you are in the company of your loving partner. However, you are choosy, and you may go off in pursuit of that special partner with whom to share your life. Once you feel that you have found your soul mate you are fearless in your determination to materialize the relationship. Often you may have a strong instinct about who is the right person.

You can also be dreamy and unrealistic, and you may also project all kinds of feelings onto your partner which don't even exist. For example, you may think that your partner is sad that you are spending an evening out with your friends, because you think he or she will feel lonely. However, perhaps these are your feelings of loneliness because he or she is not with you, and perhaps he or she actually feels happy to be on their own for a while. Communicating your own feelings to each other at these times can help you learn how you both really feel within your relationship.

With a 22/4 you may be a down-to-earth and practical person who needs material security to help you feel safe. Therefore finding a partner with whom you can build that security may be important to you, particularly when you are searching for a stable, long-term relationship. However, you are usually willing to work hard towards this goal and are prepared to put in a joint effort to make it work. You may also be seeking emotional security and you may need a partner who can nurture you and with whom you can relate intimately on this level.

Sometimes you may find that you relate to your partner physically more than in an emotional way. For example, you may physically live together, have sex and children together, and enjoy physically going out together. Being physical is also a way of connecting and communicating with your partner or soul mate. Perhaps sharing your feelings all the time is too challenging for you both.

You may be an honest and open person who enjoys the simple things in life: simple food, simple clothes, simple walks in the park with your partner. You are fiercely loyal in love, reliable and dependable, and you may seek a partner who can reciprocate these qualities.

With a 22/4 influencing your sex life you are a highly sensitive person, and a considerate lover who aims to please when you are with your partner. Sometimes you may prefer just being physical with your partner, particularly if you find it difficult to let him or her get close to you emotionally. At other times your need for emotional intimacy makes for pure love-making.

PHYSICAL APPEARANCE

With a 22/4 influencing your looks you may have soft, watery eyes, a large face, delicate skin, and you may be soft and fleshy. Perhaps you also have a wide nose and large hips, or you are stocky. Your most outstanding feature may be that you have a very short neck.

CHILDHOOD EXPERIENCES

With a 22/4 you may have experienced a secure childhood in that you had all the material possessions that you could possibly need. Perhaps you were born into a stable family where there was no need to fear for your own security or survival. This may have left you feeling safe to relax and enjoy your childhood, and to go out into the world feeling confident and secure.

Perhaps you were a placid plodder, who simply took each day as it came, and got on with your routines in a practical step-by-step way. For example, you may not have dived into your school work to get it done as quickly as possible, but carefully and conscientiously ploughed through it in a slow but determined way. You probably worked very hard towards your goals, such as exams, and you may have taken your school work very seriously indeed.

With a 22/4 your childhood may have been very painful emotionally because you were so acutely sensitive to people around. But you learned how to survive and to live with your feelings inside. Sometimes you cut off from your feelings, and at other times your intense emotions exploded out. However, you may have learned that getting on and doing something positive and practical, like school work, playing or sport, may have focused your attention outwards, and also helped you survive.

Children with a 22/4 may often be dreamy and float around in the clouds. However, by listening to what they have to say about their dreams you may be able to encourage them to take some practical steps towards materializing some of them.

WELL-BEING

With a 22/4 influencing your health you may be prone to problems with your legs or feet (which is associated with you being 'grounded'). You may also suffer from skin problems, or breathing difficulties such as asthma.

CAREER CHOICE

With a 22/4 influencing your career you may take up work where you can relate to others and use your sensitivity to help people. You may work as a counsellor, therapist, nurse or doctor, or perhaps you may choose a career as a diplomat, peacemaker, politician or civil servant.

However, you may also be landed gentry and manage your estate, or be a caretaker, or work in real estate. Perhaps you are a builder, farmer, financier or accountant, or even work in the creative field, as a writer, artist or musician.

FAMOUS CHARACTER ANALYSIS

Giacomo Puccini Born 22 December 1858

Puccini was a famous 19th-century Italian musician who composed and presented many wonderful operas. Puccini must have been extraordinarily sensitive, because his music often sounded heavenly and dream-like. However, Puccini materialized his dreams into reality, step by step and with a tremendous amount of effort and hard work.

Puccini opened up the field of opera to many people who may not have normally been attracted by its intense emotion. For example, one of his masterpieces was the 'light' opera *Madame Butterfly*, which was extremely popular at the time. He was clearly able to portray his operas in a simple way, to which people did and can relate.

With a 22/4 Puccini was a peace-loving person who was passionate about his life and music. He must have been able to feel deeply. His audiences may have felt as if his music wrapped around them, touched their hearts and filled up their senses. Puccini gave himself and shared himself through his work and his dreams.

Puccini died on 28 November 1924, having laid the foundation for a whole new generation of opera-lovers. The whole date adds up to a 1, so perhaps he was seeking a new direction at that time. The day adds up to a 28, or another 1, so clearly he was ready for a new start.

NUMBER
23/5

PERSONALITY

GENERAL TRENDS FOR NUMBER 23/5 PERSONALITY

With a 23/5 influencing your Personality you have the gift of imagination, and a deepest yearning to express your dreams. You are a dreamer, but you are able to implement discipline and effort, and work towards making them real. You have the most vivid imagination, and therefore you like to add a lot of 'colour' to your life when you are creating your dreams. For example, you may dream of building a beautiful house for yourself and your family. In your life it is almost real, in a beautiful design, with beautiful fabrics and furnishings, plenty of natural light and a dreamy garden, similar to the one in your imagination.

People may be surprised that despite being so dreamy you are able to materialize so much in your life. However, it is precisely because you believe in your dreams, and because you expect them to happen, that some of them naturally do, no matter how 'big' or unrealistic they may seem.

You may often catch yourself staring into space and day-dreaming. Sometimes you have vivid dreams when you sleep, and writing them down and interpreting them when you wake up may help you to learn more about yourself. You may also be psychic, and some of your dreams may give you information about your friends and family; you may also have premonitions at times.

Your dreams may seem very 'real'. For example, you may dream that you were visiting your brother in Australia and you were having a conversation with him and his wife about your family. If you were very close to your brother, he may actually 'remember' having the conversation with you too, and when you talk to him about it on the telephone the next day, he may say, 'You've already told me that!' Hence you may have a keen interest in and curiosity about mysticism. However, even when you are awake you are able to contact your intuition easily, and receive clear information which can help you with your life.

With a 23/5 you often have a child-like simplicity, and you can be 'read' like an open book; you feel safe to express yourself openly and honestly with people. For example, you may feel safe to ask directly for what you want, which people may find threatening at times because there is nowhere for them to hide. Sometimes people say 'yes' to your requests because you are so genuine, and they may want to give you what you want; at other times they may say 'yes' simply because you asked.

You are often full of laughter and joy, and you can always find something to smile about; you have a lovely, sunny nature which brings warmth to others. You can also be very gentle and soft, thoughtful or passive at times, and you may thrive off affection and physical warmth. You are a harmonious person, and you like to feel at peace with those around you, and you will work hard on co-operating with others to achieve a calm and caring environment.

With a 23/5 influencing your Personality you are a very sensitive person and you like to share your feelings with those closest to you. You like to be able to relate to people and to communicate with people emotionally. However, you are so 'open' that people instantly know how you feel anyway.

You are carefree and uninhibited and you feel free to express yourself. You are laid-back and relaxed and you are naturally at ease with life. You are a real charmer too, and your magnetism draws all kinds of different people to you, everywhere you go. You love being with people and you explore many opportunities that come your way: visits to art galleries, dinners, parties, celebrations, and travelling. You have a gregarious and adventurous side to your Personality which is always on the look-out for more action-packed activities and excitement.

With a 23/5 you can sometimes get serious about life, and have serious ambitions and want to have serious fun too. With your magnetism, your openness and your abundant creative gifts, you may be able to create all the situations necessary to make a great success of your life. You are motivated by your desires, and with your powerful imagination you can make them come true.

You enjoy sports as part of your social life: skiing, tennis, racing, riding, sailing, water-skiing and swimming.

CHALLENGES

With a 23/5 influencing your Personality you may be immature at times, and refuse to face reality by taking your responsibilities seriously. For example, you may be so laid-back that you forget to take your purse when you go out for dinner, and so someone else has to pay. Or you may neglect responsibilities for your children sometimes. Perhaps you even try to literally run away from your responsibilities, and change relationship, job and house in order to escape. You may simply go through life without a care in the world, leaving a mess behind you. Perhaps you may want everyone else to take responsibility and look after you, or you may think that love is measured by the amount of things people can do for you.

However, although people may go along with you for while, eventually they may get bored of playing games with a 'child' instead of having fun and sharing life with a grown adult. So if you want others to take you seriously, learning to take responsibility for yourself may be a good way to start.

At times you may not be deliberately irresponsible, but it may be simply that you just don't think, or perhaps you are off in your own dream world. Disasters may happen at these times; for example, if you lose concentration when you are in an important meeting, or when you are baking cakes. However, it is your responsibility to make sure that at times when you do feel a little 'out of it' you make the effort to pay extra attention to where you are. Sometimes grounding yourself by taking a walk, having a warm drink or hugging someone may help.

With a 23/5 influencing your Personality you have a strong mind and a vivid and creative imagination, which can help you to materialize your dreams. However, when you think negative thoughts or are thinking deeply about your fears, you may externalize them and contribute towards making them real. So it may help you to be aware of your thoughts and to be careful what you dream about.

Sometimes you may live in your own little dream world and attract similar people to you too, who are happy to go along with your dreams for a while. However, life catches you out; for example, when you forget to pay bills and you receive demanding letters. Or you may be surprised when people let you down, because everything always works out fine in your dreams. However, having these 'knocks' may help you to learn to be more practical and grounded, and may encourage you to learn to live in the 'real' world.

The facts of life and reality are sometimes too much for you, and you may tell lies to make life more interesting, or exaggerate the truth to make life more exciting. For example, you may tell your friends at work that you have a boyfriend who is a prince (although not many people would fall for that one!), or you may tell people that you have millions in the bank (take off a few zeros!). However, people around you may seek proof of your lifestyle, as they easily spot that you are not telling the truth and once again you may be forced to face reality.

With a 23/5 you often like to run around and give everyone the slip; you enjoy your freedom. You may not like to be pinned down to making decisions and if you are you may feel trapped and find yourself making commitments which you cannot keep. For example, if your boss wants you to make a quick decision about whether you are prepared to go to work in Paris for six weeks, you may say 'yes' and then not turn up at the airport on the day. However, learning to be honest with yourself about what you really want from your life may help you to lead an even more carefree life, by not needing to lie to yourself or hide your true feelings from others.

You may like to burn the candle at both ends in your desire for adventure and fun. Perhaps you try to push things just a little too far, and eventually you may even burn yourself out and suffer from exhaustion. By learning to find a balance between your needs (food, rest, work), and your desires (whatever they may be), it may help you to be more relaxed, and perhaps heal your life. Sometimes living the simple life for a while may be all you need to help sort yourself out and to bring harmony to your whole life.

ROMANCE AND SEX

With a 23/5 influencing your relationships you have a dreamy imagination and you may be looking for your ideal 'dream' partner to share your life with. Perhaps you are looking for your soul mate, and you may keep on until you do. You love life, and may love to experiment with lots of different partners. But finding that 'special one' with whom you can feel the power of your whole being, and with whom you can deeply connect, may be your optimum goal.

Generally you are an expressive person who gossips freely about your love life with all your pals. But in relation to your soul partner 'still waters run deep', and you may feel like savouring the moments, rather than revealing your antics or what you both feel to others. Once you have found your 'dream' you are happy to commit to him or her for 'real'.

You love to play, and you revel in sensual delights. You may even find another 'playboy' (or girl) who likes the freedom to roam around all day, simply being a 'good time babe'. You have an incredible ability to make life fun, and with your vivid imagination you can be creative in making your partner's life more interesting too. With a 23/5 you are flirtatious, vivacious and out for adventure – you'll try almost anything once. So finding a partner who likes the adrenalin boost may really help to inspire you. You have an impulsive nature and you may get restless easily, so your partner may need to be strong to keep you from running off, or may enjoy being spontaneous with you too.

With a 23/5 influencing your relationships you are genuine, and you give a lot of love and consideration to your partner, and to his or her needs. You may particularly like to share your feelings openly with your partner and to hear how he or she feels. However, you can be over-sensitive and vulnerable at times, or be very emotional too. You may try to pick a fight with your partner, or get irrational. So finding a partner who can comfort and care for you, and who can understand your moods, may help to bring you closer together.

Romance is high on your list, and you may spare no expense on things which make you feel good: chocolates, flowers, clothes, and holidays in the sun with your partner. Perhaps your partner lavishes all these things on you. However, although you love the stimulation of romance you are a bright and intelligent person too, and you may also be turned on by bright conversation; an intellectual or spiritual person may fascinate you.

With a 23/5 influencing your sex life, you are a sensual person who may enjoy being fed grapes or rubbed with oil as part of your play-time, before delving into sex games with your partner. Your affectionate nature makes you a very warm dream lover, and your zest for adventure and your wild imagination makes you creative too. Whether you are romping around on a waterbed or in the 'mile-high club' on a plane, you simply revel in your sexuality, and you may enjoy a lot of loving sex.

PHYSICAL APPEARANCE

With a 23/5 influencing your Personality you may have large dreamy eyes, an upturned nose, and have a 'ruddy' complexion or freckles. You are of medium height with straight shoulders, and you may be pear-shaped. Your outstanding features are your long and shapely legs.

CHILDHOOD EXPERIENCES

With a 23/5 influencing your childhood you may have been a very expressive child with a brilliant sense of humour, and you may have spent your time entertaining your family and friends. Perhaps you took acting classes or went to a theatrical school, or to a school specializing in your talents along with conventional education.

Perhaps you had a happy-go-lucky childhood, and one where you were spoiled with love and affection. You may even have been too spoiled at times, and quickly learned how to sulk and stamp your feet when life didn't deliver all your wants or needs. However, you were probably very generous and shared your toys with your friends and family. You may have loved holidays, and the excitement of travelling on boats, trains and aeroplanes. You may have liked swimming, snorkelling, skating and riding, and perhaps you were inspired by the circus too.

You may have been a dreamy child who was always 'disappearing' into your imagination, for security and comfort, and for creative ideas. You may have been angry and frustrated at not being able to express your dreams to your friends and family and to be able to share with them what you 'see'. Perhaps your imagination was also an escape route for you when life got too serious or when there were too many distractions around.

Children with a 23/5 may need to be encouraged to explore their mind to their heart's content because the key to their future lies here, in their creative imagination. They may also need to be encouraged to express some of their dreams into reality.

WELL-BEING

With a 23/5 influencing your health you may be prone to throat or thyroid problems, asthma, eczema, skin rashes or allergies. You may also have mental or emotional stress sometimes.

CAREER CHOICE

With a 23/5 influencing your career you may take up work as a secret agent, detective or spy, or you may work in the public sector. You may also work as a lawyer, an agent of any kind, barrister, peacemaker, book-keeper, or even in PR, sales, marketing, advertising or travel, or you may work as a computer expert or scientist.

You may also 'work' as a socialite, playboy or playgirl, or as a carer, therapist, writer, actor or entertainer, or you may be a film or television director, or an imaginative designer. You may also work with children in some way. A career as a teacher or ski instructor may also appeal.

FAMOUS CHARACTER ANALYSIS

Samuel Pepys Born 23 February 1633

Samuel Pepys was an English writer and socialite whose diaries were published after he died; they contained accurate and fascinating insights into British life around 1660 to 1669. He kept his diaries avidly for nine and a half years, and they form factual historical accounts rather than a record of his dreams and desires.

Pepys was committed to his work and found solace in his ability to express himself through his writing, and hence by communicating to the world. He was a teacher too, educating the world about Britain and society.

Pepys explored many of the typical qualities of the 23/5: he was energetic, witty and creative, with a bright mind, and he was obviously fascinated by people. His ability to listen carefully to people enabled him to write descriptively about them, and he was very observant too. Pepys escaped into his mind when he wrote his diaries, and withdrew into his imagination even when he was recording facts.

Samuel Pepys died on 26 May 1703, having completed a full cycle of nine years of journals. The whole date adds up to a 5, so perhaps he had described enough social changes in Britain and was seeking a change for himself, at that time. The day is a 26 or 8, which is a number for karma, and like others who died on an 8, he had fulfilled his karma – for this lifetime.

24/6

GENERAL TRENDS FOR NUMBER 24/6 PERSONALITY

With a 24/6 influencing your Personality you have a musical gift and a deepest yearning to be able to make the most of your time. You may be someone who is extremely aware of time, and perhaps you are always looking at your watch, or trying to find the 'best time' to do something. You are systematic and organized, generally, and you may keep appointments to the exact time allocated, because you have so many other things to do. You realize that 'time flies by' quickly, and in order to materialize all the things that you need to do with your life you allocate a certain amount of time for everything.

You may also be very aware of 'timing', and you may feel that everything happens in its own time; you are not someone who manipulates life your way, but you simply work to make the most out of the experiences on offer. However, you may feel that there is a 'right' time to go for something, and that you need to make the most out of the time slots allocated to you. For example, you may be looking for a new job, but you are not quite ready to leave your old one yet because you may feel insecure. After six weeks of looking, a fantastic job comes your way, but you may not feel ready to leave. But after three months, when another exciting job in a super company is offered, you take it; to you this is the 'right' time to leave. However, there were two opportunities or two time slots when you could have left, but you opted for the second. Each opportunity leads you in a different direction along your path in life.

With a 24/6 you may also be aware that time is not just relevant to one lifetime, and that there are other time systems operating in the world, of which linear time is only one. There are other dimensions to time, and one lifetime is simply a flicker.

With a 24/6 influencing your Personality you are a practical, efficient person with your feet planted firmly on the ground. You are also methodical, and you like everything to be in its place. You may also organize your life brilliantly, by making lists and ticking things off as you go through the day in a systematic way. You may love methodically working through things and through life, and achieving the goals you set for yourself each day.

Generally you are a hard worker, and you work in a purposeful and constructive way; you like to think that everyone around you can benefit from your input. You often take your duties, responsibilities and commitments very seriously, and you are a loyal person who sometimes pushes yourself aside to help others. You are a communitarian. You are also a 'provider' and you may be particularly devoted to providing material security for your family by working hard. You are also a warm and affectionate human being, with a deep sense of caring, and you are also able to provide emotional security for your family (and your friends).

You have a natural wisdom and a big heart, and you are often able to help people by listening to their problems, or in a practical way. Indeed, you are generous and giving, and seeing people happy or fed helps to enrich your life.

With a 24/6 you may be a gentle soul, who likes peace and quiet and harmony in your home and in your life. You are also a peacemaker, and you like to sort out life's challenges in a co-operative way. For example, there is a dispute about a parking space outside your home, and three people are claiming the space as theirs. You are able to see the whole picture, and you are able to negotiate an agreement diplomatically with all those involved. You are a careful decision-maker, and you do not generally jump into anything without due consideration and tact.

You are a sensual person who appreciates warm people, lovely surroundings, good food and wine, beautiful clothes, art and music, and you may lead the 'good life' too. You are an idealist and a romantic, but you are a practical person and you are down to earth too.

With a 24/6 you may listen to music or play a musical instrument, for relaxation. You may also love yoga, walking, cycling, and working out in the gym.

CHALLENGES

With a 24/6 influencing your Personality you may take your duties and your responsibilities too seriously at times, and you may become burdened down with emotion. You may even feel depressed because you feel that you can never 'do enough' to fulfil all the duties you need to perform. However, you are normally good at sharing, and at these times you may be able to share your responsibilities with others in order to lighten your load. You may also like to express how you are feeling to others, and ask for their help at these times.

Alternatively, when the emphasis on matters of duty and responsibility falls at the other extreme, you may be an irresponsible person who always depends on others to make you feel good and to make your life go right. You may want others to provide you with emotional support and material possessions, and depend on them working hard to provide these things for you. However, although it's great to have someone looking after you, earning your own money, sorting out your own emotions and taking responsibility for yourself can really make you feel good, and take the pressure off others to provide for your needs.

With a 24/6 influencing your Personality you may be very emotional and needy, and get carried away with your emotional demands at times. For example, you may be upset about a problem at work, and you may expect your partner, friends, family and, indeed, anyone who is prepared to listen, to give you their time and support. Sometimes you may go too deeply into your emotions and get obsessed about your feelings and thoughts. However, considering the whole problem, and always looking at the whole group's needs, may take the focus off what *you* are feeling and bring wholeness to the situation.

You can be moody at times and sulk when people try to ask you for help. You may even resent 'having' to help them, but you may feel obligated to do what you can, particularly if they are a relative. However, by being open and honest with people, and by making a conscious decision to choose to help, or whether or not to do things for people, you are taking responsibility for yourself. There is then no need to blame or resent others, or feel guilty for not helping them.

With a 24/6 influencing your Personality you may be passive, lazy and too laid-back at times, and you may not always handle life in a realistic way. Sometimes you may be over-occupied by what your instincts are telling you, and lose a grip on reality. However, life has a habit of bringing you back to reality: for example, by giving you a huge bill to pay or a problem with a leaking roof, or something even larger to worry about, like a divorce. Tackling life in a step-by-step way can help you to carry on each day.

Sometimes, no matter how hard you work, you may be unable to provide the material security for yourself and your family. You may even sacrifice yourself by going without food, clothes or social activities in order to meet others' needs. You may feel inadequate or frustrated about this, at times. However, perhaps by providing more of their emotional needs – love, nurturing, affection, support – it may help you to feel better about the situation, knowing that you are doing all you can.

You love glamour and the 'good life', and you may be particularly taken in by how beautiful somebody is, how well they are dressed, whether they live in a 'good' area, or how prestigious their job is. You may be impressed by all their superficial 'glitter', or you may try to impress others by glamorizing your life too. However, your emotions run deep and you may sometimes want to dive deeper into life instead of swimming around on the surface. For example, you meet somebody at a cocktail party who is a beautiful model, and for a while you lead a life of parties with him or her. But eventually you may want to get to find out what he or she is really like within. Superficiality is a hollow characteristic, and you may lose your interest, as glamour alone cannot keep the spark going in any relationship.

With a 24/6 you may have no sense of 'timing', or you may say the wrong things (unless it was a Freudian slip!) at the wrong time. However, by learning to be responsible about your comments, and diplomatic in what you say, you may avoid these awkward situations.

ROMANCE AND SEX

With a 24/6 influencing your relationships you are a loving and responsive person with an open heart and an ability to express your love generously to your partner. You are demonstrative, and you like to feel the warmth of a companion next to you, and for you, love is the most important element within a relationship. Therefore finding a partner with whom you can enjoy emotional intimacy and nurturing, and even share your practical responsibilities, may be helpful, or essential.

Generally you like to settle into a long-term relationship which gives you the emotional security and stability that you need. You may like to build your nest with your partner, and you may contribute financially towards building a solid foundation, and to provide material security for you both too. However, you may be a strong provider and want to provide for your partner and family, or you may want your partner to provide for you.

You may possess a strong sense of duty towards your family, and your extended family too. Sometimes these duties may eclipse your relationship with your partner, and he or she may feel resentful towards the time they take up. For example, if you have children he or she may be jealous of the amount of time you lavish on them, and so on. You may also be resentful when your family takes up more of your attention and time than you desire. Perhaps you may be only too aware of your need to balance the time pressures between your family, your work and your social life.

With a 24/6 influencing your Personality you are very aware of timing within your relationship, and you like to sit down and discuss the best time to do things with your partner, rather than spontaneously jump into things. For example, if you want to move house, get married, start a family or go on holiday, then you carefully find the best possible time for you both. You take practicalities and your strong instincts into consideration when making these decisions.

You like to pay a lot of attention to the clothes you wear; you love sensual colours and fabrics, and you like to feel comfortable. You always like to look your best (for your partner too), but you may look glamorous even when you are only wearing an old scruffy pair of jeans and T-shirt! You exude warmth and your inner beauty really shines through. You may be laid back about what your partner looks like, because love holds the key to your heart.

You are a nurturing person and may love to bake 'love cookies' and prepare 'love potions' as aphrodisiacs for you and your partner. Indeed, food may be an important key to your heart too. You can be romantic at times, and a wonderful meal at a candlelit restaurant may be your idea of heaven.

With a 24/6 influencing your sex life you may enjoy sex as a physical release, but emotional intimacy and sharing and physical affection are very high on your list of needs. You may also seek a partner who can be useful to you in a practical way, by sharing in the equation to provide for a family, for example.

PHYSICAL APPEARANCE

With a 24/6 influencing your Personality you may have a heart-shaped face with big round cheeks, large watery eyes, a straight nose and large breasts or chest. Your outstanding feature may be your overall appearance, which is solid, or round.

CHILDHOOD EXPERIENCES

With a 24/6 influencing your childhood you may have felt pressured by the heavy duties and responsibilities within your (extended) family. For example, perhaps your parents had to look after a sick relative, which put more responsibility onto you. Or perhaps your parents were diplomats and so you had extra family duties and functions to attend. This means you may have been a rather serious child, who was perhaps full of your own sense of purpose.

You may also have been a dreamy child, who was very sensitive to your environment and the people around you, and at times you may have been easily hurt. For example, if a school friend made a nasty comment to you, then you may have really taken it to heart. However, you may have felt anger and resentment towards your friend, and perhaps you even tried to get your own back by being spiteful towards him or her.

With a 24/6 you were probably a wise child, and although you were dreamy at times you were practical too. For example, you expressed yourself openly to people, and they may have been surprised by your insightful remarks. You may have not thought too much about what you were saying, because it was your natural healing abilities and instincts which helped you express your wisdom.

Children with a 24/6 are often so responsible that they blame themselves and feel guilty for things that go wrong within their family or school group. They may feel like it is up to them (even when they are very young) to sort things out. However, explaining to a child the part the whole group has played in creating a situation can help them to release their burdens.

WELL-BEING

With a 24/6 influencing your health you may be prone to hormonal imbalances or hearing difficulties, or get bronchitis, asthma or eczema. You may also have problems with your legs or feet.

CAREER CHOICE

With a 24/6 influencing your career you may work as a diplomat, lawyer or peacemaker, or as an agent in any field. You may also work as a therapist or marriage guidance counsellor, or work in the medical profession. You have creative talents, which you may express as a musician, an artist or as a flamboyant writer.

Perhaps you take up a career as a scientist, physicist, geologist or archaeologist. You may also like to work in a disciplined and structured environment, for example within a government body, or as a solicitor, working within the confines of the law.

FAMOUS CHARACTER ANALYSIS

Henri de Toulouse-Lautrec Born 24 November 1864

Henri de Toulouse-Lautrec was a highly imaginative and famous artist who had almost an obsession with painting Montmartre nightlife – brothels, cafés, bars – and everyday earthy scenes. Indeed, he was obviously more interested in this than in painting 'pretty' pictures of famous people for example; one could say that he may have slightly glamorized his models in brothels, because it seemed like they were icons to him.

It is said that Toulouse-Lautrec loved the 'good life', and drinking in particular. Some also said that he became too open about the company he kept. However, his interest in culture drove him on to experience life for himself, instead of simply being a passive observer.

With a 24/6 Toulouse-Lautrec was an incredibly sensitive and emotional person at times, so it is no surprise that he preferred painting as the medium for his creative expression. The colours he used were also sensual, and full of life.

Toulouse-Lautrec died on 9 September 1901, having explored the love of his life – painting. The whole date adds up to 29 or 2, so perhaps he was looking to make some new decisions about his life at that time. The day adds up to a 9, so perhaps he was discriminating about his future, or perhaps he felt complete with his life in some way.

NUMBER
25/7
PERSONALITY

GENERAL TRENDS FOR NUMBER 25/7 PERSONALITY

With 25/7 influencing your Personality you have the gift of patience and a deepest yearning to be able to communicate to the world. You may express yourself through speech, and very often you will be good at it, and like the sound of your own voice. You may communicate by computer, which you love to use to send messages to people all around the world, or by writing 'papers', books, poetry or songs, so that you can communicate to others through words. However, there are many other ways by which you communicate, and expressing your feelings may be one of them.

You are a highly sensitive and deeply emotional person, and you like to be able to relate (and communicate) with others through this medium. For example, having a chat about your feelings with your best friend can help you to feel close and connected to him or her. Indeed you love to share your feelings and to hear how others are feeling too, and there may be nothing you like better than to stay up all night having an intimate tête-à-tête.

Sometimes your sensitivity helps you to help others in all areas of your life. For example, when there are problems at work you are able to sense them, often before anybody says anything, and you may take steps to rectify or defuse 'situations' before they arise. You are also a good listener, and when people come to you with their problems you may be able to feel exactly what needs to be done to help them. You may also have strong gut feelings and intuition, and perhaps you have learned to trust these faculties to help guide you through life.

With a 25/7 influencing your life you have a logical brain and a clarity of mind, and this may be why you are such a successful communicator. You also have a technical brain, which has a fascination for detail, so that in your work, in your relationships and at home you like to know the ins and outs of everything, or have everything worked out. Indeed you are an analytical person, and you may spend a lot of time 'in your head' trying to work out the finer details in life.

You also have a scientific mind, and you may like to know all the facts about a situation, for example, before making decisions, although you may like to listen to your instincts too. You are a good decision-maker, and sometimes you make spontaneous decisions – you can be quick-thinking at times. However, you generally like to think things through, and are careful about the decisions you take, and once you have made a decision you like to stick to it.

With a 25/7 you are analytical about life and yourself, and you can be an introspective person. Indeed you need space to go into your 'shell' for your personal growth. It is said that you can find everything you need – inner peace, happiness, wealth, love, support – 'inside yourself', and your need for introspection makes this doubly so. Indeed you have a strong need to find your own identity and your 'inner truth' about who you are; you can be philosophical at times. When you connect with your inner self you may also feel more connected to others, and be clearly able to see truths about them and the world at large.

With your strong imagination and clarity of mind, and your ability to instigate things in a practical way, you may be able to manifest your goals and your dreams easily. Communication may play a large role in your success, and your natural and gentle powers of persuasion may mean that you make things happen around you, without hardly doing a thing. Indeed, miracles may seem to occur as a result of your magic touch and your ability to materialize things out of thin air.

With a 25/7 influencing your Personality you are a patient person and you like to trust the process of life. You may think that although life doesn't always bring you what you want, it certainly brings you what you need. You are outgoing, adventurous, magnetic and energetic, and you like to make the most of the opportunities that come your way. You love to meet new people, to dance, to sing, to travel the world, and with your minute observation about life you drink in every new thing. You thrive off change, and you magnetically draw in to you many new experiences to stimulate your mind, body and spirit.

You may love swimming, walking, skiing, roller-blading, ice skating or fencing, or gentle exercise such as yoga, meditation or tai chi, for relaxation.

CHALLENGES

With a 25/7 influencing your Personality you may be a complex person who likes peace and harmony in one respect, and yet likes to create a fuss by drawing attention to yourself in another. Sometimes you may even feel confused about what you want, with your mind saying one thing and your emotions another. Indeed you can be a contrary person, and people may react to your ambivalence and unpredictable nature with great frustration and even anger, because they don't (like you) know where they stand. However, change helps to keep you on your toes and can teach you, and them, to be adaptable to life. But by spending a little time each day going 'inside', or meditating, you can allow your mind to quieten your emotions, and it can help you to get balanced and centred again. Listening to your inner self may also help you to get clarity about what actions you need to take, or what you need to do with your life.

Sometimes you may be changeable so that you don't need to make or keep commitments in your life. For example, you may fear your emotions, so you may change friends and partners to avoid relating to them in that way. Or you may be like a nomad moving from place to place, or rent instead of buying a property in which to live, to avoid that kind of commitment. However, although it may be fun to go through life fancy-free for a while, you love to materialize your goals and your dreams, and only by making commitments can they become real.

You may restrict your life because you are fearful of change, and you may procrastinate and put up with a lot before you make any moves. For example, you may restrict yourself to one difficult relationship with someone who is incompatible, and put off looking for someone new. Perhaps your boss is a 'dragon', but you stay put because you think that you will never get as many financial benefits in another job. However, you become very dependent when you are fearful of losing something, and sometimes the unexpected happens to push you away from those things and may bring changes for the better.

With a 25/7 influencing your Personality, you sometimes hear your intuition and feel your instincts, but you don't follow them through. For example, you may be planning an outing to the beach and your instincts are telling you to drive along the scenic route, because the highway is full. However, your logical mind says, 'The highway is always quicker' as you head off into long queues of traffic to start your summer break. In hindsight you wish that you had listened to the local radio to see if there were any traffic delays, or that you had trusted your intuition.

You may spend too much time 'in your head', worrying about problems or what is to come. This can be destructive because you go in too deep, get over-anxious and get lost in a dream world. You also have a strong imagination and things may get out of perspective when they go round and round in your head. Luckily you also possess a logical mind, which can bring you down to earth by encouraging you to face the facts of life. It may also help you to find a goal, or something positive to keep your mind occupied.

With a 25/7 you may be an outgoing person who is always out exploring the world, having fun and adventures, and at these times you may neglect spending quiet time in contemplation. Paradoxically you also have the potential to be dreamy and too introspective, so that you isolate yourself from the outside world; or you may think too much and not spend enough time actively doing things and participating in the 'real' world. However, you can help to bring harmony to your life by balancing time spent outside – having fun – and inside, by having times of introspection so that you get the most out of both worlds.

At times you can be over-sensitive and react to life by being touchy or defensive, or you may torment others because you feel hurt, perhaps because you had been gullible and you have been let down. You may also be over-emotional, or wallow in doom and gloom, or be irrational sometimes. Perhaps you deliver verbal torture or you are deliberately rude or cruel to people. Sometimes the pain of living in physical reality is too much for you, or you may have low self-worth and have an inferiority complex. However, by using your quick mind to calm your emotions you may learn to react to situations more positively, which may create more happiness around you and keep your life running more smoothly.

With a 25/7 your sensitivity is your gift, and by learning to appreciate and love who you are, you may grow stronger in your identity and learn to accept your imperfections.

ROMANCE AND SEX

With a 25/7 influencing your relationships you may be a conventional person, and you may seek a similar partner to share your life with – someone who is courteous, well mannered and polite. You may be someone who 'just gets on with life' and who uses your mind more than your emotions to relate to people in life. So perhaps your partner is intellectual and has a bright mind. You may be a private person, and perhaps you are a private couple who lead an isolated life together away from the hustle and bustle.

However, you may also be freedom loving with a zest for life and a yearning for adventure. You may find a partner who has that extra 'sparkle' and joie de vivre, and who can keep your restlessness at bay. Perhaps your partner is very creative and communicative, and together you can have fun and wild times doing unusual things. You may love travelling, and perhaps you become an international jet-set couple who travel (or live) in many exotic places around the world, always on the move.

With a 25/7 you can be a restless person who finds it hard to settle down and make a big commitment to your partner. You may often take a long time to commit yourself because you like to be sure of yourself and to really trust your partner, perhaps because you have been naïve and gullible in the past and are trying to avoid emotional pain. However, you can be unpredictable and, at times, make fast and furious decisions, taking the plunge spontaneously. For example, after going out with a new partner a few times you may suddenly decide to move in; sometimes you lose and sometimes you win, but you always gain from the experience.

You may also have a calm, placid and gentle side to your nature, and you may be looking for the 'simple life' with an equally nurturing and loving partner. Perhaps you are seeking your soul mate, and you may be able to intuitively recognize him or her when you meet. You also have a strong interest in spirituality and perhaps you seek a partner with whom you can travel to a spiritual retreat, or travel the journey of life with, by exploring your spirituality together in your minds, and in relationship. You may even have a telepathic link which helps you, for example, to find out when he or she is going to be home late from work!

You may be a dreamy person who plays out your relationships in your head, at times. For example, you may prefer to connect with your partner by telepathic communication, instead of meeting with him or her and experiencing the relationship in 'real' life. Or you may make up scenarios in your mind to make the relationship into something 'special' instead of facing the ordinariness of life.

With a 25/7 influencing your sex life you may seek that perfect partner or soul mate to satisfy your sexual desires or fantasies. You may be intense in your need for sex and be addicted to it at times. Perhaps you may be happy to simply engage your vivid imagination sometimes to make your sex life more interesting and exciting.

PHYSICAL APPEARANCE

With a 25/7 influencing your looks you may have soft features, large, watery, sparkling eyes, clear skin, a small mouth with lips down turned at the edges, and a long straight nose. You may have a medium- to high-pitched voice, and your outstanding feature is that you may look androgynous.

CHILDHOOD EXPERIENCES

With a 25/7 influencing your childhood you may have been a fussy child who was always tidying your room and smartening up your clothes, and you may have liked a clinical environment in which to live. You may not have enjoyed getting your hands dirty and indeed you may have acted like a little prince or princess at times. Perhaps everyone used to run around you, and fetch and carry things for you too, and you may have carried yourself with great deportment and with an aloof air.

However, you may have experienced a strict upbringing where manners were the order of the day, and where you were taught to respect others, and to have dignity. You may have attended a strict school too, perhaps with spirituality or religion playing a part in your upbringing there.

With a 25/7 you may have found childhood a challenge because of your acute sensitivity to people and the sometimes unexpected events which came your way. Perhaps you withdrew into your imagination or focused all your energies into sport or into your creativity. You probably loved to read science fiction, and science too, and things which could stimulate your mind and keep you preoccupied. With a 25/7 you may have been a sickly child, or with your strong mind created a headache or some imaginary illness when you wanted to get out of doing things.

Children with a 25/7 may not make friends easily because they are withdrawn, or because they have an inferiority complex. However, showing them appreciation, or making a fuss of them and the things they can do, may help them to overcome their fears and bring them slowly into life.

WELL-BEING

With a 25/7 influencing your health you may be prone to asthma, eczema, skin allergies or even panic attacks. You may also have thyroid imbalances, or create illusionary illnesses (as you may be a hypochondriac).

CAREER CHOICE

With a 25/7 influencing your career you may work in the travel industry or as a public relations, marketing, technical sales or advertising executive. You may also work as a journalist or as a television or radio presenter, or as a researcher in any field.

You may take up a career as a teacher of any kind, linguist or translator, or you may work as a psychologist, counsellor or therapist. Perhaps you work with your intuition, by becoming a mystic or a private detective. You may also take up work as a lawyer, an agent of any kind, or work in the financial sector.

FAMOUS CHARACTER ANALYSIS
Guglielmo Marconi Born 25 April 1874

Guglielmo Marconi was the Italian Inventor who constructed the first wireless telegraph at the beginning of the 20th century. He used radio waves as a practical means for communication. He sent long-wave signals from Cornwall (England) to Newfoundland (Canada), and proved his theory that radio waves could bend around the earth, for which he received the Nobel Prize for Physics.

Marconi had a vivid imagination, a clear intuition and a bright scientific and technical mind, and he made the world a 'smaller' place. He brought great change to the world; his glorious invention gave many people their freedom of expression and communication.

With a 25/7 Marconi was an instigator, and a loner at times, and he probably spent much of his time 'in his head'. He obviously trusted his ideas and concepts; he experimented to satisfy his curiosity, and life must have felt like one big adventure to him. He must have also trusted his instincts to lead him to produce something that was greatly needed.

Guglielmo Marconi died on 20 July 1932, having materialized the dream in his head successfully. The whole date adds up to a 29 or 2, so perhaps he felt he had achieved balance in his life by communicating his knowledge. The day is a 20 or 2, so at last he could experience peace and harmony within himself, and with the world at large.

NUMBER
26/8
PERSONALITY

GENERAL TRENDS FOR NUMBER 26/8 PERSONALITY

With a 26/8 influencing your Personality you have the gift of compassion, and the deepest yearning to feel emotionally secure. For example, you may be a very loving, kind and generous person who gives a lot of emotional support to others, and when people need you it makes you feel more secure, such as when you know that you are loved by your partner, friends and family, or liked by the people at work. However, you also love yourself, and you are able to nurture and look after yourself, and you like to take responsibility for keeping yourself happy and balanced.

You are a warm and open person, and approachable too, and people often come to you with their problems because you are able to patiently listen to them and talk things through. You love relating to people emotionally, and you are able to express and share your feelings with them easily too. Sometimes when things go 'wrong' and you feel hurt by people's actions and words, you are able to let go of the situation by expressing to them how you feel, and then to move on.

With a 26/8 you are a peacemaker and you have a natural ability to listen to things that people say, and to see the whole picture, and to draw your own conclusions before you make any decisions or put people in the picture about where they 'stand'. For example, you are a manager and at work three of your co-workers are locked in a dispute about their positions of authority. You may sit them around a table and diplomatically listen to each one, without taking sides, and encourage them to co-operate with each other and to reach a peaceful settlement.

With a 26/8 influencing your Personality you are a kind person with an enormous heart and enough love for everybody. You are a natural carer with the stamina to keep on helping people, and you are gentle and soft. You have a particular affinity and bond with children, and children feel safe and secure with you. You have a wonderful warm sense of humour which shines through, and you make learning fun, and show children how to learn from fun too. Perhaps you are also interested in issues surrounding children and work for a children's charity or in helping under-privileged children. You are a wise person and you have learned from your experiences many things which you love to share with others, and children can also learn from your wisdom too.

You are extremely practical and responsible and you are willing to work hard to make a success out of your life. That is, you put in a lot of effort into your relationships and career, and you may work hard to maintain your fitness and health. You are usually talented in business and can generally make a success out of what you do. Perhaps you are a leader of an organization, or an authority on a particular subject, or on what you do. Like all 8s, you may even achieve great recognition from your talents and your gifts and you may often be famous in your field, or the world over, for your contribution. With a 26/8 you may enjoy material possessions and may also be financially rich.

With a 26/8 influencing your Personality you may love taking on responsibility and particularly enjoy caring for others, or helping them in business. Perhaps you empower people to be successful and to stand on their own, and to be diplomatic and respectful with whoever they meet. You have strength and determination and you inspire others with your organizational skills. Perhaps you are also aware that some of the situations in life bring up karmic responsibilities from the past; that is, things which you have not faced up to before come back for you to deal with in your present life.

You are strong, because you are a spiritual person and you exhibit inner spiritual strength to the world. You may meditate, follow some religious philosophy, or simply feel a strong spiritual connection to people around you, or to the world. With a 26/8 you are able to see the larger picture, and you listen to the international news, or perhaps you have made friends in all parts of the globe. You may have friends in politics, business, the arts, or in the healing professions. You are a true communitarian, and you understand your duty to serve the world; you are not taken in by the glamour of all the money, famous friends or the status that you may hold.

For relaxation, you may particularly enjoy gentle walks, stretching exercises, or meditation and Hatha yoga in a peaceful environment. You may also love aerobics, squash and tennis, riding or rigorous exercise routines at times, which help to keep you in shape. You may also participate in competitive sports too

CHALLENGES

With a 26/8 influencing your Personality you may be an insecure person who needs people to say, 'Yes, you are OK,' or say, 'Haven't you done well!' every day. Sometimes this develops into a greater need for attention and success to help you get through life or even through each day. For example, you may crave power, authority and status externally, or you may try to make yourself famous (or even infamous) to gain the enormous amounts of attention you request. The more people tell you that you are great, and the more you achieve, the more it boosts your ego and makes you feel on top of the world. However, no matter how much stardom you achieve, the important thing is to feel at rest 'inside'. Perhaps connecting to your inner spirituality and finding your inner strength may help you to feel secure within yourself, instead.

You may be very grumpy and serious at times, and get heavy and intense. Sometimes you may get obsessed about how you feel and get lost in your emotions, and at other times you may throw tantrums or scream and shout at whoever's about. Sometimes you may even be violent and throw things, as you release emotions which may have been blocked for quite some time. However, 26/8 is an extremely karmic number and sometimes you are releasing karma in your tantrums, and you may also be karmically linked to the person towards whom you direct your outbursts. However, it may help you to use your mind to steady your emotions, and to take responsibility for your actions. Perhaps by putting yourself in others' shoes at these times you can use your famous diplomacy and tact to help express your emotions calmly and clearly instead.

With a 26/8 influencing your Personality you are a very sensitive person and you can be aggressive and vindictive, and hold grudges against people when you feel that they have hurt you in some way. You have a delicate ego, and hurt pride may make you tyrannical and even brutal in your revenge. Perhaps you may persecute people until the bitter end, until they have paid back their karmic debts and paid for the suffering and pain which you felt. However, even if you harass people or become obsessive in getting even with the world, the continual emotional input may be hurting you more than them. By going into your mind and thinking it through, you may find out what part you played in creating the situation. Perhaps you may find an inner resolve and avoid those actions or behaviour again.

Whoever you are, in whatever position, you may demand, instead of earn, respect from people around you, and perhaps you demand responsibility as well. Perhaps you are 'hard work' for people as you constantly test their patience, but they know deep down inside that you are a kind person, and you are only doing what you think is best for them most of the time. Sometimes you test people because you feel insecure, but it may also be because you want the best for the whole group, and for everyone involved.

Sometimes you listen to people's problems, but instead of remaining impartial tell them what you think they ought to do. However, by allowing them the freedom of their own choice, you may in fact agree with what they decide is best for them to do, rather than interfering in their lives and adding to your karmic debts.

With a 26/8 influencing your Personality you may be an egocentric person who loves to drive around all the best places in town in your convertible, or to be seen out with the most beautiful and successful people. However, it may never be enough, and sometimes you manipulate others to get more power or the status for yourself. You may be selfish in your pursuits and exploit people too. However, again you get back what you give out, so karmically you may become a doormat and someone who people don't respect. It is wonderful to go for your desires, but respecting yourself by respecting others along the way may really help you to feel your 'inner' power and strength, which is much more important.

You may belong to a large family, work group or community group, but you may sometimes lack a sense of duty or responsibility towards them. Perhaps you do not view everyone as part of the whole, but as little isolated pieces; but in the same way that each cog helps to make the wheel go round, when one piece is missing it is difficult for the whole to function. By finding your individuality, but recognizing the power of your group, or society, it can help you to feel connected to your spirituality, to life and to others too.

ROMANCE AND SEX

With a 26/8 influencing your relationships, personal responsibility may be of great importance to you, and you may seek a partner who has their own career, their own social life, and who can materially stand on his or her own two feet. You may seek a partner who has a strong backbone, and who is independent, who also does not depend upon you emotionally, most of the time at least. However, although you may both have an independent streak you may be happy to give and take, and of course love coming together and being open and sharing yourselves fully.

You may feel insecure and uncomfortable when you first meet a new partner, and it may take a while before you feel safe to open up, as you sometimes have sensitive and fragile emotions. You may put on a brave face, but you may get cold feet and opt out of a relationship for fear of failure. In commitment however, you may feel safe to open up.

You are highly romantic and you love hearts and flowers, to be serenaded over dinner, and to be taken on cruises up the Seine. However, until you feel sure of yourself with your new partner, and sure of how you feel, you may seem cool and detached and the last person on earth to be moved by beauty and romance. Others may be surprised that 'in love' you may be all soft and gooey and be fond of using intimate terms of endearment.

With a 26/8 influencing your Personality you may be a passionate person who loves to dress in sensual clothes, or to look smart, and you may take great pride in your appearance, and like to dress to please your partner. You expect your partner to look good too, particularly if you are going out on the town together; looks are not the most important element for you, but you definitely like him or her to make an effort for you.

You exude warmth, and your love and compassion for the world glows from your open heart. You may be a communitarian, and therefore you may seek a partner who has an interest in the world at large, and who is intelligent and can think about things other than him- or herself. Perhaps you may work together in some charity projects, or work together in business. You are also a home lover, and you love to provide care for yourself, your partner and children, or for all the little ones around you.

The 26/8 is a strongly karmic number and you may attract partners with whom you have strong karmic links from the past, and you may also find your long-lost mate, or soul mate, to share your journey throughout life. You may not be seeking a partner of this kind, but you may draw this person to you with your strong animal magnetism; destiny has its own mind.

With a 26/8 influencing your sex life you have a strong desire for pleasure, and you like to feel powerful and in control with the partner with whom you sexually connect. Perhaps you play power games for foreplay and have erotic leather, suede, silks and velvets around you to turn you on. Affection and commitment may play a large part in enabling you to enjoy intimacy and to feel safe to open up to your partner sexually.

PHYSICAL APPEARANCE

With a 26/8 influencing your looks you may have course hair, long eyelashes, and eyebrows which meet in the middle. You may have soft features, rounded shoulders and a forward stoop. Your most out-standing feature is your figure, which looks rounded, and you may look like an authoritative parent.

CHILDHOOD EXPERIENCES

With a 26/8 influencing your childhood you may have been an exceed-ingly caring child with a natural wisdom, which you expressed by your understanding of life and your ability to accept life as it was. You may have also been psychic and could 'see through people' at a glance. However, you were no doubt blessed with practical common sense, and perhaps you were dutiful too, and the first to offer your help to people and around the house. You may have been a responsible and capable child who always seemed to know what to do practically, even when you were very young.

You probably liked to care for your dollies and teddies, or nurture your brothers, sisters and friends. You may have really understood the power of giving and found pleasure in helping others, but you enjoyed being looked after and having kisses and cuddles too.

With a 26/8 you could be horrid and very naughty sometimes, and you may have thrown tantrums, perhaps because you were spoiled or because you were karmically throwing off events from the past which had revisited you. You may have tested your parents too, because you felt insecure and wanted to see if they would still love you no matter how much you put them through.

Children with a 26/8 may feel frightened by their psychic powers, or by the power of their emotions at times. Helping them to keep their feet on the ground, by doing chores and participating in 'ordinary' everyday life, may help them to feel safe and comfortable within themselves.

WELL-BEING

With a 26/8 influencing your health you may be prone to problems with your knees or your spine, or you may suffer from hormonal imbalances or breathing difficulties such as bronchitis and asthma. You may also be prone to dyslexia, or TB, malaria or any kind of rare or unusual illness may occur from time to time.

CAREER CHOICE

With a 26/8 influencing your Personality you may take up work as a diplomat, negotiator of any kind, therapist, or work in the medical profession. You may also be a social worker or health visitor, or work with children (as a nanny or midwife, for example). Perhaps you are a compassionate leader or a communitarian, or a good samaritan.

With a 26/8 you may work in the field of business, or as an accountant, or even take up a career as a horse breeder!

FAMOUS CHARACTER ANALYSIS
Mother Teresa Born 26 August 1910

Mother Teresa was a 'living Saint', and one of the most compassionate, caring and selfless human beings of the late 20th century. She was known for her caring of the sick in Calcutta, India, where she had her order of helpers to share her gruelling work. Indeed she worked with lepers and 'untouchables' and people with sometimes strongly karmic illnesses, although she did not suffer from any of those afflictions herself. But it was obviously her karma to carry out her work.

She led a hard life, and used her stamina, and spiritual strength to help get her through. She was devoted to her work, and used her wisdom to help people, and she had great humility and sought no reward for herself. She was always thinking of her community and paid little attention to her personal needs.

With a 26/8 Mother Teresa probably held extremely high standards, and was a powerful person who liked people to do as she said. Perhaps she threw tantrums at times, because of the enormity of the task ahead of her. No doubt she was a shrewd woman, and she was highly ambitious with her work, in her own way.

Mother Teresa of Calcutta died on 5 September 1997, of a heart attack. The whole date adds up to a 4, which emphasizes that she had laid solid foundations for the work ahead. The day is a 5, so perhaps she needed her freedom to go into the next life, and to work somewhere else as one of God's helpers.

NUMBER

27/9

PERSONALITY

GENERAL TRENDS FOR NUMBER 27/9 PERSONALITY

With a 27/9 influencing your Personality you have the gift of understanding and the deepest yearning to expand your knowledge about life. You find inner knowledge or 'knowing' from your mind and deep inside yourself, and you have learned about life by experiences in the past. You also seek out knowledge from others, and you recognize that everyone has something to teach you about life. But you have a studious mind and you may seek knowledge from books, from specialist courses in subjects of interest, or from travelling, where you can gain knowledge about people and life first hand.

You are a highly intuitive person and even though you have a strong logic, which you apply to help you with your life, you also trust your intuition, which sometimes sways you in your decision-making. You trust your inner 'truth' and at times when you have ignored these messages you may have regretted it later. For example, if you have an intuitive flash that your body needs more iron and you ignore this, then you may not be surprised when the doctor advises you upon the results of a blood test that you are anaemic. You also have strong instincts and feelings, and you may get psychic dreams or hunches particularly about people you are close to. However, emotions are not always predictable and you can be wrong about things at times too.

You may be deeply connected to your spirituality, and you may meditate, do yoga classes, or find other ways of introspecting, at times. Perhaps you connect by going out into nature, or by living in the countryside, or by connecting with people too. You have an understanding of people, and people sense this and draw to you for help. You are a kind-hearted person, and you can feel their need, and you like to help them out in any way you can.

With a 27/9 influencing your Personality you are a light, fun-loving and warm person with a passion for life, and you are usually very respectful and caring of people and your environment. For example, when you visit people's houses you are courteous and well-mannered and take care to be a perfect guest, and you may ring or write to say 'thank you' to your host. Perhaps you are also careful to give your partner space around your home. You are sensitive to your environment too, and you easily pick up on the atmosphere wherever you go. You like a peaceful environment to live in and you may even go as far as to restrict visitors who may disturb this peace. With a 27/9 your home is your haven and you may love entertaining people with lavish suppers and cocktail parties; perhaps you enjoy cooking all the food yourself too, and making sure that every aspect is 'just right'.

With a 27/9 you have an appreciation of beauty; life to you is a gift, and is indeed beautiful. You have a positive mind and you like to remain optimistic even during stressful and challenging times. You may love fine art and antiques, beautiful clothes and classical music, and you may also find beauty in literature. You have an intellectual mind, and you are highly creative, and you may be keen to have 'beautiful' people around to stimulate you.

You have a discriminating mind and you are usually able to work out fact from fiction. For example, you may listen to the team you lead at work and you may understand their problems and can tell when they may be exaggerating the truth, or see through their illusions and see reality. You may be a wonderful leader, and you can be diplomatic and tactful, and you weigh up situations carefully before making any decisions or taking any actions. You are generally a considerate person who enjoys negotiating with people, and encouraging them to co-operate with each other. You are also a 'fair' person and you may encourage compromise, or see to it that 'in your eyes' justice is done.

With a 27/9 you may possess a vivid imagination and you are able sometimes to creatively visualize your goals in your mind. With your positive thoughts, and practical application, you may be able to materialize your goals and your dreams into reality. You may carefully consider your direction in life before making any decisions, and you may not like to 'chop and change' too much but may often set goals or long-term visions and aims. For example, you may want to materialize your dream home, perhaps high in the hills, but you may take a while to make a final decision, if it is in relation to a long-term commitment.

To keep fit you may swim, play tennis, enjoy long walks in the countryside, or partake in peaceful meditation and yoga.

CHALLENGES

With a 27/9 influencing your life your sensitivity may sometimes mean that you are prone to extreme mood swings, because you feel things so intensely. For example, if your brother is going through a crisis, you may instinctively and deeply feel what is happening to him. Perhaps when your pregnant friend is in labour you even get sympathetic labour pains too. However, you are acutely sensitive to everything that is going on around you all the time, and you may react by cutting off from your emotions or becoming over-emotional at times. You may find that you blush easily and get easily embarrassed in situations, or you may burst into tears suddenly in public. However, using your mind to focus on something positive may help to bring you back to yourself so that you can calm your emotions. For example, working on needlework which requires a lot of attention, or absorbing yourself in study or watching a television programme can help you to 'switch off' from your emotions for a while.

You may try to protect yourself from feeling pain and hurt by withdrawing from life or not getting involved in a relationship because you feel so vulnerable and sensitive sometimes. You may project a cold, uncaring and hard shell to the world because you do not want to feel your own or others' emotions at these times. However, no matter how hard you try to avoid getting hurt, it all builds up inside. Perhaps learning to open up a little and sharing how you feel even when you are vulnerable, particularly to those close to you, may help you to move through the pain inside.

With a 27/9 influencing your Personality you may be a bit of a dreamer, who literally daydreams and gets lost in illusion sometimes. At these times you may be out of touch with reality and find yourself gullible and taken in by life. For example, you may be in a daydream when you are paying for groceries and perhaps you don't notice that you are overcharged. You may also be naïve and impressionable too.

Sometimes, in this dream-like state, and with your indecision too, you may meander through life with no real focus. Even in one day you may intend to do four things on your list, but as you set out on your journey you meander and do three other things instead. Sometimes life has a way of grounding you when you are too dreamy; by giving you practical problems to sort out, or by bringing you down to earth (with a bump). However, by applying discipline so that in a day perhaps you do three things out of four on your list, you may feel a sense of achievement and feel good about yourself.

Generally you have high standards and ideals, and you are often a perfectionist, and you may be hard on yourself when you don't get things right at times. You are then likely to criticize yourself from morning to noon, and judge others in the same way, or pick on them for not being good enough. Sometimes you can be spiteful to people when they do not match your expectations, and make their lives a misery by criticizing them too. However, although it's wonderful to have high standards you may give yourself a headache by flogging yourself and others. Perhaps by realizing that life is acceptably perfect in its imperfection you can let go of worrying too.

With a 27/9 influencing your Personality you may be (or think that you are) a highly intelligent, wonderful human being with a dynamic intellect, and you may try to use these qualities to impress everyone you meet. Or perhaps you try to impress people with your psychic abilities. Perhaps you behave like this to make up for your lack of confidence, or because you are continually seeking approval from others. However, by learning to accept yourself the way you are you can let go of the need to impress people because you feel comfortable within yourself.

Alternatively you may think that you are an unintelligent person, who is pathetic and stupid and 'no good' at life. You may even worry that your way of doing things does not meet the approval of others all the time. However, whether you are intelligent or not is irrelevant because it is what you are like inside that counts. But telling yourself 'I'm stupid' too many times may send out the wrong vibes and people may start to treat you like you feel inside. So by learning to appreciate your gifts instead of reprimanding yourself, you can actually grow in confidence and attract people to you who show you their appreciation too.

ROMANCE AND SEX

With a 27/9 influencing your relationships you may be a gentle, warm and caring person, and you may be seeking a partner who you can nurture, and with whom you feel safe to open up emotionally – perhaps someone who is responsive to your feelings and doesn't take offence when you snap at him or her when you are in one of your sensitive moods. Indeed you can sulk at times, and therefore a sensitive partner who can 'read' your moods, or who instinctively knows how to bring you out of them, may help you with your life.

Generally you are a demonstrative person and you may love the feel of your partner's body heat, and you may seek a partner who is affectionate and who enjoys being physically close with you too. In a relationship you may be seeking that perfect person to share your life with, but what you see may often be your illusions about how you would like a partner to be. Life may teach you that no one is perfect. Your partner may get breadcrumbs between the sheets, or you may have to put up with him or her telling you that you have got the biggest spot they've ever seen (the honest type, of course!). However, you may search for your soul mate and, faults or no faults, you may find your perfect match. 'In love' you may find perfection as you become dreamily romantic.

With a 27/9 you may like to find a partner who is fair, and who can share joint responsibilities with you. For example, you may do the weekly shopping, and your partner does it next, or perhaps you own a joint account; you see this as only fair. Even if you don't live together you may seek a partner who is able to give and take, and share, and not someone who is selfish and with whom you couldn't relate emotionally. You may love to travel the world together, or work and play together, and sometimes you may even become inseparable, or dependent on each other too.

You may have been hurt in the past or fear it will happen again, and therefore you may try to protect yourself. You may well launch into a relationship but you may feel unsettled, and it may take a while for you to make a long-term commitment to him or her. However, once you have learned to trust yourself and your intuition about yourself and your partner you may remain faithful, and you may get protective of your joint relationship.

With a 27/9 influencing your relationships you have the ability to make your partner feel special by telling him or her how clever or wonderful they are, or how much you appreciate them. Sometimes on a first date, however, you may naïvely put your foot in it by saying something too effusive about the other person because it is in your nature to be positive.

With a 27/9 influencing your sex life you are a passionate person and you may thrive off the intimacy of connecting with your partner physically. However, that is when you have learned to trust your partner; you may feel detached otherwise. You can also be prudish in your desires. Perhaps your liberal side does allow you to let go sometimes, and you may be willing to explore many sexual variations, like playing out each other's fantasies

PHYSICAL APPEARANCE

With a 27/9 influencing your looks you may be tall, with red hair, freckles, a long face, high cheekbones, and a bobble or bulbous nose. You may have a high voice, with small hips and a large chest or breasts. Your outstanding features are your legs, which are often long.

CHILDHOOD EXPERIENCES

With a 27/9 influencing your childhood you may have seemed ethereal as a child, because you were very intuitive and spiritual and you may have been 'off with the fairies' much of the time. Perhaps you loved to escape to your imagination because you found reality, and people's feelings, too much to handle at times. You may have been painfully self-conscious sometimes too.

You may have been quiet and introspective and enjoyed playing musical instruments, listening to music quietly, or reading by yourself for hours. You were probably academic, and to avoid too much attention from people at school perhaps you immersed yourself in research, your studies, and physical activities or sports. Not that you loved games, but it may have been an easy and inconspicuous way to get through life at school.

With a 27/9 you may have received a lot of discipline at home, and perhaps your parents were firm or strict with you. You probably did as you were told because you may have liked to gain their approval and acceptance.

Children with a 27/9 may feel isolated and cut off from people at times, because they get lost in their imagination. Sometimes simply giving them a hug or involving them in some joint family or group activity may help them feel like they are living in the real world again.

WELL-BEING

With a 27/9 influencing your health you may be prone to skin allergies, acne, headaches or migraines, and bronchitis or asthma. You may also suffer from anxiety or fatigue, or have problems with your knees and feet. Perhaps you have blood-sugar imbalances or hormonal problems too.

CAREER CHOICE

With a 27/9 influencing your career you may work as a diplomat, an agent, or work as a peacemaker, humanitarian, or leader in any field. You may also take up a career teaching religion, philosophy, psychology or spirituality, or you may become an art, design or history teacher.

With a 27/9 you may also work in one of the health professions, for example as a medical researcher, a medical worker or as a complementary therapist or healer. Perhaps you use your powers of negotiation, or work as a bookkeeper or an accountant. Perhaps you work as an antiques dealer or an interior designer, because of your love and appreciation of the fine things in life.

FAMOUS CHARACTER ANALYSIS
Samuel Morse Born 17 April 1791

Samuel Morse was an American Artist, who eventually became internationally famous for his invention of the Morse Code (dot-dash code) and for his work in electro-magnetic telegraphy. His invention meant that people were able to communicate with each other all over the world using this simple method.

Samuel probably used the free-thinking artistic and intuitive side of his brain to dream, and in his imagination created something that he felt would be of service to the world. He no doubt used his inner knowledge to guide him, and developed an interest in factual knowledge which could practically enable him to materialize his dream.

With a 27/9 Morse must, however, have possessed a bright and logical mind, because the dot-dash system is logical and easy to understand. However, he needed to prove to himself and to others that it would work, and it did, and perhaps he deserved to feel pride and self-congratulation at his achievement.

Samuel Morse died on 2 April 1872, having satisfied himself as an artist and an inventor. The whole date adds up to a 24 or 6, so perhaps his service to humanity was complete. The day is a 2, and he had successfully used his right creative brain and his left logical brain in his lifetime, and had found balance. Perhaps he felt in harmony with himself on the day he died.

NUMBER

28/1

PERSONALITY

GENERAL TRENDS FOR NUMBER 28/1 PERSONALITY

With a 28/1 influencing your Personality you have the gift of fearlessness, and a deepest yearning to succeed with your life, in whichever areas you choose. You, like all 1s, have the courage to go for your goals in a practical manner, and to conquer challenges that occur along the way. Challenges are there to be worked through, and you cope with them easily. You have the potential for enormous flair in business. In your eyes a part of your success will usually be measured by the level of your material possession, and by the financial rewards you receive.

You may be fiercely independent. Nobody can push you around; you have a strength of character that is always 'on call'. Like all 1s, you are a dynamic individual and sometimes you stand apart, and people may often look to you to lead.

You may also be a highly assertive human being. You have tremendous amounts of energy, are extremely ambitious, and you are bold and able to follow your dreams positively. You are generally direct in your communication, and you have the ability to focus directly on your goals. For example, you may have a goal to write a book, own a company, get married and have children … whatever it is, it is your challenge, and as far as you are concerned it is there to be achieved.

With a 28/1 influencing your Personality you have the qualities of the 2 penetrating through. You may be gentle, diplomatic in your communications and negotiations, and clearly able to see the other person's point of view. You are able to relate to people easily, and can also be an anchor for others in times of need. You may also be good at listening, and although you are highly opinionated you are open and considerate to people around you.

Sometimes your mind conjures up an abundance of ideas and concepts for you to work on. Although you like the independence of doing things on your own, you can also be a team player. At work you can even be part of a 'swat team' that thinks up creative ideas. This suits you fine, because you can assert your individuality and share your ideas with others too.

You like and value co-operation, and even when you are the boss you may not think of yourself as superior, or any different from any other member of the team. However, at times you like to steer the ship, and to steer others, and you are good at it. You also have a gift to be able to encourage and empower others to take the lead.

With a 28/1 influencing your Personality you are brilliant at conjuring up original concepts and ideas, and you are also good at introducing these to others. With your gift of diplomacy you can gently break down others' perceptions and ideas, without them feeling threatened. For example, you may have designed a new version of a particular household product and try to sell it to manufacturers. You may do it in such a way that they do not feel threatened by your revolutionary idea, nor by the fact that it could make their own product obsolete. You put your point across and really listen and relate to them until an agreement is reached. You are also blessed with common sense, and strong gut feelings that usually seem to lead you to the right doors to knock on in the first place.

With a 28/1 you have a very warm, caring and nurturing side to your Personality, and you enjoy emotional stability and the comfort of harmony in your life, particularly at home. You may be passive at times, and shy, and enjoy your own company and space. You like to re-evaluate life, and therefore you need time alone to think. Sometimes you are so busy giving to others that you may need to retreat to your inner sanctuary for peace. You are usually very caring of your environment, and like to help to make the world a better place in which to live.

With the influence of the 28/1 you may have a bright mind and can quickly make decisions. You may be intellectual and love debating, particularly about social issues, or even with your partner on simple issues such as what to eat. Your mind needs stimulation, and apart from filling in crosswords, watching documentaries and educating yourself, you enjoy reading 'whodunnits' and spine-chilling thrillers.

You may enjoy competitive sport, and you may be very successful professionally too. You may love rugby, aerobics and vigorous workout routines, and perhaps you like to set yourself daily challenges within your exercise regime.

CHALLENGES

With a 28/1 influencing your Personality you may be bold and brash in your goal-setting and goal-getting, and sometimes ruthless in your approach. You may be aggressive and dominating: 'Don't mess with me, I'm serious, I'm going for my goals whether you like it or not,' you shout. With a 28/1 in this mode, others would do well to get out of your way! Sometimes you adopt this attitude because of your enormous fear of failure, because success matters to you at all costs. However, going into this destructive pattern can help teach you about focusing, which you can eventually use in a positive way. It can also help to teach others to respect your commitment to your ideas and goals, even if you are heading for them like a tornado.

Sometimes, at the other end of the 28/1 spectrum, you may be lazy, with no particular ambitions or goals to aim for. You may lack direction, energy or drive. Alternatively, when you do have ideas you may lack the focus to carry them through. At these times you may withdraw into your own space. When people try to drag you out of yourself you can be very stubborn; you do not like being told what to do. So you may resist and bury your feet deeper into the earth and refuse to budge. If you are left alone you will come out into the world again, in your own time, having renewed your energy and focus.

With a 28/1 you may be a compulsive person who completes routines over and over again. For example, you may open the fridge door every time you are in the kitchen, even when you don't need anything from it. Compulsiveness is often associated with children because it means that you do things without making your own conscious choice. You may also be immature for your age or you may also take a long time to leave home, grow up, and face the responsibilities of adulthood.

You may not be happy making decisions for yourself even when you are acting like an adult; you may prefer others to make them for you. This is because you may doubt yourself and your abilities. Learning to make little decisions can help you to make more important life decisions for yourself eventually.

With a 28/1 you have a vile and explosive temper at times, and you can be abrasive in your speech. You are often bossing people around and giving them orders; you like to have people under your control.

You like to crack the whip and break others mentally too; you can be a real bully at times. However, this may be because you are frightened of feeling inferior and never making the grade. Perhaps someone will help you to realize your gifts and to accept yourself as you are, without needing to control others to help you feel superior.

You may be a strong leader but you tend to enforce your leadership on others rather than empower them with your help. You may place yourself on a pedestal, or you may be a dictator who 'rules the land', but with few friends, because they have all been crushed by your commands. You may learn, by experience, that humility is the sign of a good leader, and the more humble you are, the better the leader you can be. You may also think yourself so important that there is no room for anyone else at your level.

With a 28/1 influencing your Personality you can be forceful, and inconsiderate towards others at times. However, you may also want them to consider you, because you can also be very sensitive, and easily hurt by others too. You may be over-emotional at times, and cut off from your emotions. You can be passive, and people may take advantage of this; they may try to use you. However, you can also be assertive, so you may soon put a stop to unnecessary obligations.

You can be a bolshy person who battles your way through life, putting up imaginary obstacles in the way of your goals. However, sometimes you may enjoy these challenges, and whilst they can be tiring, they may actually help to spur you on.

With a 28/1 you are a procrastinator. You may withdraw as a line of defence, particularly to keep people away from you emotionally, for fear they will get too close. You may also have difficulty receiving from others, like all 1s, and at times may create spontaneous arguments to get away from people who you think have got too intimate with you.

ROMANCE AND SEX

With a 28/1 influencing your relationships you are a dynamic, creative and strong individual. You may look for a wonderful and equally strong partner. You love to relate to people, particularly emotionally, and so you may look for a partner with whom you can share your emotions, and who feels safe to respond. As with all 1s, an emotionally expressive partner can really help to open you up and to keep the communication flowing.

You may like to get deeply involved with a partner, and because you like to be successful you will want the relationship to succeed too. Getting involved to you means having a healthy sex life, sharing emotionally, and perhaps sharing an interest in intellectual or spiritual matters.

Alternatively, with a 28/1 in a challenging guise, you may also like to keep people at a distance, because you are fearful of getting involved. You may set up an obstacle like compulsively working seven days a week to avoid getting into a relationship. Or, like an ostrich burying its head in the sand, you might overwork to avoid facing challenges with your current partner. However, you will eventually come face to face with the one situation you have been trying to avoid for so long. At this point you may decide to face your inner feelings and allow yourself to get involved.

With a 28/1 you are a charming and magnetic person, and even when you are in a committed relationship you revel in the attentions of others. However, you have a compulsive nature and you may sometimes try life out on the 'other' side; you can be highly promiscuous at times. This is because you like to experience new things, and do not generally like to exclude anyone or anything from your list.

You can be immature for your age, and therefore you may prefer to find a partner who can take responsibility for you, or even to organize and take control of your life. This perhaps older figure may help you to retain your childish behaviour, and you may experience conflicts when you begin to grow up. Eventually you may learn to enjoy taking responsibility for your own life and working life out for yourself.

One of your challenges may be that you are difficult to satisfy and your partner cannot ever seem to do enough. For example, you may be emotionally needy but still want more, or sexually demanding, or demanding of your partner's time. Perhaps when you feel like this you can learn to give to your partner instead. However, taken to the other extreme, you may always be trying to please your partner, and you may need to think of number 1, and yourself for a change.

With a 28/1 influencing your sex life, sex is often like a physical workout in the gym – challenging and fun. You have a very high sex drive, particularly when you are young, and you may experiment with many lovers, compulsively seeking the 'perfect one'. Sometimes sex may seem shallow, and you feel frustrated when you don't achieve your goal of ecstasy every time. Once you have 'grown up', the security of monogamous sex often becomes the challenge within a relationship.

PHYSICAL APPEARANCE

With a 28/1 influencing your looks you may have strong muscular shoulders, sturdy hips and arms. You usually have a very short neck, high cheekbones and a heavy jaw. Your outstanding feature is that you usually look muscular and toned.

CHILDHOOD EXPERIENCES

With a 28/1 influencing your childhood you are likely to have been a doer, or been restless and unable to sit still. You may have been quite bossy and aggressive, and if you are female, perhaps a bit of a tomboy. You probably came home from school with grazes from 'scrapes' with your friends. This may have included physical fisticuffs at times, and you may have been argumentative too. You may have been very good at asserting yourself and getting your own way; you *knew* that the last piece of cake was yours, because otherwise you would scream and shout!

You may have been taught to take responsibility for yourself, by having to clear your own dishes away from the kitchen table or putting your own ironing away. Perhaps you helped your mother to bake cakes, or your father to wash the car ... even then you were shrewd, and you may have bargained and negotiated extra pocket money in return.

With a 28/1 you may have been quiet, mouse-like and studious, and paid more attention to your books than to your family and friends. Perhaps you were withdrawn at times, or preferred the company of one very best friend. You may have enjoyed parties when you weren't feeling too shy or isolated.

Children with this number influencing their lives often need to be set accomplishable goals, even when they are young, so that they can feel what it is like to achieve things. They may also need to be listened to, and encouraged to discuss their feelings, like why they feel angry or sad. Then they can feel safe with their emotions and express them in a positive way.

WELL-BEING

With a 28/1 influencing your health you may be prone to skin disorders or kidney or urinary infections (like cystitis) or you may suffer from hormonal headaches. You may also have problems with your toes.

CAREER CHOICE

With a 28/1 influencing your career, and with your creative business flair, you can make a success out of almost anything once you have set your goals. You can also excel as a dynamic public relations or marketing executive, a creative copywriter, a journalist or novelist.

You may also be a 'whiz-kid' entrepreneur with your focus set firmly on your bank balance, a sales negotiator, or even a property developer. You may take up a career in the forces, which may also appeal to the social side of your nature, and you enjoy being part of a team. With a 28/1 you may enjoy charity work, or fund-raising for a special cause.

FAMOUS CHARACTER ANALYSIS
King Henry VIII *Born 28 June 1491*

King Henry VIII was a strong and forceful character whose dictatorship brought fear to those around him. He made decisions quickly and when he wanted something – or someone – he got it. This included his six wives, two of whom were beheaded at his command. However, with a 28/1 influencing his Personality he often consulted others for their opinions, but he was stubborn and did not always listen.

King Henry's Personality exhibited many typical influences from the 28/1 energy. For example, he was assertive, direct and original (no other English king ruled with quite the same 'style'). He was also destructive at times, and did not care who he hurt along the way.

With a 28/1 he was a totally compulsive monarch who may have intensely feared intimacy; as soon as he became close to one wife he moved on to the next. He desperately wanted to produce an heir, which provided another excuse for dreaming up reasons to remove his current wife and find a new one.

Henry VIII died on the 28 January 1547, having achieved his goal of producing an heir. He indulged in life fully – sport, women, food and wine – and took his leadership seriously. The whole date adds up to 1, so he was ready for new challenges in his life. The day was the 28th, which aligns with his Personality number – a sign that he felt complete with his tasks in England, and within his life.

NUMBER
29/2
PERSONALITY

GENERAL TRENDS FOR NUMBER 29/2 PERSONALITY

With a 29/2 influencing your Personality you have the gift of persistence, and a deepest yearning to materialize your goals. You will direct enormous amounts of energy and focused concentration in order to achieve them. For example, you may get up at the break of day and work through until late at night, hardly stopping to draw breath or eat. You are passionate about your goals and about life and usually, with this dynamic flow of energy, you can create great financial rewards too.

You are a perfectionist, and every day you strive to improve yourself and make a better life for yourself and those around you. In your eyes 'second best' is what happens when you don't achieve your goals, and to you that is failure. However, you are persistent, and even when life does 'fail' you go back for more.

You are an inventive person who can continually come up with new ways of doing things, and new ideas and creations. You have a strong intuition, and an ability to sense when your ideas may work, but you also have a clear and logical mind which can help you to make sensible decisions about which are the best to pursue. You are also astute. However, with your clarity, intuition and boundless enthusiasm, you are easily able to materialize your creative inventions into reality, and often into a great success. You may even receive recognition or fame for your work.

With the influence of a 29/2 you are certainly a charismatic and attractive individual and you have no problems materializing friends, lovers or work into your life. You are an intellectual, and like to be stimulated by literature, fine art and classical music, and you may study these too. Indeed you may be very academic, possibly with an interest in the educational system and how it works.

You may also be deeply spiritual, and you may study philosophy or religion. Connecting to your spirituality is important for you because it helps you to feel centred and calm. You are also a leader and you may even pioneer an expedition to a spiritual site – a holy mountain or a temple – and help to guide others towards their spirituality too. Humanitarian issues may also interest you, and you may choose to highlight these by helping to educate others about various causes for those in need. You are a powerful person, and you can often set an example to people by the life you lead.

With a 29/2 you are inspired by life and can uplift and inspire others too. People are often inspired by your creativity, your focus, the things you create, or by your great wealth, power or status. They may be also inspired by your gentleness and sensitivity and your ability to help people, because you are also a carer. You selflessly think of others at times, and you have a genuine ability to give.

You are a bright, witty person and a good conversationalist, and you may like life in the fast lane. Your yen for perfection means that you may eat in the best places in town, buy food from the finest delicatessen, and wear stylish designer clothes that may bring you lots of attention. This all makes you feel good about yourself, and material things give you a sense of security and power. However, no matter how much money is in your bank account, you always like to buy the best you can afford. You are also, generally, meticulous in your appearance, and you like to keep a very tidy house.

With a 29/2 influencing your Personality you are an 'open' person who feels your emotions deeply, and who finds it essential to create harmony in your home environment. You can be quiet at times, and sometimes you may enjoy doing a little yoga or meditating in order to help you relax and reconnect to your spirituality at the end of the day.

You can be a very thoughtful person, and you like to negotiate with others and to arrive at co-operative agreements. You often enjoy relating to people and sharing your feelings with those close to you. With a 29/2 you may seek emotional intimacy and like to nurture this vulnerable side to your Personality.

With the moon influencing your Personality you may love water and enjoy sailing, jet skiing, snorkelling and swimming. You may also be keen on horse riding and enjoy meditating at times too.

CHALLENGES

With a 29/2 influencing your Personality you have high expectations of yourself and others, and you may feel bitterly disappointed when these ideals fall through. You may collapse, give up, sulk, or even go into depression. The bigger the expectation, the harder the fall. However, at times when you do feel that you have failed, you may have also gained in experience. For example, failure may teach you to set more realistic expectations next time, or to keep trying with the ideas you have already found.

Sometimes your need to be paid well for your work and to make financial gain in your career overrides all your other thoughts and ideas. You may think you need lots of money to help you feel safe and secure. However, spirituality is also important to you, and at times when you can't face material failure you may head off in search of spiritual paradise to help you escape from that reality. Turning towards your spirituality at these times may enable you to rediscover your energy and direct you back towards your goals in a more balanced way.

With a 29/2 you are a strong individual and an innovative creator. When you are working towards creating original ideas and concepts, or introducing new ways of doing things, you may sometimes experience disappointments along the way. This is quite natural, and these 'failures' can sometimes drive you on to work even harder at achieving your goals. Your motto may be 'never give up'.

You enjoy being competitive, because it inspires you to work even harder towards your goals. However, you can be quite cold, ruthless and manipulative, in order to get exactly what you want. Sometimes you may even feel a real one-upmanship about winning out over others. Eventually you may realize that life usually gives you what you need, and sometimes what you want, but fighting for it in a cold-blooded way may only lead you to feel the pain of a hollow victory.

You have fiery energy and you may be argumentative at times. However, you do not like getting caught in others' fights and arguments and you will do your best not to be drawn into taking sides. Arguments can make you depressed because they counteract the peace that you crave for your security and stability. You may remain tactful, discreet and diplomatic in your response, or you may say things to please people, to get them off your back. However, if you are forced into others' arguments because you are involved in some way, you may explode with intense emotion. However painful being in the middle may feel, by remaining calm and discussing your feelings openly with all concerned, you may be able to find a resolve in co-operation.

With a 29/2 influencing your Personality you are highly strung and temperamental at times, because of the abundance of nervous energy that you transmit. You are also an intense person with a feeling of 'heaviness' around you due to your high levels of concentration, and also when you are in a mood. At these times you may be insensitive to how others feel in your environment, or you may just not care – you can be self-centred. However, sometimes people need to get in contact with their own emotions by feeling the intensity of yours. At other times, it may be a case of 'give and take', and perhaps keeping your own company for a while when you feel worked up about something.

At times you may be fearful of life and create real problems from not facing these fears. For example, you may fear losing your job, and by worrying about this so much you may contribute towards creating the very thing you fear. Keeping a positive mind and focusing on things you enjoy and are good at can help you to do the best you can in life. If you were 'meant' to lose your job you would do so anyway; some things are simply out of your hands.

With a 29/2 when you are fearful you may make rash decisions, which you may regret later on. For instance, because you feel that you are going to lose your job, you may suddenly decide to leave. However, you may regret this later when your boss tells you how much you have done for the company, and how valuable you are. Sometimes such decisions come from your gut feelings, which may at times be wrong. It may help to use your discriminative mind to help you assess the facts when you are making important decisions about your life.

ROMANCE AND SEX

With a 29/2 influencing your Personality you are charismatic, and you like to feel that you are appreciated and approved of by your partner. You may go out of your way to ensure that, on your first date for example, everything runs smoothly. When you start dating you may also try to impress your partner by taking them out to the most expensive restaurant in town (even if you can only afford the starter!), and you may even hire a smart car for the evening. You also make sure that you look the part too, and you love to dress in a unique and vibrant way. However, you generally work hard (although you may have inherited wealth too), and you may have plenty of money with which to enjoy the 'good life'.

Therefore you may be very attracted to a partner who is interested in making money for him- or herself, and who is also an ambitious, magnetic and powerful person too. However, you may be only too happy to set up home and work with your partner on making money together. The more money you make, the better you feel in yourself, and the more confident you become. Money also gives you security; no matter if you have the most perfect partner, you may not feel contented, happy or complete without a certain amount of money or lifestyle.

With a 29/2 you are focused and set on your goals, and you may like to set goals with your partner. For example, 'We'll review the relationship in six months' time (to the day!) to see if we still like each other then,' you decide. You are very precise, and you have exact expectations, which you naïvely believe will work out exactly as you plan. However, remember that life often throws up the unexpected. You may also have such high expectations for your relationship that you lack faith that it can ever truly work. This may also be a way of opting out and not committing yourself. Letting go of any expectation can help the relationship to develop in its own way.

You have a strong mind and emotions, and are usually very spiritual too. You may therefore find a partner to whom you can relate on some of these levels. However, being able to relate emotionally to your partner and being able to share your feelings openly in an intimate way is really important to you. You may at times find it difficult to express your emotions because you feel too vulnerable or sensitive. You may also try to hide from your emotions by avoiding going 'in deep' with your partner. This is fine for a while, but eventually your emotions will surface or they may be expressed in some other indirect way.

With a 29/2 you may be immature for your age, and you may seek a partner to look after you and care for your every need. You are also warm and giving and love to give hugs and presents.

With a 29/2 influencing your sex life you are a passionate and thoughtful lover, and you love to be inventive in bed. Sex inspires you, but you are easily bored, so finding a special partner who is willing to explore all the positions in the *Karma Sutra* with you, may be useful. You have high expectations, but you aim to please, and you keep on trying too!

PHYSICAL APPEARANCE

With a 29/2 influencing your looks you may have a large 'baby' face, a protruding jaw, a thin nose and very high eyebrows. You may also look wiry, or if the 2 influence is strong, your outstanding feature will be your soft, watery eyes, which spellbind at a glance, or your eyes may be intense (with an 11) too.

CHILDHOOD EXPERIENCES

With a 29/2 influencing your childhood you may have been a magnetic child, who was always being invited to all the best parties around (even then!). You were probably a popular child, with lots of friends. However, you may have been spoiled, particularly by your parents, who just gave in to you to avoid your temper when they tried to say 'no' to your demands.

You may have often felt let down by those around you because you were sensitive and easily took things to 'heart'; for example, if your best friend truly forgot to bring over his favourite computer game, which you wanted. However, you got bored easily and soon found something else to inspire you and keep you focused.

Sometimes your sensitivity inspired others, perhaps by the deep feelings you put into playing the piano, singing beautiful songs, writing poetry or painting colourful pictures. You may also have used up your creative and dynamic energies by acting in the school play. However, with a head for business you probably loved to play the game 'Monopoly', to see what toy money you could make and what properties you could collect.

Children with a 29/2 may often need to be encouraged to keep trying when at first they do not succeed with their dreams and expectations. They may feel bitterly disappointed when things go wrong. However, 'failure' can lead to 'success' next time around, and being reassured about how much they are loved may make everything else seem like a bad dream.

WELL-BEING

With a 29/2 influencing your health you may sometimes be prone to blood-sugar imbalances, nervousness, tummy aches, tension headaches or hormonal imbalances. You may also suffer from breathing problems at times, or from emotional and mental stress.

CAREER CHOICE

With a 29/2 influencing your career you may use your abilities or decision-making skills as a diplomat, mediator, agent or negotiator. Perhaps you may use your wisdom and compassion as a peacemaker, humanitarian, carer or counsellor, or become an acupuncturist.

You may take up a career in big business, as a financial management consultant, financier or industrialist, or work for your own large organization. A career pioneering your own opportunities as an entrepreneur may also appeal. You may also work as an actor or actress, artist, musician or writer. However, whichever career you choose, success and recognition may be yours.

FAMOUS CHARACTER ANALYSIS

John F Kennedy Born 29 May 1917

John F Kennedy, or JFK as he was known, was the highly magnetic and attractive individual who exerted his power and leadership by becoming the President of the United States. He was very astute, and an inspiring decision-maker. He also, on at least one occasion, used his powers of negoti-ating, diplomacy and co-operation to help bring peace to a volatile diplomatic situation.

JFK was certainly a charismatic character and a popular President, who found love in his soul mate and wife, Jackie. However, his vibrant charm made him irresistible to the rich and beautiful around him and he was thought to have 'bedded' many in his time, the most famous of all (apparently) being the sex symbol Marilyn Monroe. Marilyn would certainly have matched his power and magnetism, and may even have been a challenge to him.

JFK was typical of the influence of a 29/2 in that he amassed great wealth and fortune in his life, and also that only the best would do. He was bright, witty and intelligent, but he was also vulnerable and sensitive.

JFK died on 22 November 1963, after achieving at least one of his expectations as a national leader and hero. The whole date adds up to a 7, so perhaps he was reaching deep within himself for a spiritual connection in his life at that time. The day was a 22, which is for materializing the dream, but he already had.

30/3

GENERAL TRENDS FOR NUMBER 30/3 PERSONALITY

With a 30/3 influencing your Personality you have the gift of serenity and a deepest yearning for fun in your life. This may be because you struggle along with trying to juggle so many things in your life all at once, so things may get very serious at times. You are pleasure-seeking, and according to you every second of your life should be fun! Therefore you put a lot of energy into trying to make this happen. For example, you may do the most mundane chores whilst listening to some fun music, or to a comedy on the radio or television. You also like to have people around you who are light-hearted and fun-loving too.

You are brilliant with children and really know how to entertain them with your mischievous sense of humour. You may play silly games, such as imitating people (one of your favourites), or act out little plays with them; you are a natural performer. You also love to tell stories or read out loud, and you can animate the characters so that they seem to jump out of the pages. Learning is fun with you. On the other hand, you may simply giggle away, enjoying playtime more than the children you are with!

With a 30/3 influencing your Personality you may be described as a chatterbox, although you do have your quiet moments when you may 'go inside' for peace from your (at times) over-active mind. You are a warm and friendly person and you converse easily with others, although sometimes they cannot get a word in edgeways! However, you also have a gift of communicating serious things to people, and getting your point across with humour, so that they really hear what you are saying without getting offended. For example, you tell your brother that he needs a bath because he stinks, but you make it into a joke so that he ends up laughing about it too. People take to this, and they take to you, which is one of the reasons why you are so popular. Even when you do criticize others it is usually done in a constructive and helpful way.

You are naturally an extrovert and a bubbly person, with vibrant energy that keeps you going all day long. You are also a socializer (and you may even be a socialite), and your need to be with people and to express yourself is great. You love to be stimulated by meeting new people, and you may often flit around like a butterfly at parties so that you don't miss anyone out. You are flexible; you can be superficial and light, or go into deep conversations about life. However, your humour is never far away, and you are very much in demand at social events and your diary is often full. You may also be extremely sporty, and part of your social life may be devoted to that circle of friends and acquaintances.

You are usually a confident person, and you love to express yourself by being affectionate and tactile; you have no hang-ups about hugging a stranger or holding hands with your best friend. You thrive off this kind of intimacy and connection, and being demonstrative comes naturally to you.

With a 30/3 influencing your Personality you are a doer; you don't sit around and simply think about what you want to do with your life, you go for it 100 per cent. You tend to throw yourself into life, involving yourself with lots of different projects and people. You are an expressive person, and people are often inspired by your prolific creativity. For example, you may bake three cakes at once, or paint seven pictures in a day, or write five books in a year … sometimes your output is astounding. However, you do like your sleep, even though it may not add up to more than six hours a night; you have so much to do you need all the waking hours you can get!

Your abundance of creativity, love and joy uplifts others and helps to lighten their load. You can also be light and superficial. However, this does not mean that you don't have any depth to your Personality; you do have a serious side too. When something in life catches your eye, you can go into it very deeply. For example, you may decide to take a professional qualification in colour and design, or spend time exploring a foreign country (you may even live there for years). You may feel your emotions very deeply too, and you can be quite intense at times. You are also a thinker, and sometimes you simply love to 'be,' or make time to meditate.

You may also love being out in the sunshine or riding, athletics and aerobics, or keep fit by running around all day!

CHALLENGES

With a 30/3 influencing your Personality you like to chat, but sometimes you are so busy talking at people that you fail to notice their feelings or other things happening around you. For example, you may stop to talk to the post or delivery person and forget that you left the tap running in the bathroom, or that you have left someone hanging on the telephone. It is great to express yourself to people, but chatting too much can mean you are ungrounded, or simply unaware of yourself at that time. Sometimes focusing on one thing at a time can really help to keep you 'centred' and safe, and aware of others around you.

You may enjoy being superficial and gossiping with your friends. However, you are a very critical person, and sometimes your negative attitude towards people is apparent in your vicious comments or in hurtful gossip. You may make snide remarks about the way they dress, their achievements, or who they've been dating. You may do this because you are jealous, or because it makes you feel better than them. However, this kind of gossip usually ends up hurting you more than anyone else, and you may feel really guilty afterwards. Learning to laugh at yourself and at life is a wonderful way to release stress, and helps keep you happy. But by learning to keep your comments to yourself, unless you have something positive to say, you can keep your peace of mind and keep your friends too.

Generally you love attention, but you also try to grab others' attention by gossiping about people, talking loudly, making outlandish statements, being argumentative and controversial, or wearing outrageous clothes. Everyone loves to be the centre of attention at times, but it helps to receive attention for the right reason. For example, you may feel better by getting attention for winning an award for your poetry rather than for making loud comments criticizing other poets. When you are happy within yourself you do not have a desperate need for attention; you are simply content to enjoy your life the way it is.

With a 30/3 influencing your Personality you may also be lacking in self-confidence at times, and you may not feel able to express your opinions, your feelings, your affection or your creativity in as many ways as you would like. Perhaps you would like to, but an inner voice may tell you that you will not succeed. However, you generally have a positive attitude towards life, and on days when you wake up to brilliant sunshine (inside and out) you may use this vitality to help you overcome your self-doubts.

You may experience times of great conflict and confusion in your life. This may be because you have so many things to do that you get lost in your endless list of demands and activities. Sometimes deciding which parties to attend can also create conflict – you are so popular! Conflicts may also run deep. For example, you may truly worry about how you are going to keep your partner (and children) happy, and run your own business at the same time. However, life has a habit of working itself out, and by applying your famous easy-going attitude, it can help you to take life in your stride.

You can also be too laid-back at times and get lazy, or too casual about things. This may show itself by you being untidy and messy at home, and in unprofessionalism at work; for example by sending out an important letter with coffee stains on it. You may also be casual in your acquaintances and attract problems from not being fussy enough about whom you play around with. However, when you go through the mess and destruction then you usually come out the other end with clarity and a new light on things. For example, you may eventually tidy out your drawers, tidy up your office, and learn to set boundaries when you meet people in future.

With a 30/3 you may also complain about other people's mess and blame and criticize them for their faults, or moan on and on about your own life too. However, you may eventually get so fed up with moaning about your problems that you decide to change, and take some positive actions to help make things better for yourself. For example, this may be making a telephone call, getting your hair cut or applying for a job. It may help to cheer you up, and others will be pleased to find that you have started to do something positive with your life, and it may also encourage them to do the same.

ROMANCE AND SEX

With a 30/3 influencing your love life you may often love to travel, get out and about and do things – you are an active person. Therefore it may be helpful for you to find a partner who is physically fit enough to stand the pace, or at least fit enough to listen to you gabble on about what you have been doing, who you've seen and where you've been. You don't mind travelling or going out on your own because you are like a magnet, and you usually find interesting people to talk to. You feel confident and at ease. However, you may prefer a partner who likes to socialize at least some of the time with you and the crowd too.

Usually you are an outgoing person who enjoys your freedom, so you may not take to a partner who you feel is relying on you for entertainment or is dependent upon you in a big way. Perhaps this person can't be bothered to make an effort to go out and see friends but relies on you to jolly them up all the time, or is dependent upon you to provide them with their daily bread because they can't be bothered to work. You get bored easily, and if you feel that there are too many demands placed upon you then you may well seek a change and turn to others for stimulation

However, once you have found a partner and made a commitment, you are persistent and will focus your energies on making it work. You are generally a relaxed person and your lightness and joy radiate out. Therefore you may at times be an easy person to live with, and a lovely person to have around.

With a 30/3 influencing your relationships you may seek a practical and down-to-earth partner who can help to steady you. You are also a romantic who likes candlelit meals, romantic walks, and boxes of chocolates and flowers delivered to your door. You can also be sentimental at times too, as you coo about old romantic photographs, or reminisce about your last night of passion in front of a glowing fire. Therefore finding a partner who enjoys the thrill of romance may be an essential ingredient that keeps you staying around for more.

You may be an intellectual person, and you may like to find a partner who can inspire you with his or her bright mind and stimulating conversation. You can be serious at times and may enjoy deep discussions with your partner or friends, or time alone to think, rather than bounding around at loud parties. However, you also have a wicked sense of humour and an incredible sense of the ridiculous, which can keep your partner entertained all day long. You may also like to keep your partner 'guessing' by teasing and flirting (in a fun-loving way) with anyone around.

With a 30/3 you generally have a high sex drive and you are prolifically creative in or out of bed. You are also generous with your love and affections. You may like spontaneous sex with a partner with the stamina to keep going, and with the energy to then serve you breakfast in bed!

PHYSICAL APPEARANCE

With a 30/3 influencing your looks you may have large bushy eyebrows, a high forehead, a large mouth, and possibly a small nose. You may also have a heavy midriff and legs. Your most outstanding feature is your muscular body which, when toned, makes you look fit and healthy.

CHILDHOOD EXPERIENCES

With a 30/3 influencing your childhood you may have been very active and hardly found time to sit down. You may have been a doer who flitted from one thing to another in an attempt to pack as much into your day as you possibly could. For example, you may have been out to the museum with your family, then enjoyed tea with your friends, then played games in the garden, then went home and read. You may also have been a talkative child who loved having lots of different friends to communicate with, because you had a variety of interests.

You may have also been creative with your hands. For example, making clothes for your dolls, building matchstick toys, painting, sculpting, writing or cooking. However, you probably possessed a bright mind too, and you may have enjoyed studying and going to school, where you were stimulated by lots of different subjects.

With a 30/3 you may have been an extrovert and gregarious child, who was full of fun and laughter. Perhaps you were the joker in the family who was always telling jokes (or making up your own). However, you may also have been serious, emotional or moody at times, like when you were being reminded that it was time for bed.

Children with a 30/3 often have so much energy going out to so many different things at once that they may lose their focus, and can get clumsy, drop things or have accidents. By being aware when a child is getting out of their depth, you may encourage them to stop what they are doing and be still for a while, or perhaps take a rest.

WELL-BEING

With a 30/3 influencing your health you may be prone to muscular aches and pains, or blood-pressure imbalances. Sometimes, you may also be accident-prone and sustain injuries as a result of your loss of concentration and focus.

CAREER CHOICE

With a 30/3 influencing your career you are a lively person who may take up work as a professional party organizer or a socialite, or you may work in the travel industry where you can meet a variety of different people and travel. You may also be a comedian or entertainer, uplifting others with your humour and wit.

You may work as a photographer, massage therapist, artist, sculptor, writer, designer, interior designer or feng shui consultant. You may also be drawn to mysticism, and if you are psychic you may work using your instincts to help others, as a tarot reader or palmist.

FAMOUS CHARACTER ANALYSIS
Christopher Columbus Born 30 October 1451

Christopher Columbus typically demonstrated the qualities of his 30/3 Personality because he was a traveller who loved to sail off into the horizon in search of fun, adventure and stimulation. He was probably a mystic too, with his own strong instincts about his life and what he was meant to do. Perhaps he knew how to follow the stars and how to 'read' the seas. Maybe as a child he even had psychic dreams of sailing to new lands across the ocean.

Columbus travelled constantly; having experienced the excitement of reaching new land, he was soon off navigating the open water in search of more adventure. He loved challenges and he didn't give up. Indeed, considering his unsophisticated method of transport you could say he was 'protected' to have achieved his dreams.

With a 30/3 Columbus was a communicator, who brought with him information about his own land and the places he had visited, and took it on to somewhere new. He led a truly inspiring life, and his discoveries have helped to form the present-day history of the world.

Christopher Columbus died on 20 May 1506, having navigated his instincts and his dreams. The whole date adds up to a 19 or 1, which refers to status, power and leadership, and a searching for a new direction. The day was a 20, which represents peace, so perhaps he was at peace with himself and knew that his pioneering days were over.

31/4

GENERAL TRENDS FOR NUMBER 31/4 PERSONALITY

With a 31/4 influencing your Personality you have the gift of courage, and a deepest yearning to be at ease with life. However, people may often say that you are courageous, but it is natural for you to go for your goals and for life in a totally dynamic way. You do not generally stop to worry about whether your goals are difficult or how enormous the challenge of creating them is, you simply follow your instincts and get stuck right in. You may be a pioneer, and often in breaking new ground – whether with an idea, an attitude or with an invention or goal – you pave the way for others. Sometimes whilst being courageous and following your goals, you may find yourself standing out from the crowd. For instance, you may open up a medical centre in an under-privileged area, and in so doing you may attract masses of attention from the media. As a result, hue sums of money are donated to your centre, and a good cause receives the attention it deserves.

You are a born leader and you carry responsibility conscientiously; you do not expect others to do your work for you. You are a down-to-earth and practical person and you will often work hard towards materializing your goals. Once you have made a commitment you have an incredible determination to follow it through until the very end. For example, one of your hobbies may be designing and making clothes for yourself, and you may want to make a suit. You draw the pattern out, cut it up, and begin to sew the suit together piece by piece, and you do not stop until every last buttonhole is complete. You may at times hardly sleep as you are inspired to focus so intently on your goals.

With a 31/4 you possess an incredible amount of drive and

ambition, which flows through your abundant creativity and out into the world around you. For example, you may be an artist, and your home is filled with a wealth of inspiring paintings and vibrant colours. There may be an earthy kitchen brimming over with food, and a warm, caring atmosphere – it's a lovely place to be. You may have built a solid foundation in your life from the money you have earned from grounding your creative energies.

You need to feel secure, and you are persistent in your pursuit of attaining material security by constantly working towards your goals. However, very often you may choose a career which actually seems like play because it flows so easily. For example, you love to entertain others with your bubbly, bright sense of humour, so you may choose work as an entertainer, where you can work and play all day!

Generally you like to keep yourself busy by doing lots of different things at once. For example, there's family life, your social life, working, playing sport, and travelling, before all the other *ad hoc* projects that you like to fit in. Sometimes you can be deadly serious as you try to focus on too many things at once, and you realize that if you lose concentration for a second everything will fall apart. However, you generally manage to keep it all together with your brilliant organizational skills and your creative flair.

With a 31/4 influencing your Personality you have a strong mind, and at times you may withdraw into your world of thoughts, pondering upon spirituality, mysticism, religion or life. However, you may explore the unearthly territories of your mind sometimes for philosophical ideas and seek answers to your earthly problems. You may also be interested in finding answers to mankind's problems, for example how to find harmony from age-old religious or political conflicts, or how to feed the world, and so on. Then you may help these causes in a practical way, in reality.

You have an outgoing and gregarious side to your personality, and you love to socialize, entertain others, and to get out and about; you love to travel. You may, for example, enjoy trekking through the Himalayas, walking through woodlands, or attaching a rucksack to your back and taking off into the great unknown. You have a zest for freedom, and whether alone or with others, on holiday or otherwise,you like to wander around with not a care in the world.

With a 31/4 you are a tactile and earthy person. You enjoy playing many different sports, cycling and riding, and you may be a brilliant long-distance runner, where your iron will and your physical stamina carry you through to the very end.

CHALLENGES

With a 31/4 influencing your Personality you are someone who likes to dive into life and explore new opportunities that come your way. You like to have variety and you may soon get bored if you are bogged down in too much routine. However, sometimes you have so much to do that your energies scatter. For example, you may be rushing from one appointment to the next and so are unable to relax or pay full attention to what is needed at any of them. However, somewhere in your personality you do have organizational skills, and by utilizing these to decide on the most important things you need to do each day you can materialize results. You may also like to set your boundaries clearly. For example, at the beginning of your meeting you can say, 'I have forty-five minutes to spend with you, because I need to leave for …' This can then help the other person to focus on what needs to be achieved at the meeting too.

You may feel at times that you simply cannot finish things; you only read half a book, you start to bake a cake but abandon it in the bowl after ten minutes, and so on. Similarly you may have lots of work but never get to the bottom of it, sometimes because you have taken on too much, and at other times because you are simply too disorganized or lazy. However, learning to follow through on your commitments and being realistic about what you take on, may help you to achieve success in any area of your life.

With a 31/4 influencing your Personality at times you may work so methodically but so slowly towards your goals that you may feel like you are never going to get there. At these times, you may think, 'I give up'. Sometimes all you have to do is to keep working methodically towards them. However, if you have been focusing too much energy directly onto one goal, for a long time, then your concentration may eventually begin to waver, and your energies may drain away from the very thing you desire. Sometimes taking your attention elsewhere, or changing your routine in some way for a while, may actually help to re-focus you. For example, by going out dancing, or having fun with your friends at a party, or taking a weekend break, or having a massage. These can help you to revitalize and, within the context, help you to materialize your goals.

You are a hard worker, and you may require others around you to match your pace because you are a leader and you expect them to follow. Perhaps you may even drive them into the ground by giving them too much work, or too many directions to follow at once. Sometimes you may even be too serious when you are focusing on work that needs to be done, or goals that need to be achieved. By learning to apply a little of your carefree energy to lighten you up and lighten your load, you may find that more work gets done, because with your relaxed attitude the work can simply flow.

Sometimes you take your leadership very seriously and like to feel that you are 'special', and even superior to others. You may also be loud and expressive, and over-opinionated, and full of your own self-importance. However, you may resort to this behaviour when you are feeling insecure, or when you don't feel good enough, and you may try to over-compensate. Eventually you may learn that everyone is special in their own unique way, and that everyone has a special gift. Perhaps then you can learn to accept that you are 'good enough' without needing to prove yourself, or prove a thing.

With a 31/4 you may lack confidence at times and withdraw into a corner (at parties for example) and feel unable to express yourself easily. Again, by learning to relax and adopt a more carefree attitude towards your situation, you may be able to loosen up and simply learn to enjoy the atmosphere and the people you are with.

At times you may lack the courage of your convictions. For example, you may tell everyone that you can climb mountains, but on the way to the airport, with your team of hikers, you chicken out. Sometimes, at least by making an effort you can feel satisfied knowing that you gave it your best shot, even if you do fail. However, not trying may mean that you don't get the opportunity to find out.

With a 31/4 you sometimes jump into things too quickly, without any consideration or due thought of the consequences. However, the fastest way to learn is through experience, and there is no point getting depressed or regretful over spilt milk.

ROMANCE AND SEX

With a 31/4 influencing your love life there is a part of you that enjoys being superficial, and you may not like to find yourself 'in too deep' within a relationship. For example, you may prefer to go out with lots of different people at once, because you like variety. Or perhaps you may like to connect with your partner physically, but not want to get too close or intimate emotionally, and remain superficial on that level. However, relationships can work in many different ways. A part of you may like to settle into the security of a long-term relationship with one person, and you may find it easy to follow through on your commitments and to settle down when it feels 'right.'

Sometimes you can be superficial and fun; you can be a dream to have around, and you may keep your partner happily entertained for hours. This really helps to lighten the atmosphere on days when you both have challenges to face, or when your partner is unhappy too. Laughter can really help to get you both through.

With a 31/4 you are freedom loving, and no matter whether you are in a short- or long-term relationship you may still need to feel your freedom and be able to explore available opportunities. In a brief encounter you may feel free to express yourself in a more extrovert way, knowing that you have no ties. In a long-term relationship, simply setting aside time for yourself during each week, where you feel free to do what you want, may be all that you need. However, finding a partner who understands this need may be essential for your compatibility.

You may also be free with your love, and you may not be hung up about your body either. For example, you may be happy to dress in clothes that reveal your figure, or feel comfortable to parade around on beaches with little or nothing on. You are also a tactile and warm person, and you feel free to be affectionate with others too.

With a 31/4 you may like to find a partner who is down to earth and who enjoys the conformity of a relationship where you can set definite boundaries with each other, along with respecting each other's freedom. You may enjoy working with your partner to build unity within the relationship, and also to materialize your joint goals together.

You may be very psychic, and like to follow your instincts about what is needed within your relationship. You can really 'feel' your partner and feel his or her needs. You are also sensible, and you do not allow your feelings to run away with you; you have your feet firmly on the ground and therefore like your partner to discuss his or her feelings too.

With a 31/4 influencing your sex life you usually have a high sex drive, as you are very physical, and you have the stamina to go on and on. However, friendship is very important to you, and once you feel you have found loyalty with your partner, you may experiment with the intimacy of tantric sex too. Security is the most important aspect to a happy and healthy sex life for you.

PHYSICAL APPEARANCE

With a 31/4 influencing your looks you may be of a small to medium height, with a high forehead, and have a long face with an extended jaw, and you may look muscular and hardy. Your most outstanding features are your hands, which are usually small and strong.

CHILDHOOD EXPERIENCES

With a 31/4 influence you may have experienced an unusual childhood in that you may have stood out from the crowd, for example by being brilliant at your school work or with some particular gift. Perhaps you had parents who were famous or who were unconventional in some way. For whatever reason, a lot of attention probably came your way.

You may also have been an active child who loved to work hard, and also to devote your attention to playing, and to your hobbies and interests. For example, you may have loved to put on plays with your friends, build things, play musical instruments, or perhaps you liked to write 'pretend' speeches and deliver them to your friends. You may have loved sports; indeed, you may have spent more time outdoors than in.

With a 31/4, you may have been brought up with a solid and secure background, where you felt safe and comfortable and were able to express yourself freely. Alternatively there may have been a lot of conflict or confusion in your household, and perhaps life was too hectic and chaotic. Sometimes you may have felt unsettled, with seemingly too many activities going on around you all at once. Perhaps you were literally unsettled and moved home or schools more than once. You were probably a conscientious child who liked to plod on, whatever was going on around you.

Children with a 31/4 may often feel like they are totally free and therefore may not understand their boundaries, such as going to bed on time, or returning from a friend's house on time, and so on. However, applying discipline to these children may help them to adapt to their environment.

WELL-BEING

With a 31/4 influencing your health you may be prone to headaches or problems with your circulation. You may sometimes suffer from muscular aches and pains, or from weaknesses in your legs. You may have a tendency to overdo things, which can result in physical exhaustion at times.

CAREER CHOICE

With 31/4 influencing your career, you may work as a farmer, massage therapist, cook, gardener, artist or writer. You may also work as a herbalist, healer or midwife, or in the medical field, and you may be particularly interested in Eastern or Tibetan forms of healing and medicine.

Perhaps you may work as a political or humanitarian leader, and help to solve people's problems. You may also work in education, or as a director or a television or radio presenter, or even as an entertainer, or you may have a successful career in sport.

FAMOUS CHARACTER ANALYSIS
Dr Maria Montessori Born 31 August 1870

Dr Montessori was a pioneer in the field of education, and she became the first woman in Italy to receive a medical degree, in 1894. Indeed she was typical of the 31/4 influence, as she created a breakthrough and waved the flag for women's rights and for education. Maria was a strong and bright individual, and she invented her own 'Montessori methods' of teaching and education, and set up her own school. She formalized her own structure, which encouraged creative development and play as much as formal education, and allowed children to feel free to learn in a more informal atmosphere. Today the Montessori schools and system of education are used all around the world.

Maria was a courageous leader who helped to break down old structures and implement positive physical change in the field of education. She must have worked very hard to make herself heard and to get enough attention for her work to be taken seriously. She certainly was determined and persistent, and she was practically able to follow through on her commitments to fully materialize them.

Dr Montessori died on 6 May 1952, having achieved her goals of highlighting education in the world. The whole date adds up to a 28 or 1, so perhaps she was ready to move on to new things at that time. The day is a 6, which indicates that her communitarian responsibilities had been achieved and her service to humanity was complete.

LEARNING MORE ABOUT NUMEROLOGY

TAKING IT FURTHER

Learning about the number(s) which influence your Personality – the day of the month on which you were born – is essential if you wish to understand how you function and learn about your psychological patterns of behaviour. Your Personality is your 'space suit', which shapes your whole life. Without this space suit you would have no individuality and could not interact with the world around you. That is why this book has chosen to focus on such an important aspect of your chart.

When you know and understand the functions of your Personality and the influence of its number(s), you can go on to find out more about your Life Path through your Life Path Number, which is given by adding up your whole date of birth, and your soul work and karma, which are revealed in your names. All the aspects contained within your numerological chart blend together and offer potential.

Words are powerful. They produce sounds and vibrations, and their numerological meanings influence us greatly. For example, as mentioned in the introduction, the name of the city or country in which you live in can be 'added up' to reveal its influence over your life. It is also interesting to note the sequence of numbers in a word. For example, let's consider the name Susan. There are three 1s in it, which will make the influence of its qualities stronger in Susan's life. The name of the country Japan also has three 1s, so perhaps Susan may be especially attracted to all things Japanese, or, alternatively, she may actively resist its culture. Any word can be 'translated' into its numerological correspondences. The following table shows the numerical significance of each letter in the alphabet.

There are many ways to find out more about numerology. You may learn a tremendous amount of information about yourself by reading

ALPHABET CORRESPONDENCE CHART

1	A	J	S
2	B	K	T
3	C	L	U
4	D	M	V
5	E	N	W
6	F	O	X
7	G	P	Y
8	H	Q	Z
9	I	R	

books on the subject. Books are wonderful methods for learning because they are usually easy to obtain and offer information at your finger tips. You can scout through them to find the information you require – about yourself, your friends and family. You can read books at your own leisure, and you can read and re-read them so that you can get clarity about the information they contain. Of course, you can also read 'between the lines' or 'behind the numbers' and let your intuition guide you to teach you about life.

You can also visit a numerologist for a chart reading, which will give you information about your health, your relationships, your career, or about any challenging situations you find yourself walking through on your path in life. A Numerologist can highlight your hidden potential in all areas of your life, and bring together an overview of your Personality, your Life Path, your soul work, karmic influences, and so on. The advantage of a personal chart reading with a numerologist is that it is objective, and can mirror back to you information which might seem subjective when you are 'reading' information about your own chart.

If numerology wraps around your mind and grabs your attention, and it fascinates you enough to inspire you to search for further information into these wonderful little digits, then professional training may be for you. On any numerology training course you will work on your own personal development as well as learning how numbers relate to the world at large.

However, once you have understood a little about the qualities and cycles contained within each number, the quickest way to learn is to let life teach you. Observe how numbers influence your life and the life of those around you every day, and the experiences they create.

Numbers can enrich your life, and once you begin to open up your mind and your intuition to them they start to 'speak' to you, teaching you about the inner mysteries of life.

GROWING INTEREST IN NUMEROLOGY

Numerology has been around since the beginning of time but today it is extremely popular owing to people's awareness of the more material aspects of numbers; that is, the numbers in your pay-packet, numbers in the Lottery, lucky numbers, and so on. People are gradually realizing that numbers really do run their lives. Numerology is also gaining popularity because it can reveal so much about every aspect of our lives.

In the media there is increased interest in numerology, be it in business gazettes, health journals, or in women's magazines. Even large organizations and businesses consult numerolgists to help them with their work.

However, with the entry into the second millennium people have become more aware of how that 2 – in 2000 – has affected their lives, and how it feels different to living with the influence of the 1 and 9 of the 90s. These feelings may be heightened by the effects of the leap in the 1–9 numerical cycle and by the effects of other numbers, such as your Personal Year influence number, in your life.

Changes of numbers on a grand scale, like from the year 1000 to the year 2000, influences all life. Read on further to get a greater sense of how this happens.

NUMEROLOGY AND THE MILLENNIA

MILLENNIUM AD 1000–2000

The number 1 is a number which influences the breaking down of old ways of doing things and the invention and pioneering of new things. It is the number of new opportunities and new things. There are also three zeros in the year 1000, carrying with it strong potential and protection for the last millennium. In numerology this 1000 is a précis of what had to come.

In the last 1,000 years man has achieved rapid advancements in all areas of life (particularly during the latter half of the millennium) – for example, in medicine, in science, in the industrial world, in the arts, in communications and in consciousness. Indeed, at the end of the old millennium there was a particularly rapid movement towards spirituality and mysticism. Not necessarily in a way of going to church or to a temple every week, but perhaps more in a way of people feeling more spiritually connected with each other.

The world has literally 'shrunk' away, as more and more people travel around the world, connecting and mixing with different cultures, and are educated by different lifestyles. Even illnesses which were once only found in specific countries are now shared with many foreigners due to the open network of communications – train, bus, boat, plane. However, new illnesses always develop with each generation, but with so many more people travelling around the world meeting and interacting, other new strains of illnesses have also unfortunately developed. For example, people with some forms of influenza have in the past practically 'knocked out' isolated ethnic tribes by coming into contact with them, because these tribes had no resistance to their visitors' disease. Vice versa, those modern travellers brought back new illnesses from distant tribes to their own communities. Life is constantly moving on …

However, illnesses aside, man has forged ahead in other ways during the last 1,000 years. Perhaps the biggest challenge left from that time is the quality of intolerance: ethnically, politically and culturally. Indeed, this includes intolerance towards self, towards partners, children and friends and family. When people feel uncomfortable or lack tolerance towards others it can cause friction, disputes, fights and even wars. However, these hostilities have been necessary parts of growth, parts of history and a part of evolution.

In the last 1,000 years man has been particularly concerned with the selfish aspects of the 1, often thinking only in terms of 'me, me, me'. It is this isolation of self from others that has caused much pain and anxiety. However, we need to learn about ourselves as individuals first, before learning about others and their needs.

Indeed, the 1 influences individualization, and by learning to be alone, and 'stand' alone, mankind has learned to be with itself. The world and its people have been learning to be independent, which is why so many countries have been fighting for their rights and fighting for their independence. However, evolution may sometimes mean that countries or villages may join together, and then seek independence, as one.

MILLENNIUM AD 2000–3000

The number 2 particularly represents the emotions, and it is a number which influences balance, harmony and co-operation. Once again, with the three zeros influencing the overall picture, humanity is literally 'back to zero', 'back to basics' and 'picking up the pieces' – and the achievements – from the last millennium, to start again.

During this new millennium however, the influence must surely be on learning patience and tolerance towards other humans and the whole of nature. Tolerance means being adult and respecting each other's differences, rights and freedom, and accepting people as they are. Tolerance can also mean learning to include others in 'your' team, instead of excluding them by being superior in your actions or in your attitude.

During the current millennium there may also be more emphasis on sharing and co-operation, so that instead of people living alone, they may literally live in more close-knit communities. People may also feel more connected spiritually with humanity, wherever they live in the world. In their communities people will be able to share the good times, and share the challenges too. This possibility means that people may feel less isolated and may be more motivated by group needs, rather than thinking of themselves all the time. Perhaps by this they will also learn to relate to each other more readily, and to give and take according to the needs of the community as a whole.

In the next 1,000 years there may also be more good will and compassion amongst mankind as a whole, and perhaps people may feel more at ease and at peace with themselves and with the land. People may also be more open and caring towards each other, and be able to express themselves emotionally.

However, this millennium is all about balance and there may occasionally be some imbalance emotionally. This may also apply in a more general sense.

During this millennium there will almost certainly be an upsurge in spirituality, and in learning more about the mind and developing intuition. Perhaps numerology and psychology can help people in this direction. As people become more in touch and in tune with themselves they will naturally connect with others more easily too. Perhaps soon more people will become more telepathic, rather than using computers, telephones and faxes for communication – telepathy is even quicker than pressing a button.

Over the next 1,000 years, as people learn to live together more closely, perhaps a universal language will be used so that everyone can communicate and understand each other verbally or telepathically.

A FINAL NOTE

As we have seen, numerology can act as a guide for the ages to come. It is fascinating yet fun to practise anywhere at any time. Life is for learning, and numerology can help you do just that ... with this book your journey has only just begun.

FURTHER READING

Numerology is such a vast subject; because numbers are universal there are endless different methods of numerology, and ways in which it can be written about, from all over the world. However, the following books are simple and straightforward to read, and fascinating too.

Colin Baker, Dip. AIN, *Number Power*, Lorenz Books, 2005.

This beautifully colour-illustrated book is packed with information that stimulates thought, and reveals the truth about the numbers 1 to 9. An easy read.

Faith Javane and Dusty Bunker, *Numerology and the Divine Triangle*, Whitford Press, USA, 1979

This book offers in-depth information about numerology, from your whole date of birth and from your names. However, the highlight is that it covers the numbers 1 to 81, each with its own personal meanings, its temporary vibration meanings, and also with meanings from the tarot and astrology too. This book offers the ideal opportunity to learn about all these things at once.

Dan Millman, *The Life You Were Born to Live*, HJ Kramer Inc, USA, 1993

Dan has produced an accessible book which goes into great detail about your Path of Destiny and your Life Path. It also provides, guidelines, useful questions to ask yourself, and spiritual messages with reference to each number. This book is written with great clarity, and it is a wonderful tool for personal development.

HOW TO FIND A NUMEROLIGIST OR A NUMEROLOGY COURSE

For information on professional training workshops and readings worldwide, you can visit: www.numerology.org.uk

You can also send an SAE or International Reply coupon to: Association International de Numerologies, 8 Melbourn Street, Royston SG8 7BZ, Herts, UK

NUMBERS OF THE FAMOUS

Below is a list of the relevant numbers of the famous characters analysed in more depth within earlier chapters.

Number	Person	Date of Birth (day, month, year)	Date of Death (day, month, year)
1	Marilyn Monroe	1.6.1926	5.8.1962
10/1	Joyce Grenfell	10.2.1910	30.11.1979
19/1	Edgar Alan Poe	19.1.1809	7.10.1849
28/1	King Henry VIII	28.6.1491	28.1.1547
2	Mahatma Gandhi	2.10.1869	30.1.1948
11/2	Salvador Dali	11.5.1904	23.1.1989
20/2	Natalie Wood	20.7.1938	29.11.1981
29/2	John F Kennedy	29.5.1917	22.11.1963
3	Mary Shelley	3.8.1797	1.2.1851
12/3	Grace Kelly	12.11.1928	13.9.1982
21/3	Charlotte Brontë	21.4.1816	31.3.1855
30/3	Christopher Columbus	30.10.1451	20.5.1506
4	Percy Bysshe Shelley	4.8.1792	8.7.1822
13/4	Sir Alfred Hitchcock	13.8.1899	29.4.1980
22/4	Giacomo Puccini	22.12.1858	28.11.1924
31/4	Dr Maria Montessori	31.8.1870	6.5.1952
5	Freddie Mercury	5.9.1946	24.11.1991
14/5	Albert Einstein	14.3.1879	18.4.1955
23/5	Samuel Pepys	23.2.1633	26.5.1703
6	Sigmund Freud	6.5.1856	23.9.1939
15/6	Dame Agatha Christie	15.9.1890	12.1.1976
24/6	Henri de Toulouse-Lautrec	24.11.1864	9.9.1901
7	Madame Marie Tussaud	7.12.1760	15.4.1850
16/7	Oscar Wilde	16.10.1854	30.11.1900
25/7	Guglielmo Marconi	25.4.1871	20.7.1937
8	Elvis Presley	8.1.1935	16.8.1977
17/8	Jane Austen	17.12.1775	18.7.1817
26/8	Mother Teresa	26.8.1910	5.9.1997
9	John Lennon	9.10.1940	9.12.1980
18/9	Louis Tiffany	18.2.1874	17.7.1937
27/9	Samuel Morse	17.4.1791	2.4.1872